T0277384

Readers for Life

Readers for Life

HOW READING AND LISTENING IN CHILDHOOD SHAPES US

Edited by
Sander L. Gilman and
Heta Pyrhönen

REAKTION BOOKS

Published by
REAKTION BOOKS LTD
Unit 32, Waterside
44–48 Wharf Road
London N1 7UX, UK
www.reaktionbooks.co.uk

First published 2024
Copyright © The Authors 2024

Printed and bound in Great Britain
by Bell & Bain, Glasgow

A catalogue record for this book is available from the British Library

ISBN 978 1 78914 949 4

Contents

Setting the Scene

SANDER L. GILMAN *and* HETA PYRHÖNEN

In contemporary Western cultures a decline in reading seems to have become an ongoing cause for public concern and alarm. Although literacy is higher than at any other point in history, the crisis arises from the fact that people seem not to actively use this skill. When reading skills weaken, navigating the world becomes increasingly challenging, for our lives are shaped by deciphering multiple types of media texts. Modern surroundings are replete with texts. Given that the texts surrounding us are snippets, we find it difficult to concentrate on long texts: we have grasshopper minds, flitting from one focus to the next. This is a new type of illiteracy. E. P. Thompson, in his *Making of the English Working Class*, noted that the Methodist 'chapel' encouraged its congregants to learn to read the Bible, but not to learn to write. Literacy is a complicated thing.

While illiteracy remains a problem even in the so-called literate cultures – 21 per cent of adults in the United States can neither read nor write – our new problem lies in those who can, but cannot read longer, more complex, texts. We read in tweet-bits, with emojis instead of complex sentences. This is a newer form of illiteracy, a form reflecting an erosion of focus and patience in reading. Or at least that is the complaint of those whose romantic notion is that it was better in an idealized past, when Victorian triple-deckers were the choice of (some) in the middle class, but of course when true illiteracy was rampant.

Reading of any kind of books no longer seems to be a cherished activity. Indeed, poll after poll seems to indicate that many Americans, at least, stop reading for pleasure after the end of their schooling, whether high school or college. Even societies that praise themselves as 'reading' societies (for example, the Germans, the Icelanders and the Finns, translation cultures all) mourn the perceived drop-off of book sales and the concomitant decrease in readers. Yet the explosion of long books of fiction on the global bestseller lists (think J. K. Rowling or Philip Pullman) seems to mitigate this decline of reading long, complicated, indeed difficult texts, a decline perhaps best understood as measured not against any prior reality but against a world where the book-as-object has had a function in defining middle-class society. Reading 'serious' books from the Enlightenment to the present placed you, at least putatively, within the bounds of the bourgeois intelligentsia. Indeed, German notions of *Bildung* evolved parallel to the development of inexpensive printing, books that were then accompanied by highly ornamental bindings. These morphed into the coffee-table books of the twentieth century, placed ornamentally in a room to show the status of its occupiers. This tradition continues strongly in the world of twenty-first-century estate agents who 'stage' an apartment or house for sale by placing such books taken from their stockroom shelves to ornament their properties. and

What remains of former times is that Westerners come into contact with reading in childhood when their parents and teachers read aloud to them. This transition from an oral to a visual culture, from listening to listening while looking, marked a cultural change. It was the demand that E. P. Thompson placed in the chapel: don't just listen to the word of God on Sundays, read it and look at the images in your illustrated Bible with your children daily. They then learn to read silently to themselves. That this is a relatively recent shift has been recognized. Our recent forebears not only read aloud to their children but, when they read to themselves, spoke aloud or mouthed the words they were reading. Reading moved from an auxiliary to oral culture to its virtual replacement, a literate culture. Childhood and adolescence are the formative phases when the foundation for the later reading life is established in all cases. Listening to books, paralleled by the recent explosion of podcasts and audiobooks, seems to be ignored when we hear people bemoaning the death of reading. One wonders what the Methodist preachers in Thompson's nineteenth-century chapel would have made of audio-Bibles; we are sure they would have applauded them.

We imagine the movement always from adult to child as a form of autonomy, a giving of agency, as the child grasps the very notion that those squiggles on the page can be transmuted into language, and a language over which the child can have competence, replacing the adult. But there is no replacement for the succour that the adult provided for the child, who now has the agency to read, but in isolation, quietly to themself. For children, learning to read often feels like a veritable miracle. Alberto Manguel recounts what felt like a magical moment when he learned to read: 'Since I could turn bare lines into a living reality, I was all-powerful. I could read.'[1] Simultaneously children move from being 'read to' to reading by themselves.

Hence, literacy marks the beginning of at least some degree of freedom from parental control.[2]

Parents are strongly encouraged to read to their children from early on (in Finland, the so-called maternity box, given to each baby before its birth, includes a book in addition to clothing and diapers). Books inhabit the very earliest gifts to infants; some, like Jacqueline McQuade's *Touch the Bunny* or Eric Carle's *Very Hungry Caterpillar*, provide overt tactile training that includes the reading and looking, the listening and seeing. But books they are. Whether the claim of the firm Baby Einstein that their 'Quantum Physics for Babies' sharpens infant intellect, perhaps even when read to the foetus *in situ*, has any validity, books are ubiquitous in our age of hype. We are told that we live in the post-book era in which electronic media of all bytes is said to have nearly replaced the book. Indeed Baby Einstein sells videos of their books! Nevertheless, the exhortations to read to children are coupled with lists of its benefits: larger vocabulary, better concentration, the nurturing of cognitive abilities such as understanding of causality and metaphors, and quality time together.

This collection of essays focuses on childhood and adolescent reading as primary formative stages in a reader's life. It targets the contributors' personal histories and experiences as readers. As Marielle Macé puts it, literature seizes hold of us, kindling and touching our possibilities of being. Each of us has his or her own *reading history*, and that history still reverberates in us. This is the perspective that is missing from contemporary discussions on reading. We are convinced that promoting this idea will open fresh and rewarding perspectives to readers. This collection of essays focuses on memories of childhood and adolescent reading and their formative influence on us. The contributors reflect upon their memories of childhood reading and its impact on them as readers and writers.

In setting the scene for this collection of essays, we briefly consider the stages of reading and maturation.

Where it all starts: the reading aloud contract

Reading first takes place when someone reads stories aloud to children. Reading begins in someone's lap, in the crook of someone's arm or in cozily lying beside someone. As Maryanne Wolf nicely puts it, the child learns to associate being read to with a sense of being loved.[3] Meghan Cox Gurdon adds that the parental voice is important in neurological development. Babies hear the mother's voice in the womb and, once born, the language circuitry in their brains comes alive on hearing the parents speak.[4] At first, being read to centres on picture books, which may be textless. Picture books teach the child what Jane Doonan calls 'close looking'. It is training the eye to take in pictures and learning how pictures communicate meanings to us. Even if the child were not able to talk yet, its babblings, vocalizations and finger pointing make it an active partner in the language experience. Indeed, we can all 'touch the bunny'. Later the child moves on to illustrated books that combine pictures and text. This type of early reading lays the foundation for the development of what Wolf calls the brain's 'reading circuit'. It connects vision, language, cognition and emotions into interacting areas. The areas handling these functions overlap and are closely aligned and interdependent.[5] But even more so, the physical act of being held and touching in association with the book present a furtherance of the 'good-enough mother', the parent who is there and cares from the perspective of the infant habituating itself to the complex world beyond its immediate needs.

This description of the reading situation – the traditional mother reading to the young (genderless) child – was and is much more complex and contradictory in reality. Maria Tatar refers to the reading situation as building a 'contact zone' between adult and child: this zone houses both comfort and conflict.[6] Given that reading is seen to be in crisis, today we emphasize the comforts of this zone such as intimacy, time together, dialogue. Yet any parent recognizes the conflicts over choice of book, the endless moments of bedside reading to a restless child, the child's cranky boredom.

Yet the adult's succour in the contact zone is necessary, for no matter how scary the text and images children adapt and indeed revel in the combination of caring touch and frightening image and text. Think about Jacob and Wilhelm Grimm's *Kinder- und Hausmärchen* (1812–58), intended as a scholarly database that quickly transformed into stories for children, or Heinrich Hoffmann's *Struwwelpeter* (1845), where being read *to* and looking *with* reinforces socialization and autonomy. Certainly, the world of the bourgeoise children's books mirrored this development in the nineteenth century. Books for children begin with the invention of childhood (*pace* Philippe Ariès) in the early Enlightenment, with John Locke and the acknowledgement that (*pace* Erasmus) childhood education makes the civilized human being. For Locke reading was fundamental and it is in the late seventeenth century that books for children such as Charles Perrault's *Tales of Mother Goose* (1697) appear. Such texts were illustrated early on and by the nineteenth and early twentieth centuries publishers assumed that even sophisticated books 'for children', such as the novels of Robert Louis Stevenson and indeed the thousands of editions of 'Grimm's Fairy Tales', must be illustrated to sell well.

This is the interface between reading and being read to. This pre-literate moment is of key importance. We seem now to live in a world of passive reading; our culture since Homer has been one of passive listening. That is also the world of childhood. One perhaps now mirrored again by the pure pleasure, heightened because of the recent pandemic, derived from listening to podcasts and audiobooks. The audiobook, the podcast, places us in the twenty-first century in much the same position as Homer's listeners. With the same claims on the immediacy of the listening experience in our function as eager and passive listeners, attuned and anxious, like Scheherazade's bloodthirsty Shah, always for the next episode, we are infantilized and thus comforted. Gender, too plays a role, for parents are far from neutral players. The reading situation builds up various father-mother-daughter-son dyads. Who reads to whom, or the context in which one listens, is a determinant to no small degree of the pleasure obtained.

No better example of this as a theme in a text *for* children is to be found in Lewis Carroll's *Alice's Adventures in Wonderland* (1865), which begins with Alice attempting to read over her sister's shoulder, unhappy at not being read to and indeed distanced from the act of reading itself:

Alice was beginning to get very tired of sitting by her sister on the bank, and of having nothing to do: once or twice she had peeped into the book her sister was reading, but it had no pictures or conversations in it, 'and what is the use of a book,' thought Alice, 'without pictures or conversation?'[7]

The novel that we are reading, with its bountiful and now classic illustrations by John Tenniel, continues into a dream state, until Alice is awakened by the external world intruding on her reverie:

'Wake up, Alice dear!' said her sister. 'Why, what a long sleep you've had!'

'Oh, I've had such a curious dream!' said Alice, and she told her sister, as well as she could remember them, all these strange Adventures of hers that you have just been reading about; and when she had finished, her sister kissed her, and said, 'It *was* a curious dream, dear, certainly: but now run in to your tea; it's getting late.' So Alice got up and ran off, thinking while she ran, as well she might, what a wonderful dream it had been.[8]

But the caregiver, her sister, the surrogate mother, imagines her role as dreamer and then also as protector, a frame that does not make it into the Walt Disney film of 1951, which has very different visualizations. In a film, the narrative is primarily heard or seen. While the film provides a frame of dozing and waking, the notion of repletion from generation to generation of the act of reading and dreaming is abandoned.

But her sister sat still just as she left her, leaning her head on her hand, watching the setting sun, and thinking of

little Alice and all her wonderful Adventures, till she too
began dreaming after a fashion, and this was her dream:
First, she dreamed of little Alice herself . . . she could
hear the very tones of her voice, and see that queer little
toss of her head to keep back the wandering hair that
would always get into her eyes – and still as she listened, or
seemed to listen, the whole place around her became alive
with the strange creatures of her little sister's dream . . .
Lastly, she pictured to herself how this same little
sister of hers would, in the after-time, be herself a grown
woman; and how she would keep, through all her riper
years, the simple and loving heart of her childhood: and
how she would gather about her other little children, and
make *their* eyes bright and eager with many a strange tale,
perhaps even with the dream of Wonderland of long ago:
and how she would feel with all their simple sorrows, and
find a pleasure in all their simple joys, remembering her
own child-life, and the happy summer days.[9]

That in the end all adults in Carroll's world (and perhaps
also ours) *were* children, children who revelled in images and
texts and the solace of being read *to*, is embedded in Carroll's
admittedly quite saccharine Victorian dream in a dream of
little girls growing up and having children. Gender plays a huge
role in the patriarchal idea of reading aloud *to* another rather
than reading quietly to oneself, a rather modern convention of
reading. That Alice's dream journey takes place prompted by her
sister suggests that it may not have happened had she been the
presence of an adult. The sister's liberating position illustrates
Adam Gopnik's clever observation about the key difference

between adults and children in the contact zone of reading: 'in children's literature the grown-up wants a comforting image of childhood . . . the child wants a boat, a way out, an example of the life beyond. The parent wants to get back, the child wants to get out.'[10]

Remember how you were lectured early on not to move your lips when you 'read silently'. Interestingly that admonition, so often repeated when both editors were in school (a long time ago), has now vanished from modern pedagogy. Yet this transition remains a moment of repression when we are forced to move from 'hearing' (if virtually) to 'seeing' stories and is what Sigmund Freud refers to as 'considerations of representability'. Dreams too work in pictures – so the abstract and conflicted thoughts that might underlie the dream must be turned into a pictorial and concrete language before they can be used in a dream. Dreaming is indeed a form of reading, if, as is claimed, reading, at least silently, can be analogous to daydreaming.[11]

While at first adults largely choose the child's reading matter, the child's choices eventually begin to play a greater role. As looking, hearing and participating in reading is about learning how to assign meaning to pictures, sounds and representations, the question of the addressee is of key importance. To whom are children's books addressed? Zohar Shavit identifies a dual structure in many children's books that allows them to communicate simultaneously with both children and adults at their own levels.[12] These levels of reception imply a hierarchical organization in reading, emphasizing the adult's understanding. They are typical of the classics of children's books of which A. A. Milne's *Winnie-the-Pooh* books will here serve as an example. Milne's books thematize reading, writing and narrating in many ways. At the start of *Winnie-the-Pooh* Christopher Robin requests that the narrator 'very sweetly' recount a story about Pooh. The boy is referring to how sharing moments of reading and listening soothes and relaxes the reader and listener, creating a sense of togetherness. The story begins thus:

> Once upon a time, a very long time ago now, about last Friday, Winnie-the-Pooh lived in a forest all by himself under the name of Sanders.
> ('What does "under the name" mean?' asked Christopher Robin.
> 'It means he had the name over the door in gold letters and lived under it.'
> 'Winnie-the-Pooh wasn't quite sure,' said Christopher Robin.
> 'Now I am,' said a growly voice.
> 'Then I will go on,' said I.)[13]

This excerpt illustrates what we call *the reading aloud contract* by demonstrating one of its core features – interruption. Being read to includes the child listener's right, nay, even duty, to interrupt the reading and ask for clarifications, explanations and ponder on what has just been read. This right applies to adult readers as well, for they may want to pause to explain words, connections and give background information facilitating understanding. Often this includes linking the book to the child's own context. The back-and-forth of questions and comments shows that the parties are engaged in the reading. Reading aloud adds to and enriches children's vocabulary, improving their understanding of language. As the text has a picture of Pooh sitting in front of his house with the sign visibly over the door, the narrator's explanation is further concretized. The illustrations teach the child to link pictures with the text, further emphasizing the benefits of reading aloud. This shared attention is often confirmed by eye contact. The calming and stilling effect of reading aloud strengthens the sense of sharing and enjoying the other's presence.

In the frame narrative of *Winnie-the-Pooh*, the narrator introduces Christopher Robin, Pooh and Piglet. He plays with orthography, describing their trip to London Zoo as directed by the signs WAYIN and WAYOUT. When we are reading aloud, we may run the words together and speak them out loud. We notice that this play with language and orthography continues throughout the book. The adult's hierarchical position appears clearly in a similar scene in which the piece of broken board with the text 'TRESPASSERS W' is discussed. Piglet explains to Christopher Robin that the text refers to his grandfather, Trespassers Will(iam), while the adult links the board with an expanded meaning ('Trespassers will be prosecuted'), cherishing the humour and Piglet's clever explanation.

No one in the Hundred Acre Wood knows how to read and write fluently, although Owl and Rabbit let others understand that they do. They are not illiterate but, like most of the working-class population of Great Britain in the 1920s, semi-literate; they read the tabloids with their photographs, with their puns and elisions, not the broadsheets with their essays. E. H. Shepard's (and then Walt Disney's) images were and are an intrinsic part of the reading experience, with the misspelled and fragmentary words appearing in the images as well as in the texts. Christopher Robin's reading skills are only rudimentary, but his *looking* skills are highly developed. Everyone in the forest holds these abilities in high regard. Reading and writing are repeatedly thematized in the Pooh books. One day, Piglet notices that Pooh is tracking something in the snow. That something, perhaps a Woozle, has left paw-marks. Piglet joins his friend in the effort to catch the mysterious and potentially hostile creature. We are genetically wired for seeing and observing our surroundings. The ability to spot signs such as animal footprints and to assume a chain of events out of them – a Woozle walked this way – has been requisite for the survival of our species. The brain circuits necessary for combining sighted markings with meanings have been available to us since our earliest ancestors had to make sense of the book of Nature to survive. As the two friends continue tracking, it seems there is more than one creature on the move, and they count at least four sets of paws. Their activity echoes the practical needs of early humans, in that writing and reading partly developed from the economic desire to count phenomena (such as number of cattle) and record the results.[14] The friends' anxiety is put to rest with the arrival of Christopher Robin, who points out that they have been tracking their own footprints. The relieved Pooh admits that he has been 'foolish and deluded', for he is 'a Bear with no Brain at all'.[15] His head is filled with sawdust and it certainly does not help that Christopher Robin drags him up and down the stairs with Pooh's head bumping on each step!

Maryanne Wolf calls reading one of the single most remarkable inventions in human history.[16] The invention of writing has very different trajectories from the Mediterranean basin, with its invention of the alphabet, to the Valley of the Tigris and the Euphrates and cuneiform, to the world of the Han and the magical tortoise shells, to the hieroglyphs of the Maya. All writing systems are not interchangeable as visualization in each may be communicated through a myriad of different semiotic systems. Yet all are understood as the means when 'civilization' can transmit ideas (from simple bookkeeping to magic to literature) from distant place to distant place, from time present to time future. Reading, that is, deciphering a fixed code, is the necessary key to unlock the text. Wolf reminds us that this skill is not passed on by a genetic programme, as is, for example, sight. It is in this sense that reading is unnatural: each human being must learn to read 'from scratch'. Even though Pooh understands that a mark on the ground stands for something else, he has not fully recognized that sounds of spoken language may be represented by a finite group of individual letters. He cannot link the sounds he makes to a group of individual signs.

Wolf specifies that a brain that can learn to read needs three design characteristics. First, plasticity, which is the capacity to make new connections among old structures. This means that the brain can use, connect and integrate older structures from many systems with one another. It can simultaneously draw on and combine vision, audition, language, cognition and emotions – and it can do so automatically. Second, the capacity to form areas of exquisitely precise specialization for recognizing patterns of information; and third, the ability to learn to recruit and connect information from these areas automatically with great speed.[17] Reading depends on the brain's ability to connect and integrate various sources of information: visual, auditory, linguistic and conceptual areas.

The benefits of reading aloud are multiple and varied, and they range from physical, emotional, linguistic and cognitive effects to lifelong impressions. Reading aloud nourishes and cultivates the child's mind in many ways. In the first chapter of *Winnie-the-Pooh*, Pooh hears a buzzing noise and immediately reasons thus: 'If there's a buzzing-noise, somebody's making a buzzing-noise, and the only reason for making a buzzing-noise that *I* know of is because you're a bee.' His train of reasoning is crowned by a conclusion: 'And the only reason for making honey is so as *I* can eat it.'[18] Even a young child realizes that buzzes can issue forth from other animals or things than bees (such as a gardening tool); also, that bees do not produce honey exclusively for bears. The child notices faulty reasoning, self-centredness and greed in Pooh's thinking and actions. And it is no accident that the onomatopoeic 'bee' buzzing is also the act of associating sound with object in space, as when we learn to read phonetically and see the picture of the bee, the letter 'B' and then suddenly can sound out our first word and read it simultaneously: BEE.

For a child, the structure of narrative communication makes the Pooh books delightful. The narrator places the child almost on a par with Christopher Robin, whom he treats as a near equal – although the hierarchy between them remains – and by so doing privileges Christopher and the child as persons who see and understand much more than the toy animals. This advantage in knowledge and experience prompts the child to evaluate the animal characters' opinions, actions and interactions. Thus children learn to reason, to fill in missing information and to monitor and correct their possibly faulty inferences and expectations. For example, they can notice the ungrounded boasting of Owl and Rabbit as regards their reading and writing skills. Being read to teaches a child about language and literature and the registers and devices of literary language.

Further, it entices him or her to read between the lines, to spot what is not said, and to go beyond the text.

The House at Pooh Corner ends with Christopher Robin's departure from home and, although it is not directly stated, it marks the start of his education in a boarding school. He will learn to read and write properly and be inducted into the British upper-class way of life. The ending is strongly elegiac and nostalgic with a lingering sense of wistful sadness, for Christopher Robin is embarking on a new phase of life. This change is expressed as an adieu to the world of childhood:

> Sitting [in the only place in the Forest where you could sit down carelessly] they could see the whole world spread out until it reached the sky, and whatever there was all the world over was with them in Galleons Lap . . . So they went off together. But wherever they go, and whatever happens to them on the way, in that enchanted place on the top of the Forest, a little boy and his Bear will always be playing.[19]

The reading aloud contract includes characteristics that address primarily the adult reader. The hierarchy between adult and child is rarely undone. As we have seen, the structure of communication is at its core a structure of hierarchy and it affects the reading aloud contract by placing the adult in the position of the subject-supposed-to-know, with an advantage of knowledge and insight. Tatar calls the adult's monitoring of the child during reading the adult's 'bifocal vision'. The adult is reflecting on the text but also observing the child's reactions.[20] The reading aloud contract includes the expectation that whatever the child will ask about the reading, the adult can provide an answer. In cases of uncertainty or ignorance, the safe option is to turn the question around and query how the child understands the issue at question. This strategy enables developing a shared answer. For the adult, the contract involves estimations about the child: what kinds of explanations can the child receive and how much can the adult draw the child into verbal interactions. For example, *Winnie-the-Pooh* introduces a situation in which two strangers, Kanga and her baby Roo, enter the community and Rabbit objects to them, wanting to make them go away, because they are uncommon: 'We find a Strange Animal among us. An animal of whom we had never even heard before! An animal who carries her family about with her in her pocket!'[21] This scene invites the child and the adult to think about how to handle difference and, potentially, moves their discussion to wider issues. The first picture of the pair shows Roo to be even smaller than Piglet, which casts an ominous light on Rabbit's scheme.

Significantly, reading aloud also entices the adult reader to read between the lines, to spot what is not said, and to go beyond the text. The adult may wonder why A. A. Milne decided to portray community life and an individual's position in it through animals, or why animals were chosen to represent different personal dispositions, characteristics and emotions such as envy, self-centredness, rivalry and vulnerability. The adult may connect these choices with the Western cultural tradition of seeing children and emotions in terms of animality and primitivity. No better example is the trajectory from Winnie-the-Pooh, a child of the insouciant 1920s, to his most extraordinary cousins, Margret and H. A. Rey's *Curious George* (1941), as a response to the rise of fascism and the fall of France, through George Orwell's *Animal Farm* (1945) responding to the Stalinism of the 1930s and '40s, and then to the seemingly benign post-war universalism of the 1950s in E. B. White's *Charlotte's Web* of 1952. Alternatively, the adult may fasten on the nature of Milne's characters as toys, linking them to what Donald Winnicott called 'transitional objects'. They often are plushy toys that soothe and comfort a child during his or her gradual stages of growth. They are the safe 'other' whose presence makes separation from the mother tolerable. The child often talks to them. The interaction among the toys helps Christopher Robin to deal with his various emotions. The toys exist in the fiction, but, in our world of capitalism, they exist as transitional objects for sale beyond the text. Disneyfied dolls of Winnie the Pooh (without his hyphens), Eeyore and Tigger as well as Wilbur, from *Charlotte's Web*, are purchased with or after the book and provide an immediate transitional object, here between read experience and lived experience. Unsurprisingly, no dolls of Snowball or Napoleon (pig) from *Animal Farm* seem to have had any circulation, as we are reminded 'All animals are equal, but some animals are more equal than others.'

These examples illustrate that engaged reading aloud also provides the adult reader ample food for thought and reflection. Furthermore, reading aloud reverberates with the adult's earlier stages of reading, calling forth emotions and transporting them to previous reading experiences. To briefly return to the ending of *The House at Pooh Corner*, its description of the forest as an enchanted place is grounded in Milne's and our shared vision of childhood as the golden, blessed foundation of life. That Pooh promises never to forget Christopher Robin, even when the boy is a hundred years old, speaks of this nostalgic and idolized notion of childhood. There is no escaping from the fact that children's books reflect adults' understanding of children and childhood. Part and parcel of that reflection is the nostalgia the narrator expresses at the point of Christopher Robin's departure from the forest.

This nostalgia infuses the play with language and orthography. Although Pooh is illiterate, he turns out to be the only poet in his world who composes catchy ditties:

> I could spend a happy morning
> Seeing Roo,
> I could spend a happy morning
> Being Pooh.
> For it doesn't seem to matter,
> If I don't get any fatter
> (And I don't get any fatter),
> What I do.[22]

Pooh's poetry is of the moment. His ditties suggest a joyful receptivity to language and improvisatory capabilities. He simply feels a poem coming on to him. He is completely without the kinds of worries and inhibitions that typically characterize adult writing. The poems express a fantasy of carefree, easy access to creativity. No wonder the Pooh books have given rise to various life-skill books. Pooh is proud of his artistic gift, for his creative talent singles him out as special. This loving lingering and Pooh's ditties pay homage to the idea of childhood as involving flights of fantasy and imagination. It suggests that we may think of the childhood books we love the most as *transitional objects for life.* They frequently are the books we return to in adulthood, for example in moments of crisis. They continue to provide us consolation, reassurance and safety, making our ageing tolerable.

Readers change as they age

Learning to read liberates the child to make independent choices regarding reading matter. J. A. Appleyard subscribes to a developmental notion of reading, arguing that maturation brings on changes in reading. Therefore, he relies on various psychological accounts of development such as Jean Piaget's. His study is partly based on his interviews of sixty adults about their reading. The changes in reading are affected and shaped by many variables such as gender, educational opportunities, race, class status and communities. Appleyard, however, does not analyse their effects, but emphasizes that future research ought to focus on the effects of these variables of reading. Each Western literate person engages in various stages of reading and employs multiple acts of reading.[23] This developmental view of reading is based on two key assumptions. First, it is assumed that reading progresses along a regulated sequence, steered by cognitive maturation, cultural expectations, education and communal reading practices. Second, it is proposed that the later stages are qualitatively superior to the earlier ones.[24] Appleyard concedes that readers may move between stages, adapting their reading strategies to fit a book or a phase of life. A reader can always fall back on an earlier strategy of reading. What shapes the analysis further is Northrop Frye's *Anatomy of Criticism*, as Appleyard relates the main stages of reading to Frye's literary modes of romance, tragedy, irony and comedy.

Instead of analysing reading strategies, Appleyard identifies the roles readers take at various life stages. This choice stems from his transactional notion of reading, inspired by Louise Rosenblatt. For her, reading is both a cognitive and affective transaction between readers and a text. As active participants, readers come straight from life, bringing their cultural contexts to meet with those of the texts. Rosenblatt claims that readers 'must broaden the scope of attention to include the personal, affective aura and associations surrounding the words evoked and must focus on experience, live through the words, scenes, situations being created during the transaction'.[25] Appleyard concurs with Rosenblatt in emphasizing reading as combining cognitions and emotions: 'The underlying and real source of energy with which we experience literature is emotional, because [literature] really deals with the profound desires and fears we have for ourselves.'[26] Consequently, literature provides a *living through*, not just knowledge about, the issues treated. It is this *efferent reading* (from Latin *effere*, to carry away) that provides readers with means and modes for life and living.[27] The roles Appleyard assigns to various stages of reading are constructed to capture the primary benefit and psychodynamics of each stage. He maintains that readers go through five stages: young children as players, literate children as heroes or heroines, adolescents as thinkers, young adults as interpreters and mature adults as pragmatic readers.

The reader as player is the preschool children's role, one during which they mostly listen to reading. They gradually gain mastery of language as a means of expression and creativity. Also, they learn to recognize the constituents of narrative and various genres, and to distinguish literary language from other types of discourse. The main task of this stage addresses gaining confidence in learning to immerse oneself in fictional worlds, to navigate there and to organize and control fictional material. This ability builds on the adoption of the player's role. Children become adept at managing fantasy through symbolic play. When a stick can be a horse or a doll can be a child, they learn what objects may be substituted for what roles. And here even the tattiest dolls, the Winnie the Pooh from Disney World, can play a vital role. Child readers also master the ways in which representations work within the play's rules. Simultaneously, children become adept at distinguishing between fictional and pragmatic worlds. This skill includes the ability to occupy simultaneously the roles of participant and spectator. Readers as players immerse themselves in the worlds of fiction yet retain an awareness of make-believe.

Once children learn to read, reading acquires new functions. It is the primary means for gaining and organizing information about the world and finding out about how it works – or, at least, it used to be the primary means. Significantly, as readers they now have freedom to choose their reading matter. In books written for prepubescent children (ages seven to twelve) the role of illustrations lessens, the stories are longer, with lots of dialogue, the language is often uncomplicated and the action fast. Given that the narrative structures build on problems, journeys or dangers to be overcome, they suggest the possibility of a tragic ending, one of failure or even death. Therefore, not only are emotions deeply engaged but the awareness of the differences between literary worlds and actual life are strengthened. The role prepubescent children adopt while reading is that of the *hero or heroine*. This role is based on identification.

The typical literary mode at this stage is romance, 'because it is the simplest version of the fantasy of competence, a story about having one's wish to be successful come true because of the way one acts'.[28] Identification with the protagonist draws on idealization: the protagonists are what the children would want to be. Philip Pullman's *His Dark Materials* series provides rich opportunities for such identification, as readers of the original trilogy may side with either Lyra or Will, or, rather, both. They are brave, honest, persevering, resourceful and playful. They tackle insurmountable obstacles with brazen directness. They are our best selves. Appleyard argues, however, that at this stage of a person's development, playing the hero evokes the child's growing awareness of the restrictions that reality places on their fantasies. Thus the shift to the new role that maturation brings involves some nostalgic longing for the former self's ability to entertain an omnipotent fantasy of itself.[29] Tatar specifies that identification does not mean treating characters as second selves or living in their skins; rather, readers silently witness and observe them. Readers like certain characters and empathize with them because these characters have traits that the readers want to imitate or they have values that the readers also hold. Moreover, they enjoy having entry into the minds of characters they like.[30]

The role of hero or heroine has multiple benefits for children. Meeting various challenges together with the protagonist enables readers to practise their world-building skills and capacities of evaluating actions, behaviours and motives of characters. No one understood this better than C. S. Lewis. His evangelical texts proselytizing a more moderate and less comfortable Christianity in his writings (and successful BBC programmes) from the 1930s and '40s shaped *The Chronicles of Narnia* (1950–56) and its adventurous children in a world of sacrifice. Like *Winnie-the-Pooh* and *Charlotte's Web*, the Narnia books have been popularized on stage, TV, radio and cinema, maintaining Lewis's clearly Christian message in secular form. Evaluating motives builds up understanding of the psychology of characters. This helps readers to understand effective agency. The fast-paced events of Pullman's novels compel Lyra to assess her parents' actions and their designs for her. She must conclude that her parents' ideas of what is best for her may not coincide with her own estimation. For Appleyard, the most significant benefit at this stage is emotional. The literary structures deepen the treatment of themes, and it is emotional engagement that impresses them on the minds of readers. Pullman, like Lewis, relies heavily on Christian mythology in and for an overtly secular age and readership. Even if a young reader were not fully familiar with it, this mythology infuses our narrative patterns, images and modes of thinking, drawing the reader's attention to this author's adaptive riffing on it that makes it powerfully new.

The roles and strategies of reading change for adolescents for whom school provides an important site of reading. Given that they are in the process of creating and consolidating a sense of self, they effortlessly take up the role of *the reader as thinker*. This is the stage when adolescents mull over fundamental questions such as life's meaning, values, beliefs and ideals worthy of commitment. Given that the school system promotes reading as a primary strategy for accessing information and gaining knowledge, this role may overlap with the previous one. Robert Scholes identifies three types of response at this stage: identification, realism and thinking.

Although rapport with characters is familiar to the adolescent reader from earlier stages, it now acquires new dimensions. A central discovery in adolescence is the differentiation between an inner and an outer self: the former is one's unique personality while the latter is the social role one adopts. Pullman's introduction of daemons, animal-shaped manifestations of a human's soul, provides a delightful perspective to thinking about the self. Although the daemon Pantalaimon is integral to Lyra, he often is at odds with her. Lyra's discussions with him dramatize in an appealing way the processes and benefits of self-reflection. Identification fosters immersion in the book one reads to the point of diffusion of the subject-object divide. At this stage, however, readers tend to retain and even cherish the awareness of one's simultaneous division into a participant in the book's events and a spectator of them. This is what Rosenblatt calls the reader's own angle of refraction.[31] Appleyard maintains that rapport with characters is at its deepest whenever the reader retains awareness of being a spectator to them.[32] This double consciousness befits the adolescent's evolving self-reflexive capabilities.

As for the adolescent reader's valuation of realism, it is grounded in the growing awareness of life's realities. Now readers embrace tragedy as reflecting the possibility of quests ending in loss and catastrophe. It involves a growing awareness of life's possibilities and limits. These readers value characters, evaluating their resemblances and differences from fictional people. At this stage, readers are aware of the multilayered nature of meaning, but do not yet master developed skills of interpretation. In keeping with Rosenblatt's notion of efferent reading, Appleyard maintains that readers who engage emotionally with texts are better at appraising the actions, ideas and values texts promote. Unless readers have engaged with Lyra and Will's mutual respect, admiration and love for each other, they cannot understand the integrity and heroism with which they accept their lasting separation into different worlds. They agree to reunite in their separate worlds in a garden once a year on Midsummer's Day to celebrate their love for each other. Yet they know that it is possible for them to fall in love with someone else and get married. The crux of the matter is to be cheerful, for the treasure of their shared experiences and love will carry them through life. Emotional engagement helps readers to connect texts with their lives. Such connection cannot be achieved solely through an account of a reader's private response or the formal analysis of textual strategies – emotion ties reading to its psychic and social context, making it matter.

Once the young finish school there takes place a split among readers into two groups: one getting higher education, the other moving on from secondary or high school. Although this split has far-reaching consequences, Appleyard maintains that it is best to think of people having 'alternative routes to adult reading style'.[33] *The reader as interpreter* illustrates the interests of young adults who approach literature as a system of knowledge with its own conventions, rules and practices. One may say that at this stage even bookworms realize that they need to learn new skills of reading. This role involves acquiring sophisticated skills of interpretation as well as talking and writing about literature analytically. Readers as interpreters tend to make several key realizations as regards the texts they read. First, they exchange the notion of realism to an understanding of the text as an artefact. Second, they become aware of the multiplicity of meanings they can read off a text. Given that a text may support many values, and meanings, readers learn to adjust to this multiplicity. Finally, the learned techniques become internalized, and readers find literary designs pleasurable. At this stage readers would probe into Pullman's use of mythologies intertexts such as John Milton's *Paradise Lost* and C. S. Lewis's Narnia books, if they had not read or watched the latter already. Indeed, we can imagine individuals who may well start with complex texts, such as Bible stories, before reading Pullman and Lewis as the reinforcement of such earlier childhood reading. They would be interested in probing the use to which Pullman puts all these various building blocks of his trilogy and the meanings they together create.

The last stage Appleyard identifies is that of *the pragmatic reader*. It includes the greatest amount of freedom, as readers freely choose among the strategies they have learned. They may fit these tactics according to the purposes and goals of their reading. They may wish to savour the aesthetics of a text, to learn new things, to find comfort and wisdom, or simply to escape. Adult readers make conscious and pragmatic choices about the kinds of purposes and goals their reading serves.

Although Appleyard emphasizes the role context and gender play, he nowhere considers them in detail. Consequently, all readers are curious blank slates. Also, it does not seem plausible that readers start interpreting what they read as late as in their teens and early adolescence. The essays in this book counter that argument. Adrienne Kertzer objects to Appleyard's disregard of the role that education plays in reading. For her, different responses to literature rely on readers' choices of different theoretical models.[34] However, what escapes Kertzer is Appleyard's deliberate refusal to accord higher education a key role in assessing the significance of reading for adults. His aim is to provide a general view of how reading benefits us. The uniting theme in his study is the primary role emotions play in reading: if a reader engages only cognitively, but not emotionally, reading will not stick. If reading is to have significance, it must touch readers in ways that they can connect with and transport to their internal and external lives. This means learning to read for life.

What makes reading stick?

When we think of the theoretical models taught at levels of higher education, the primary approach is often *close reading*, examining closely the language and form of a literary work or a section of it. In characterizing its significance, Jonathan Culler remarks that it 'has been something we take for granted, as a *sine qua non* of literary study, a skill that we expect our students to master and that we certainly expect of job candidates, whatever other sorts of critical activities they may flamboyantly display.'[35] As a reading practice, close reading draws on what Paul Ricoeur calls the 'hermeneutics of suspicion'.[36] This stance regards all phenomena that may be treated as texts with wariness, because it holds that beyond the surface lie causal forces that explain the overt and conscious phenomena. Hence, the true meaning of these phenomena lays beneath them. This strategy of reading is familiar from Freudian psychoanalysis that interprets slips of the tongue, physical symptoms and dreams as expressing the subject's repressed desires and wishes. Identifying them provides the subject with deeper self-knowledge, possibly freeing him or her to act in accordance with his or her needs. Yet Freud also acknowledges the power of lived experience, of the quotidian, of what he calls early on 'day residue' in shaping our imaginative lives. We dream in images; those images are clothed in the world of vision, of the pictures in children's books, accompanied by the voice of the parent and the closeness of the experience, or conversely the distance and harshness that can also be attributed to these moments, in acknowledging that our mental lives are not separate from but clothed in our daily lives.

Given that literary texts are replete with gaps, omissions and inconsistencies, close reading has for long been infused with a strategy that looks for that which texts do not say. Textual inconsistencies and gaps serve as symptoms of that which is not – or cannot – be said in a text. According to this symptomatic tactic nothing in a text is as it seems to be, and everything may be highly significant. For example, when Pooh asks Christopher Robin how Kanga and Roo came to the forest, the boy answers, 'In the Usual Way, if you know what I mean.'[37] Pooh has no clue but acts as if he does. Reading closely, we may link this enigmatic answer either with Kanga and Roo being gifts to Christopher or as an indirect admission of their status as of non-British origin, 'strangers' in the sense of immigrants from elsewhere in the Empire, as nationality is a layer of implied meaning in the Pooh books. Close reading infused with the hermeneutics of suspicion has been typical of various practices of ideological critique, such as Marxist, post-colonial and feminist approaches, interested in unravelling the ways in which textual discourse intersects with various ideologies. And yet each unravelling is simultaneously an obfuscation, as all reading is individual not collective, is collective and not individual – is always in the interstices of that contradiction.

Useful and indispensable as close reading strategies are, they have lately come under criticism. Rita Felski points out that academic reading practices are infused with negative emotions, as texts are diagnosed and criticized for faults and shortcomings.[38] This is a misplaced approach, as the majority read for leisure and pleasure. Shoshana Felman asks, 'Does not reading involve one risk that, precisely, cannot be risked: that of finding in the text something that one does not expect? The danger with becoming a resistant reader is that we end up, in effect, resisting reading.'[39] What, then, would be reading tactics that make reading take hold in a reader's mind and life?

In *Uses of Literature* Felski writes passionately about alternative ways of engaging with literature. Her aim is to foster a dialogical and listening stance in reading. She holds that readers' engagements with texts are varied and complex. She maintains that we read to reflect on who and what we are. She identifies four goals shaping much reading: enchantment, recognition, knowledge and shock.[40]

Emma Bovary and Don Quixote, but never mind Tristram Shandy, are regarded as failed readers, for all throw themselves into fictional fantasies, identifying with fictional characters to the point of confusion. Unable to distinguish fact from fantasy, these characters cannot sustain the double consciousness characterizing reading. When we find ourselves immersed in reading, we cannot keep distance, for we surrender to the text and experience vivid sensations. Enchantment blurs the distinction between reader and text. We enjoy being drawn into experiences, situations and emotions greater than ourselves. This reaction may also be evoked by style, sound and language. Felski maintains that the capability of being enchanted encourages an open and generous attitude to the world. Although on finishing a ravishing book the return to daily life may feel dreary, readers do not lose the awareness of being engaged with an 'imaginary spectacle'.

Reading has for long been the primary means of gaining knowledge. This goal persists in adulthood: we read to learn things, to get in contact with things we would never have access to in any other way. For example, partly based on real-life experiments, Karen Joy Fowler's *We Are All Completely Beside Ourselves* lets readers get in touch with what it is to grow up with chimpanzees, while an experiment based on the imagination, Hugo Hamilton's *The Pages*, narrated by a novel, shows us how this book experiences its life in being carried around in bags, in changing hands, in being lost and misplaced.

What is of special interest is the access to fictional minds and bodies, ways of thinking, feeling and being in the world. This is a way of expanding, enlarging and deepening our sense of how things are. An important motive is to gain a deeper sense of everyday life and the forms of social life. This stance does not treat literature as a true-to-life window to the world but remains aware of the verbal and textual medium. In fact, it regards genres as forms of knowing, heavily influenced by narrative structures, styles and thematic concerns.

Many of us read in order to gain knowledge. A crucial component in reading for knowledge is the experience of being connected with what one reads in the sense of recognizing oneself in the book: in its characters, settings, themes discussed, ways of being in the world. The text addresses us in ways that are familiar, yet simultaneously fresh and revised for us. Felski explains that we recognize something we already know, but in a new fashion. For some readers, literature may be the only medium that treats their worlds, situations and ways of being in the world. Recognition acquires the sense of acknowledgement, as reading confirms that the reader is not alone. There are others who think, feel and experience in the same way as he or she does. Such self-intensification provides solace and encouragement. Thus reading may serve as a lifeline for those without other forms of public acknowledgement.

A further facet of recognition is that it invites readers to explore what it means to be a person. In seeing ourselves in a character, we are aware of dissimilarity, for we perceive ourselves in another light. Given that modern societies prize self-fashioning and self-reflection, reading provides readers models for self-scrutiny. It may cause us to be aware of failures of self-scrutiny by, for example, making us aware of our shortcomings and prejudices. Consequently, it provides understanding, insight and self-knowledge. Elaine Castillo reminds us that there still are what she calls unexpected readers whom an author could not imagine, or who are unimaginable. That is, the envisioned audience (the so-called authorial audience) does not provide any foothold of complicity or address for such a reader. There are readers whose life conditions and experiences lie beyond anything that has been written so far. They are still waiting for books in which they can recognize themselves.[41]

We may crave thrilling rides for the duration of reading; they break the monotony of daily life. We may crave to be shocked, shaken and shattered by reading about intensely exciting or excruciatingly cruel events and deeds. The art of violence and violation bespeaks a wish to experience transgression, disturbance and disgust. Yet there are real differences in how such experiences are staged. Readers who are addicted to detective fiction may love the hardboiled texts of Raymond Chandler and Walter Mosley, while those who revel in cosy mysteries are horrified by those darker, more cynical texts and retreat into the worlds of Agatha Christie and Richard Osman instead. Children raised on the violence and horror (yes, they are there) of 'Grimm's Fairy Tales' can move in either direction as the creative act of imagining the world is individual, not collective.

Finally, it is worth noticing that reading may work on us directly, without filters as it were. Frederick Clarke Prescott observed that 'the mind can receive the truth of the poem without interpretation, imaginatively and unconsciously . . . the thought need nowhere to be formulated; the fable is instructive without the moral; and the parables of Christ were edifying even though they were not rationally comprehended.'[42] Mystical as this may sound, Simon O. Lesser emphasizes that reading invariably takes place at two levels at least: 'it says one thing to the conscious mind, and whispers something quite different to the unconscious.'[43] Scholars such as Lesser and Norman Holland demonstrate that we can try to unravel that which we unconsciously receive with the help of psychoanalytic theories, for example. What they emphasize is that the result does not simplify the reading, because each individual's psyche is unique. This idea is taken up here because reading does entail magic and wonder that we never can fully explain. Reading activates things below our awareness. What we read reverberates in us not only during reading, but afterwards, giving us what Maryanne Wolf calls its most precious gift – time to think.[44]

The idea for this collection started from our shared understanding that all literate persons have their own reading histories. Some are long and thick, others short and thin, but no matter what kind they are, they define us as persons. This idea seemed worth probing into. What delighted us was the positive character of this idea and we felt that, amid all the worry about reading and its fate, there should be happy and attractive perspectives to talking about reading. Indeed, whenever we mentioned this project to anyone, the person started reminiscing, coming up with multiple memories of books read, moments shared, feelings and experiences stored in memory and body. We felt that something deeply personal had been ignited in our interlocuters, and it reverberates in them even in adulthood. We also noticed that nostalgia does not explain their reactions. These reactions appear to mirror what Daniel Schwarz says about reading: 'it calls upon us to respond fully, with every dimension of our being.'[45] We are convinced that promoting this idea of a personal reading history will open up fresh and rewarding perspectives to readers and reading. Encouragingly, some contributors started really reading later than early childhood and, nevertheless, found in literature and reading, and in writing, their calling.

We asked authors and academics to share their early reading experiences in essays for this collection. We gave them freedom to decide for themselves how to approach and convey their experiences. The essays provide insight into the kinds of possibilities, directions and styles of being that reading has opened up for these writers. Inspired by Macé's views, we hold that reading provides mental, social and tangibly practical means and styles for life. We hope that this volume will promote reading for personal reasons, pleasures and joy!

1

Ask Yourself Which Are the Books You Truly Love

SALMAN RUSHDIE

Before there were books, there were stories. At first the stories weren't written down. Sometimes they were even sung. Children were born, and before they could speak, their parents sang them songs, a song about an egg that fell off a wall, perhaps, or about a boy and a girl who went up a hill and fell down it. As the children grew older, they asked for stories almost as often as they asked for food.

The children fell in love with these stories and wanted to hear them over and over again. Then they grew older and found those stories in books. And other stories that they had never heard before, about a girl who fell down a rabbit hole, or a silly old bear and an easily scared piglet and a gloomy donkey, or a phantom tollbooth, or a place where wild things were. The act of falling in love with stories awakened something in the children that would nourish them all their lives: their imagination.

The children made up play stories every day, they stormed castles and conquered nations and sailed the oceans blue, and at night their dreams were full of dragons. But they went on growing up and slowly the stories fell away from them, the stories were packed away in boxes in the attic, and it became harder for the former children to tell and receive stories, harder for them, sadly, to fall in love.

I believe that the books and stories we fall in love with make us who we are, or, not to claim too much, the beloved tale becomes a part of the way in which we understand things and make judgements and choices in our daily lives. A book may cease to speak to us as we grow older, and our feeling for it will fade. Or we may suddenly, as our lives shape and hopefully increase our understanding, be able to appreciate a book we dismissed earlier; we may suddenly be able to hear its music, to be enraptured by its song.

When, as a college student, I first read Günter Grass's great novel *The Tin Drum*, I was unable to finish it. It languished on a shelf for fully ten years before I gave it a second chance, whereupon it became one of my favourite novels of all time: one of the books I would say that I love. It is an interesting question to ask oneself: which are the books that you truly love? Try it. The answer will tell you a lot about who you presently are.

I grew up in Bombay, India, a city that is no longer, today, at all like the city it once was and has even changed its name to the much less euphonious Mumbai, in a time so unlike the present that it feels impossibly remote, even fantastic. In that far-off Bombay, the stories and books that reached me from the West seemed like true tales of wonder.

Hans Christian Andersen's 'The Snow Queen', with its splinters of magic mirror that entered people's bloodstreams and turned their hearts to ice, was even more terrifying to a boy from the tropics, where the only ice was in the refrigerator. 'The Emperor's New Clothes' felt especially enjoyable to a boy growing up in the immediate aftermath of the British Empire.

Perhaps tales of elsewhere always feel like fairy tales. But for me, the real wonder tales were closer to home, and I have always thought it my great good fortune as a writer to have grown up steeped in them.

Some of these stories were sacred in origin, but because I grew up in a non-religious household, I was able to receive them simply as beautiful stories. When I first heard the tale in the great epic *Mahabharata* about how the great god Indra churned the Milky Way, using the fabled Mount Mandara as his churning stick, to force the giant ocean of milk in the sky to give up its nectar, 'amrita', the nectar of immortality, I began to see the stars in a new way.

In that impossibly ancient time, my childhood, a time before light pollution made most of the stars invisible to city dwellers, a boy in a garden in Bombay could still look up at the night sky and hear the music of the spheres and see with humble joy the thick stripe of the galaxy there. I imagined it dripping with magic nectar. Maybe if I opened my mouth, a drop might fall in and then I would be immortal, too.

This is the beauty of the wonder tale and its descendant, fiction: that one can simultaneously know that the story is a work of imagination, which is to say *untrue*, and believe it to contain profound truth. The boundary between the magical and the real, at such moments, ceases to exist.

We were not Hindus, my family, but we believed the great stories of Hinduism to be available to us also. On the day of the annual Ganpati festival, when huge crowds carried effigies of the elephant-headed deity Ganesh to the water's edge at Chowpatty Beach to immerse the god in the sea, Ganesh felt as if he belonged to me too; he felt like a symbol of the collective joy and, yes, unity of the city rather than a member of the pantheon of a 'rival' faith.

When I learned that Ganesh's love of literature was so great that he sat at the feet of India's Homer, the sage Vyasa, and became the scribe who wrote down the *Mahabharata*, he belonged to me even more deeply; and when I grew up and wrote a novel about a boy called Saleem with an unusually big nose, it seemed natural, even though Saleem came from a Muslim family, to associate the narrator of *Midnight's Children* with the most literary of gods, who just happened to have a big trunk of a nose as well. The blurring of boundaries between religious cultures in that old, truly secularist Bombay now feels like one more thing that divides the past from India's bitter, stifled, censorious, sectarian present.

It has to be admitted that the influence of these tales is not always positive. The sectarian politics of the Hindu nationalist parties like India's ruling Bharatiya Janata Party uses the rhetoric of the past to fantasize about a return to 'Ram Rajya', the 'reign of Lord Ram', a supposed golden age of Hinduism without such inconveniences as members of other religions to complicate matters. The politicization of the epic *Ramayana*, and of Hinduism in general, has become, in the hands of unscrupulous sectarian leaders, a dangerous affair.

———

I want to return, however, to that childhood self, enchanted by tales whose express and sole purpose was enchantment. I want to move away from the grand religious epics to the great hoard of scurrilous, conniving, mysterious, exciting, comic, bizarre, surreal and very often extremely sexy narratives contained in the rest of the Eastern storehouse, because – not only because, but, yes, because – they show how much pleasure is to be gained from literature once God is removed from the picture.

One of the most remarkable characteristics of the stories now gathered in the pages of *The Thousand Nights and One Night*, to take just one example, is the almost complete absence of religion. Lots of sex, much mischief, a great deal of deviousness; monsters, jinn, giant Rocs; at times, enormous quantities of blood and gore; but no God. This is why censorious Islamists dislike it so much.

In Egypt, in May 2010, just seven months before the revolt against President Hosni Mubarak, a group of Islamist lawyers got wind of a new edition of *Alf Laylah wa Laylah* (the book's original Arabic title) and brought an action demanding that the edition be withdrawn and the book banned because it was 'a call to vice and sin' that contained several references to sex. Fortunately, they did not succeed, and then larger matters began to preoccupy Egyptian minds. But the fact is, they had a point.

There are indeed in that book several references to sex, and the characters seem much more preoccupied with having sex than being devout, which could indeed be, as the lawyers argued, a call to vice, if that's the deformed, puritanical way you see the world. To my mind, this call is an excellent thing and well worth responding to, but you can see how people who dislike music, jokes and pleasure would be upset by it. It is rather wonderful that this ancient text, this wonderful group of wonder tales, retains the power to upset the world's fanatics more than 1,200 years after the stories first came into the world.

The book that we now usually call *The Arabian Nights* didn't originate in the Arab world. Its probable origin is Indian; Indian story compendiums too have a fondness for frame stories, for Russian doll-style stories within stories, and for animal fables. Somewhere around the eighth century, these stories found their way into Persian, and according to surviving scraps of information, the collection was known as 'Hazar Afsaneh', 'a thousand stories'.

There's a tenth-century document from Baghdad that describes the 'Hazar Afsaneh' and mentions its frame story, about a wicked king who kills a concubine every night until one of these doomed wives manages to stave off her execution by telling him stories. This is where we first see the name 'Scheherazade'. Sadly, of the 'Hazar Afsaneh' itself not a single copy survives. This book is the great 'missing link' of world literature, the fabled volume through which the wonder tales of India travelled west to encounter, eventually, the Arabic language and to turn into *The Thousand Nights and One Night*, a book with many versions and no agreed canonical form, and then to move farther west, first into French, in the eighteenth-century version by Antoine Galland, who added a number of stories not included in the Arabic, such as the tales of 'Aladdin and the Wonderful Lamp' and 'Ali Baba and the Forty Thieves'.

And from French the stories made it into English, and from English they journeyed to Hollywood, which is a language of its own, and then it's all flying carpets and Robin Williams as the genie. (It's worth noting, by the way, that there are no flying carpets in *The Arabian Nights*. There is a legend that King Solomon possessed one that could change its size and become big enough to transport an army.)

This great migration of narrative has inspired much of the world's literature, all the way down to the magic realism of the

South American fabulists, so that when I, in my turn, used some of those devices, I had the feeling of closing a circle and bringing that story tradition all the way back home to the country in which it began. But I mourn the loss of the 'Hazar Afsaneh', which would, if rediscovered, complete the story of the stories, and what a find that would be.

Perhaps it would solve a mystery at the heart of the frame story, or rather at the very end of it, and answer a question I've been asking myself for some years: did Scheherazade and her sister, Dunyazad, finally, after one thousand nights and one night and more, become murderers and kill their bloodthirsty husbands?

How many women did Shahryar, monarch of 'the island or peninsula of India and China', and his brother Shah Zaman, sovereign ruler over barbarian Samarkand, actually kill? It began when Shah Zaman found his wife in the arms of a palace cook. Shah Zaman chopped them into several pieces and headed for his brother's home, where he found his sister-in-law, Shahryar's queen, in a garden in the company of ten ladies-in-waiting and ten slaves. The ten and ten were busy gratifying one another; the queen summoned her own lover down from a tree.

Ah, the malice and treachery of womankind! Shah Zaman told his brother what he had seen, whereupon the ladies-in-waiting, the slaves and the queen all met their fates. (The lover of Shahryar's late queen seems to have escaped.)

King Shahryar and King Shah Zaman duly took their revenge on faithless womankind. For three years, they each married, deflowered and then ordered the execution of a fresh virgin every night. Scheherazade's father, Shahryar's vizier, or prime minister, was obliged to carry out Shahryar's executions himself.

This vizier was a cultured gentleman, a man of delicate sensibilities – he must have been, must he not, to have raised such a paragon of a daughter as Scheherazade? And her sister, Dunyazad, too, another good, smart, decent girl.

What would it do to the soul of the father of such fine girls to be forced to execute young women by the hundreds, to slit girls' throats and see their lifeblood flow? We are not told. We do know, however, that Shahryar's subjects began to resent him mightily and to flee his capital city with their womenfolk, so that after three years there were no virgins to be found in town. No virgins except Scheherazade and Dunyazad.

By the time Scheherazade entered the story, marrying King Shahryar and ordering her sister, Dunyazad, to sit at the foot of the marital bed and to ask, after Scheherazade's deflowering was complete, to be told a story, Shahryar and Shah Zaman were already responsible for 2,213 deaths. Only eleven of the dead were men.

Shahryar, upon marrying Scheherazade and being captivated by her tales, stopped killing women. Shah Zaman, untamed by literature, went right on with his vengeful work. One thousand and one nights later, the death toll stood at 3,214.

Consider Scheherazade, whose name meant 'city-born' and who was without a doubt a big-city girl, crafty, wisecracking, by turns sentimental and cynical, as contemporary a metropolitan narrator as one could wish to meet. Scheherazade, who snared the prince in her never-ending story. Scheherazade, telling stories to save her life, setting fiction against death, a Statue of Liberty built not of metal but of words.

Scheherazade, who insisted, against her father's will, on taking her place in the procession into the king's deadly boudoir.

Scheherazade, who set herself the heroic task of saving her sisters by taming the king. Who had faith, who must have had faith, in the man beneath the murderous monster and in her own ability to restore him to his true humanity, by telling him stories.

What a woman! It's easy to understand how and why King Shahryar fell in love with her. For certainly he did fall, becoming the father of her children and understanding, as the nights progressed, that his threat of execution had become empty, that he could no longer ask his vizier, her father, to carry it out. His savagery was blunted by the genius of the woman who, for a thousand nights and one night, risked her life to save the lives of others, who trusted her imagination to stand against brutality and overcome it not by force but, amazingly, by civilizing it.

Lucky king! But (this is the greatest unanswered question of *The Arabian Nights*) why on earth did she fall in love with him? And why did Dunyazad, the younger sister who sat at the foot of the marital bed for one thousand nights and one night, watching her sister being fucked by the murderous king and listening to her stories – Dunyazad, the eternal listener, but also voyeur – why did she agree to marry Shah Zaman, a man even deeper in blood than his story-charmed brother?

How can we understand these women? There is a silence in the tale that cries out to be spoken of. This much we are told: after the stories were over, Shah Zaman and Dunyazad were married, but Scheherazade made one condition – that Shah Zaman leave his kingdom and come to live with his brother, so that the sisters might not be parted. This Shah Zaman gladly did, and Shahryar appointed to rule over Samarkand in his brother's stead that same vizier who was now also his father-in-law. When the vizier arrived in Samarkand, he was greeted by the townspeople very joyfully, and all the local grandees prayed that he might reign over them for a long time. Which he did.

My question is this, as I interrogate the ancient story: was there a conspiracy between the daughter and the father? Is it possible that Scheherazade and the vizier had hatched a secret plan? For, thanks to Scheherazade's strategy, Shah Zaman was no longer king in Samarkand. Thanks to Scheherazade's strategy, her father was no longer a courtier and unwilling executioner but a king in his own right, a well-beloved king, what was more, a wise man, a man of peace, succeeding a bloody ogre. And then, without explanation, Death came, simultaneously, for Shahryar and Shah Zaman. Death, the 'Destroyer of Delights and the Severer of Societies, the Desolator of Dwelling Places and the Garnerer of Graveyards', came for them, and their palaces lay in ruins, and they were replaced by a wise ruler, whose name we are not told.

But how and why did the Destroyer of Delights arrive? How was it that both brothers died simultaneously, as the text clearly implies, and why did their palaces afterward lie in ruins? And who was their successor, the Unnamed and Wise?

We are not told. But imagine, once again, the vizier filling up with fury for many years as he was forced to spill all that innocent blood. Imagine the years of the vizier's fear, the one thousand and one nights of fear, while his daughters, flesh of his flesh, blood of his blood, were hidden in Shahryar's bedroom, their fate hanging by a story's thread.

How long will a man wait for his revenge? Will he wait longer than one thousand nights and one night? This is my theory: that the vizier, now ruler of Samarkand, was the wise king who came home to rule Shahryar's kingdom. And the kings died simultaneously either at their wives' hands or at the vizier's. It's just a theory. Maybe the answer lies in the great lost book. Maybe it doesn't. We can only . . . wonder.

At any rate, the final count of the dead was 3,216. Thirteen of the dead were men.

———

The stories that made me fall in love with literature in the first place were tales full of beautiful impossibility, which were not true but by being not true told the truth, often more beautifully and memorably than stories that relied on being true. Those stories didn't have to happen once upon a time either. They could happen right now. Yesterday, today or the day after tomorrow.

Animal fables, including talking-dead-fish fables, have been among the most enduring tales in the Eastern canon, and the best of them, unlike, say, the fables of Aesop, are amoral. They don't seek to preach about humility or modesty or moderation or honesty or abstinence. They do not guarantee the triumph of virtue. As a result, they seem remarkably modern. The bad guys sometimes win.

The ancient collection known in India as the *Panchatantra* features a pair of talking jackals: Karataka, the good or better guy of the two, and Damanaka, the wicked schemer. At the book's outset they are in the service of the lion king, but Damanaka doesn't like the lion's friendship with another courtier, a bull, and tricks the lion into believing the bull to be an enemy. The lion murders the innocent animal while the jackals watch.

Many of Aesop's little morality tales about the victory of dogged slowness (the tortoise) over arrogant speed (the hare), or the foolishness of crying 'wolf' when there is no wolf, or of killing the goose that laid the golden eggs, seem positively soppy when compared to this Quentin Tarantino-like savagery. So much for the cliché of the peaceful, mystical East.

As a migrant myself, I have always been fascinated by the migration of stories, and these jackal tales travelled almost as far as the 'Arabian Nights' narratives, ending up in both Arabic and Persian versions, in which the jackals' names have mutated into Kalila and Dimna. They also ended up in Hebrew and Latin and, eventually, as 'The Fables of Bidpai', in English and French. Unlike the 'Arabian Nights' stories, however, they have faded from modern readers' consciousness, perhaps because their insufficient attention to happy endings made them unattractive to the Walt Disney Company.

Yet their power endures; and it does so, I believe, because for all their cargo of monsters and magic, these stories are entirely truthful about human nature (even when in the form of anthropomorphic animals). All human life is here, brave and cowardly, honourable and dishonourable, straight-talking and conniving, and the stories ask the greatest and most enduring question of literature: how do ordinary people respond to the arrival in their lives of the extraordinary? And they answer: sometimes we don't do so well, but at other times we find resources within ourselves we did not know we possessed, and so we rise to the challenge, we overcome the monster; Beowulf kills Grendel and Grendel's more fearsome mother as well, Red Riding Hood kills the wolf, and Beauty finds the love within the beast and then he is beastly no more. And that is ordinary magic, human magic, the true wonder of the wonder tale.

The wonder tales taught me that approaches to storytelling were manifold, almost infinite in their possibilities, and that they were fun. The fantastic has been a way of adding dimensions to the real, adding fourth, fifth, sixth and seventh dimensions to the usual three; a way of enriching and intensifying our experience of the real, rather than escaping from it into superhero-vampire fantasyland.

Only by unleashing the fictionality of fiction, the imaginativeness of the imagination, the dream songs of our dreams, can we hope to approach the new, and to create fiction that may, once again, be more interesting than the facts.

The fantastic is neither innocent nor escapist. The wonderland is not a place of refuge, not even necessarily an attractive or likeable place. It can be – in fact, it usually is – a place of slaughter, exploitation, cruelty and fear. Captain Hook wants to kill Peter Pan. The witch in the Black Forest wants to cook Hansel and Gretel. The wolf actually eats Red Riding Hood's grandmother. Albus Dumbledore is murdered, and the Lord of the Rings plans the enslavement of the whole of Middle-earth.

We know, when we hear these tales, that even though they are 'unreal', because carpets do not fly and witches in gingerbread houses do not exist, they are also 'real', because they are about real things: love, hatred, fear, power, bravery, cowardice, death. They simply arrive at the real by a different route. They are so, even though we know that they are not so. The truth is not arrived at by purely mimetic means. An image can be captured by a camera or by a paintbrush. A painting of a starry night is no less truthful than a photograph of one; arguably, if the painter is Van Gogh, it's far more truthful, even though far less 'realistic'.

The literature of the fantastic – the wonder tale, the fable, the folk tale, the magic-realist novel – has always embodied profound truths about human beings, their finest attributes and their deepest prejudices too. The wonder tale tells us truths about ourselves that are often unpalatable; it exposes bigotry, explores the libido, brings our deepest fears to light. Such stories are by no means intended simply for the amusement of children, and many of them were not originally intended for children at all. Sinbad the Sailor and Aladdin were not Disney characters when they started out on their journeys.

It is, however, a rich age in literature for children and young-hearted adults. From Maurice Sendak's place where the Wild Things are to Philip Pullman's post-religious otherworlds, from Narnia, which we reach through a wardrobe, to the strange worlds arrived at through a phantom tollbooth, from Hogwarts to Middle-earth, wonderland is alive and well. And in many of these adventures, it is children who grow into heroes, often to rescue the adult world; the children we were, the children who are still within us, the children who understand wonderland, who know the truth about stories, save the adults, who have forgotten those truths.

2

Portable Magic

MARIA TATAR

As a child, I read to ward off loneliness, finding in the public library a private, enchanted corner where I could marvel at the sly feats of Tom Sawyer, rejoice in the antics of Pippi Longstocking and weep with the Little Mermaid. I remember once being busted by a librarian who caught me in the library's main building (at that time, for adults only), a stack of books by my side. Knowing that I had not yet reached the age of biblio-emancipation, she challenged me to pronounce the name of the volume I was holding, and quickly – and defiantly – I responded by saying, 'Dan-ish (to rhyme with "vanish") Fairy Tales'.

My parents had immigrated to the United States in 1952, and we settled in an affluent suburb in Highland Park, Illinois. At the age of six I had a laminated card identifying me as a 'resident alien' and as a 'displaced person' who was required to report any change of address to the Immigration and Naturalization Service or risk deportation. 'Deportation' – that word still sends a chill up my spine today even if at the time there was really no risk of that happening. Books were my comfort, a reminder that the consolations of imagination are not imaginary consolations.

Later in life, I fled, through books, what felt to me like the stultifying dullness of suburbia to a place where I could find friends more exciting than the amiable ones I had made at school. As Jhumpa Lahiri has put it, books 'let you travel without moving your feet'. Nancy Drew, Jane Eyre and Scout kept me company and became my companions, shaping my identity in ways more powerful than people in real life ever could. Later I read for education and enlightenment, admittedly at times to become an 'intellectual', as I moved from the Middle West to the ivy halls of the East Coast. And now the treasures that line the bookshelves in my house feel like portals to somewhere over the rainbow, talismanic objects that can whisk me away, at a moment's notice, to the Congo with Marlow, to London with Sherlock Holmes, or to Kerala with Rahel and Esthappen. During the global pandemic they took me from the here and now into safety zones, places that had nothing to do with constructing identity or acquiring knowledge but had everything to do with losing myself in the beauty of a good story. Escapist? Not at all. They opened an escape hatch into Elsewhere from which I returned armed with strategies for navigating the very real anxieties and perils of the ordinary world.

'Books are not absolutely dead things but do contain a potency of life in them,' John Milton wrote in *Areopagitica* (1644), a tract opposing censorship. They may not contain the kind of wizardry found at a place like Middle-earth, Wonderland or Narnia, but they preserve the distilled genius of their authors and can work a kind of magic. Portable magic, as Stephen King tells us. Some months ago I was asked to write about five books that had shaped my identity. I expected the exercise to be an easy one. After all, I have been a bookworm all my life, a bookish child who always had her nose in a book (why have we invented so many ways to insult those who love to read?). And so I accepted the assignment, eagerly, with the expectation that it would not make me sweat.

As it happened, I was stumped. The exercise turned out to be far more time-consuming and challenging than I imagined. After much handwringing and soul-searching, I came up with my five volumes, books that had served as my guides over the past decades. First, there was *Alice's Adventures in Wonderland*, a book that I still value for its subversive energy and contrarian spirit. I recall a tug-of-war over it with my third-grade teacher, who insisted that I save it for when I was older. I can still see the stern features of Miss White as she towered over me, leaning in to remove the book from my desk as I shielded it from harm with my hands. Then there was George Eliot's *Middlemarch* – and I am moving here chronologically – a book that incomprehensibly became a favourite in my high school years. Its hymn to heroism and its final sentence (more on that in a moment) still has the power to bring tears to my eyes.

Next came Thomas Mann's *The Magic Mountain*, a volume that led me to German literature and its obsession with death, disease, decadence and dissolution. Only later in life did I embrace the life-affirming pleasures of fairy tales via Angela Carter's *The Bloody Chamber and Other Stories*, a book that demystified tales like 'Bluebeard' and 'Little Red Riding Hood' and taught me the importance of reinventing them and making them new and relevant. Then came Ralph Ellison's *Invisible Man*, which transmitted the terrors of dislocation and alienation at a time when I was writing a book about African American folk tales and the cultural work they did for the disenfranchised, disempowered and marginalized.

Today, I would add a sixth volume to that inventory: *The Arabian Nights*, which gives us a thousand and one tales in a single volume. It is something of a talking book, with a narrator named Scheherazade, who tells stories to save her own neck, spare the lives of other women in the kingdom and change the culture in which she lives. She was the inspiration for *The Heroine with 1,001 Faces*, a book that I wrote in 2021 to challenge Joseph Campbell's *The Hero with a Thousand Faces* by constructing a counter-narrative, or rather a supplementary narrative, identifying the features that constitute a feminine model of heroism.

Rounding up my favourites, the talismanic treasures that had turned pandemic solitude into a gift, led me to think hard about what reading books does, not just for us and to us, but also with us. Lately there has been a lot of talk about reading as a moral technology and about how fiction promotes empathy and other forms of prosocial behaviour. An article published in *Science* reported that subjects assigned to read literary fiction showed impressive improvement on empathy tests. Those assigned to read non-fiction, popular fiction or nothing at all did not get a boost in their scores.

Back in 1859 George Eliot had more or less affirmed that novels promote empathy when she wrote, in a letter to a friend, that 'If Art does not enlarge men's sympathies, it does nothing morally.' To be sure, the conditional phrasing can give us pause, but any reader of *Middlemarch* will have no trouble identifying that the novelist comes down on the side of art promoting empathy.

Almost exactly a century before Eliot's pronouncement, Jean-Jacques Rousseau had denounced reading as the plague of childhood and expressed his concern about sentimental feelings as substitutes for action: 'In giving our tears to these fictions, we have satisfied all the rights of humanity without having to give anything more of ourselves.' Our feelings change but the real world remains untouched. 'Unfortunate people in person would require attention from us, relief, consolation, and work,' he added, something that would truly put us in touch with their 'pain' and require 'sacrifice'. So much for reading as a moral technology.

Not to be cynical, but empathy has become something of a commercial mantra and selling point. 'Why empathy is good for business – and how to improve it,' we read on the website for the World Economic Forum. 'In a professional context, improving empathy can reduce stress, build more positive relationships, and even boost revenues' is found in one bullet point, with the clear weight of the message on monetizing empathy.

For years now I have been fretting about empathy. Of course, I have faith in its power, but, like many of my generation, I rebel against orthodox pieties, especially those that try to control and regiment affect. Which is why I finally put my foot down after watching an advertisement that opportunistically recruited empathy to sell Lexus's luxury LS 500 vehicle, with a motivational speaker touting the benefits of moving out of your comfort zone from the seat of a luxury vehicle.

———

You don't have to read Paul Bloom's *Against Empathy*, Fritz Breithaupt's *The Dark Sides of Empathy* or Namwali Serpell's essay 'The Banality of Empathy' to understand that cultivating empathy may in fact not be such a great thing. In a piece written for *Vulture*, Kathryn VanArendonk coined the phrase 'empathy tourism' to capture the pleasure we derive from revisiting sensational cases of trauma from a safe perch and comfortable remove. And perhaps my own personal rebellion against empathy has something to do with resistance to instrumentalizing fiction and turning it into a tool for promoting virtue. In a sense fiction does no more and no less than what our encounters in real life do for us. In another sense, though, it is not so much about what reading does to us as about what it does *with* us.

In his *Lectures on Literature*, delivered at Cornell University in the 1940s and '50s, Vladimir Nabokov described a radiant moment when author and reader discover each other, meet and embrace: 'Up a trackless slope climbs the master artist, and at the top, on a windy ridge, whom do you think he meets? The panting and happy reader, and there they spontaneously embrace and are linked forever if the book lasts forever.' It is, of course, a meeting of the minds more than anything else but Nabokov conveys its rapture with a bodily embrace. I'm reminded of how I longed to meet the writers behind the books I loved, little realizing that I had already encountered them in ways so powerful that a real-life meeting could only disappoint.

There are dissenting voices, and Joan Didion, an essayist known for her deadpan cynicism, tells us that the act of saying 'I' is a way of 'imposing oneself upon other people, of saying listen to me, see it my way, change your mind'. She goes on to fret about how 'setting words on paper' is the tactic of a *secret* bully, an invasion, an imposition of the writer's sensibility on the reader's most private space'. In other words, those sneaky authors are anything but your confederate.

I prefer Nabokov's scene of reading to Didion's, even if he doesn't have it exactly right. Readers and authors don't just embrace; they have the chance to start a conversation, and that's exactly what I value about the experience of reading a good book. A few weeks ago I opened the pages of one of those books, Jason Mott's *Hell of a Book*, and what did I discover in it but what Henry Louis Gates Jr calls the talking book. Its protagonist (slyly named 'Author') seamlessly weaves the facts of his own life (what it's like to go on a book tour) with a fantasy animated by the Black Lives Matter movement. Author is haunted by the spectre of a boy who lost his father to police violence.

Hell of a Book is what I like to think of as a metacognitive novel, a work of fiction that is also an exercise in thinking about thinking. As I was reading it, I could not just hear the author (Jason Mott, not 'Author') speaking to me but also see inside his mind in ways that we never can in real life. And it was through that exercise in mind-reading that, presto! I suddenly understood the sorcery of a good story. The author lets us get inside his mind but inside ours as well.

I am reminded of what the writer Tim Wynne-Jones called the 'deep-read', for his description of that practice captures exactly what happens when we climb up Nabokov's trackless slope:

> The deep-read is when you get gut-hooked and dragged overboard down and down through the maze of print and find, to your amazement, you can breathe down there after all and there's a whole other world. I'm talking about the kind of reading when you realize that books are indeed interactive . . . I'm talking about the kind of deep-read where it isn't just the plot or the characters that matter, but the words and the way they fit together and

the meandering evanescent thoughts you think between the lines: the kind of reading where you are fleetingly aware of your own mind at work.

The talking book transports us, moves us and provides an immersive reading experience even as, and perhaps because, it gives us a piece of *its* mind. That knowledge of how others think turns inward to translate into how *we* think and arms us with a powerful tool, one that we can use to navigate the choices we face in real life.

It is a truth universally acknowledged that stories give us mentors and role models. Fiction gives us everything under the sun . . . and the moon and the stars, with heroes, anti-heroes, outlaws, tricksters, villains and scoundrels. All those characters talk to us, revealing their deepest secrets, their motivations, their fears and desires, as well as how their minds work. They whisper 'Choose me' between the lines, and that is part of their magic.

Our choices change over time. There was a time when Achilles, Hector and Hercules spoke to me, all those powerful warrior heroes with their drive for glory and immortality. But at some point, and I locate that moment in 2020, at the beginning of the global pandemic, I began to realize that I was worshipping false gods. What were those three heroes from ancient times but a trio of natural-born killers! And suddenly I began listening to other figures from times past, Philomela, Arachne and a host of other women, along with those who had been sidelined and traumatized. Philomela uses the conspiratorial crafts to tell her story, and Arachne weaves a tapestry that broadcasts the criminal assaults of the gods – warning and revenge wrapped in one tidy package.

Women may not have had access to weapons, but they deployed words and stories – sometimes sewn, woven or knit into fabric to make textiles – to speak truth to power. Today we are listening to their voices and discovering their stories in novels like Pat Barker's *The Silence of the Girls* (2018), Natalie Haynes's *A Thousand Ships* (2019) and Madeline Miller's *Circe* (2018). And suddenly we realize that there is a backstory that has been suppressed, as is the case with Cassandra, who was cursed for her resistance to Apollo's advances when the god gave her the gift of prophesy and the curse of possessing no credibility at all. Her story can be read as an allegory of women's speech through the ages, how, for centuries now, it has been discredited and dismissed.

The power of reading was more evident than ever during the pandemic, when it began to dawn on me that our models for heroism are not at all fixed and immutable. They are always changing, infused with the values prized by successive generations. After all, the pandemic gave us new forms of heroism, and suddenly we discovered that health *care* workers and *care*givers, along with scientists working in the field of medicine, had become our cultural protectors and rescuers. Driven by curiosity and care, they were invested above all in healing.

In 2021 the United States began replacing statues of Confederate soldiers with monuments honouring the enslaved and with memorials dedicated to emancipation. A statue of the civil rights leader and educator Mary McLeod Bethune replaced a Confederate general in Statuary Hall in our nation's Capitol. Bethune may not have answered Joseph Campbell's famous call to adventure, but she quietly earned her medals elsewhere, outside the spotlight.

Authors often invoke the old saw about how they have been writing a certain book all their life. This was certainly true of *The Heroine with 1,001 Faces*, a book in which I processed and tried to make sense of a lifetime of reading. And what did I discover? That books had been not just a lifeline but also a way of defining who I could be, should be and might be. There they were, all my family, patiently waiting for me to reread their stories and discover who they once were to me and who they are to me today. And, serendipitously, I picked up George Eliot's *Middlemarch*, a book that I had no business reading in high school (Virginia Woolf called it the only British novel for adults) but that tempted me to pick it up again after a conversation with a young man from Mumbai who was enchanted with the novel and berated me for being mystified that he had it in his backpack.

Eliot famously ends her long novel with a sentence that pays tribute to the heroism of ordinary people, heroism with a lower-case 'h'. She tells us about the ripple effects of Dorothea's presence in the world and how her kindness and care have improved our own lot: 'The growing good of the world is partly dependent on unhistoric acts; and that things are not so ill with you and me as they might have been is half owing to the number who lived faithfully a hidden life, and rest in unvisited tombs.' Dorothea's story, which consists of 'unhistoric acts', has now made history, and her quiet legacy, fictional though it may be, continues to ensure that things are not so ill with you and me.

3

The Dream of an Intenser Experience

PETER BROOKS

Les vrais paradis sont les paradis qu'on a perdus.
Marcel Proust

I decided in my fifties that it was time to write a novel; by my sixties I had written two. Writing them was both a test of what I thought I had learned from my study of novels and a challenge to inventiveness: sitting down each morning to pull out of myself the next episodes, the next thoughts of my characters. Reviews of my productions were mixed (I still treasure those that seemed to understand what I was up to), and neither was a commercial success. Both were based on historical events: the first, on a sketchy journal left by a volunteer on Admiral Bougainville's voyage around the world on the *Boudeuse*, in the course of which the French 'discovered' Tahiti; the second on what the French call the *'retour des cendres'*: the voyage to the island of Saint Helena, more or less in the middle of nowhere, to bring the body of Napoleon back to France for interment in Les Invalides. There were lots of things culled from my reading at work in these books – the second, for instance, included Henri Beyle, pen name Stendhal, as one of the principal characters, and derived in good part from his journals. The first was written in good measure from the memoirs of Bougainville and his shipmates, especially the naturalist Philibert Commerson, an admirable representative of the Enlightenment.

But as I was writing both novels, there was one book that was constantly soliciting me, a book profoundly engrained in my understanding of *story*, of narrative and how it should be paced, how it should move forward. This was Robert Louis Stevenson's *Treasure Island*. Strange, perhaps, that after all my thinking about Stendhal, and Balzac, Flaubert and Proust, Henry James, Conrad, Woolf and Faulkner, that *Treasure Island* should remain such a strong tug, a template for how any narrative should proceed. What drew me to *Treasure Island* was my belief that it was, it is, the perfect adventure story, and that any novel, whatever its subject, should be an adventure. My two novels both included long sea voyages, though these weren't their central matter, and I delighted in imagining those months on shipboard. (I am a sailor, but of small boats that never go anywhere.) That world confined to the perimeter of a small wooden ship in the midst of the vast sea with nothing on the horizon both appealed to me and appalled me. Why did those on board not all go mad? And certainly the voyage of the *Hispaniola* in Stevenson's novel was on my mind, though its progress is never recorded in much detail.

Adventure is not confined to ocean voyages and pirates, as Henry James was at pains to point out in his Preface to *The American*, in which he in fact evokes his friend Stevenson before going on to consider the nature of the 'romantic' as that which 'can reach us only through the beautiful circuit and subterfuge of our thought and our desire'.[1] James of course is interested in inner adventures:

There are immense and flagrant adventures that are but sordid and squalid ones, as we feel, tainting with their quality the very defiances they provoke; while there are common and covert ones, that 'look like nothing' and that can be but inwardly and occultly dealt with, which involve the sharpest hazards to life and honour and the highest instant decisions and intrepidities of action.

The point, for James, is to make the ordinary yield a sense of adventure and danger comparable to the hunt for buried treasure and the combat with pirates.

'Adventure' is a key term also in the reflections of Jean-Paul Sartre's character Roquentin, in the novel *Nausea* (*La Nausée*), in the contrast he posits between life and the telling of life. In a novel, even the most apparently insignificant incidents in the life of the fictional character herald adventure, significant events that are to come, that are to have shape and meaning. Everything he does is 'gilded by the light of future passions'.[2] The plot of adventure refers us to the future, the *ad-venire*: that which is to come, so that present actions are shaped and given meaning by future ones, eventually by the outcome that sets the final seal of meaning on everything. By the time he wrote his autobiography, *The Words* (*Les Mots*), Sartre had abandoned the novel as genre precisely because its shaping of life as adventure seemed false, a denial of the human freedom that must be exercised at every moment of life, without the constraint or the foreknowledge of the plotted story.

Treasure Island remains to me the archetype of how adventure is done, a template of the interesting, engaging story that I cannot quite get beyond. Stevenson called the novel 'a book for boys', and that gendering may limit its range. But woman-lessness seems characteristic of many classic books for children. Or rather: they are characterized by a voyage away from women, possibly followed by return to them. 'I said goodbye to mother and the cove where I had lived since I was born,' Jim Hawkins tells us on the verge of his setting sail for Treasure Island.[3] Perhaps, as the French psychoanalyst Marthe Robert claimed in the case of the folk tale, the young hero must leave home to avoid the threat of incest: true most obviously for the young princess of the Grimms' 'All-Kinds-of-Fur', whose father wants her to replace his dead queen.[4] But more simply: adventure must mean severance from the comforts and certainties of home.

Whatever layers of meaning accrue to leaving home, it is where adventure really begins. Jim Hawkins bids farewell to the maternal and to life on shore. The voyage out begins. Not long after, we have this magnificent paragraph on their progress:

> We had run up the trades to get the wind of the island we were after – I am not allowed to be more plain – and now we were running down for it with a bright look-out day and night. It was about the last day of our outward voyage, by the largest computation; some time that night, or, at latest, before noon of the morrow, we should sight the Treasure Island. We were heading s.s.w., and had a steady breeze abeam and a quiet sea. The *Hispaniola* rolled steadily, dipping her bowsprit now and then with a whiff of spray. All was drawing alow and aloft; everyone was in the bravest spirits, because we were now so near an end of the first part of our adventure.[5]

A passage to invigorate any imagination. And it is at this moment that Jim goes below to get himself an apple from the apple barrel. He has to crawl in bodily to reach the few apples left in the bottom of the barrel. There he falls asleep, rocked by the movement of the ship, only to wake up to hear Long John Silver and his pirate associates plotting their mutiny. 'I understood that the lives of all the honest men aboard depended upon me alone.'[6]

I could go on quoting happily. They reach the island: 'The plunge of our anchor sent up clouds of birds wheeling and crying over the woods; but in less than a minute they were down again, and all was once more silent.'[7] And as the Captain and the Doctor and the loyal men abandon the ship to take refuge in the stockade: 'We made our best speed across the strip of wood that now divided us from the stockade; and at every step we took the voices of the buccaneers rang nearer. Soon we could hear their footfalls as they ran, and the cracking of the branches as they breasted across a bit of thicket.'[8] And then, as Jim waits to set out on his trip, alone, back to the ship in Ben Gunn's homemade coracle: 'Down I sat to wait for darkness, and made a hearty meal of biscuit. It was a night out of ten thousand for my purpose. The fog had now buried all heaven. As the last rays of daylight dwindled and disappeared, absolute blackness settled down on Treasure Island.'[9] And then perhaps the most memorable moment of the book, Jim's nearly involuntary shooting of the coxswain Israel Hands, who has pursued him into the crosstrees of the ship and threatens him with his dirk:

> back went his right hand over his shoulder. Something sang like an arrow through the air; I felt a blow and then a sharp pang, and there I was pinned by the shoulder to the

mast. In the horrid pain and surprise of the moment – I scarce can say it was by my own volition, and I am sure it was without conscious aim – both my pistols went off, and both escaped out of my hands.

They did not fall alone; with a choked cry, the coxswain loosed his grip upon the shrouds, and plunged headfirst into the water.[10]

After this great moment of involuntary heroism (one must not kill with intent), Jim is alone upon the ship, with the sole responsibility for her safety.

One more moment, the finding of Captain Flint's treasure:

That was Flint's treasure that we had come so far to seek, and that had cost already the lives of seventeen men from the *Hispaniola*. How many it had cost in the amassing, what blood and sorrow, what good ships scuttled on the deep, what brave men walking the plank blindfold, what shot of cannon, what shame and lies and cruelty, perhaps no man alive could tell.[11]

These passages are touchstones to me in the creation of a sense of adventure, thanks of course to Stevenson's perfect understanding of pitch and rhythm, his graceful mastery of English prose. I must admit too that the written record of adventure was enhanced for me by N. C. Wyeth's illustrations – the greatest, I think, ever to accompany a children's book. Each of the colour plates in the *Treasure Island* I was brought up on – in the Scribner's Illustrated Classics – became a part of my vision of the world, visual templates of high adventure. That moment where Jim Hawkins confronts Israel Hands high up on the mast of the grounded *Hispaniola*, done by Wyeth from a vertiginous perspective up in the air, as Jim aims his pistols and Hands reaches back to throw his knife, remains with you forever.

Wyeth has selected 'perfect moments' (I don't know if he or someone else was responsible for the choices) and made them visually memorable. I am reminded again of *Nausea* (Sartre is one of the best theorists of fiction), of the notion of '*moments parfaits*' elaborated by Roquentin and his sometime girlfriend Annie. First there is the 'privileged situation', *situation privilégiée*, which, handled with the proper care, gives birth to the perfect moment. Annie's idea derives from the illustrated edition of Jules Michelet's *History of France* she read as a child, and a reflection on the scenes chosen for illustration within this history. There must be something very special about them that they should have been selected, from all the thousands of other possible moments, to be assigned for illustration. The sixteenth century, for instance, has only three such moments, each full of grandeur.[12] Studying Eugène Delacroix's history paintings many years ago, I discovered that he worked in a similar fashion, seeking to determine the perfect moment for illustration in his paintings. He then would append a short paragraph, or a few lines, to the entry on the painting in the exhibition catalogue, the *livret de salon*, explaining its significance.[13] A number of his subjects are already mediated through literary representation: in novels by Walter Scott or Chateaubriand, for instance. Delacroix twice chose a scene from Scott's *Ivanhoe*, 'The Abduction of Rebecca'. The first of these, from 1846 (the other is dated 1858), was accompanied by the legend: 'Rebecca is abducted on the order of the Knight Templar Boisguilbert, in the midst of the sack of the castle of Frontdeboeuf./ She is already in the hands of two African slaves charged with taking her far from the theatre of combat.'

The 'privileged situation' of the sack of Frontdeboeuf and Rebecca's capture is specified and illustrated in the 'perfect moment' the artist has chosen, where she is slung on the back of a horse by the two slaves. Or one more example, from Chateaubriand's *Atala*, a painting that takes its title from the American Indian tribe of the novel *Les Natchez*. When exhibited in the Salon of 1835, the painting was explained by Delacroix: 'Fleeing the massacre of their tribe, two young savages go up the Mississippi. During the trip, the young woman has been seized by the pangs of labour. The moment is that where the father holds in his arms the newborn baby, whom they both look at tenderly.' Note Delacroix's 'the moment is . . .', indicating the care he has taken in choosing the perfect moment, that which best illustrates the meaning of the whole narrative.

I pondered endlessly over Wyeth's illustrations to *Treasure Island*, asking myself what made them the chosen moments, why they were so perfect in representation of what was most significant in the narrative. I think I could probably still today recall each of them, almost in sequence, as a vivid summary of the novel's high points.

Treasure Island remains for me the imaginative template of what a narrative of adventure ought to be. It has among other qualities a kind of limpidity in the narrative, whether in the chapters (most of them) narrated by Jim Hawkins or the few recounted by Dr Livesey when Jim has gone missing on his truant but life-saving adventure back to the *Hispaniola*. Stevenson's friends, including Henry James, considered him a master stylist. The story unfolds with a perfect economy and effect.

But my childhood reading – which before I could read was childhood listening, being read to, which remains one of the great privileges of a bourgeois childhood – had another important and complicated component, one closely related to *Treasure Island* but at a kind of tangent to it. This was Arthur Ransome's *Swallows and Amazons*, that original first title in what became a series – and then all the other books of the series: *Swallowdale, Winter Holiday, We Didn't Mean to Go to Sea, Peter Duck* and *Missee Lee* stand out most vividly in my recall. These are children's books, more obviously so than *Treasure Island*, and the children are both boys and girls (of indeterminate age). They stand in conscious imaginative relation to *Treasure Island*. I recently discovered, without surprise, that Arthur Ransome intended to write a study of Stevenson, one never completed, only well after his death published in fragmentary form.[14]

Swallows and Amazons begins with the four Walker children, John, Susan, Titty and Roger, on holiday in the Lake District, waiting to hear whether their father will give them permission to take the sailing dinghy *Swallow* to an island in the lake and camp there. The father is absent, presumably off serving the British Empire somewhere, and manifests himself only in the form of the telegram granting the children their freedom. The mother in this case turns out to be perfection: she helps to equip the expedition, she arranges with a local farm that they may row back from the island every morning for fresh milk – and otherwise grants them their freedom, even accepting to enter the game of being a 'native' on the shores that need exploration. *Treasure Island*'s 'I said goodbye to mother and the cove where

I had lived since I was born' is more complex and extended here: saying goodbye to mother takes a few chapters since she is not really being left behind (Jim Hawkins's mother never reappears after the voyage) but an absent presence on shore, following her children's doing with proper concern but a large grant of autonomy. The perfect upper-middle-class mother.

The adventure of *Swallows and Amazons* is, for the adult reader, a bit tongue-in-cheek, a tame replay of *Treasure Island*. Yet it offers full satisfaction as adventure, one of the most glorious realizations of childhood summer freedom and self-assertion. It's the third child, the girl Titty (with a name that has made later generations of readers smirk, and led subsequent film-makers to rename her), who is the most imaginative, who alludes repeatedly to *Robinson Crusoe* and *Treasure Island* – and who will in fact at the end discover buried treasure on Cormorant Island. She raises the stakes of the children's adventures, producing within the story a kind of second-degree story, a meta-story in which the lake is a wide sea bordered by unexplored lands, those on shore natives, and the Blackett sisters of the dinghy *Amazon* whom they meet, Nancy and Peggy, true pirates. The book succeeds at once at being realist and romantic, in James's terms.

The imaginative core of the book comes in Chapter Twenty, entitled 'Titty Alone'. The Swallows and the Amazons have agreed to war, with each crew trying to capture the other's ship. While John, Susan and Roger leave to sail the *Swallow* up the 'Amazon River' in order to seize the *Amazon*, Titty is left to guard Wild Cat Island. She begins to write her log, in imitation of Robinson Crusoe, beginning: 'Twenty-five years ago this day I was wrecked on this desolate island.'[15] As night falls, she becomes a lighthouse keeper, hoisting a lantern onto a high tree branch.

Then she goes to the harbour where *Swallow* usually lies and lights one of the two candle lanterns that will guide the boat back into its anchorage when her three siblings return. Back at the campsite, she wraps herself in a blanket and waits for the owl call that is to signal the return of the *Swallow*, when it will be time to take the second candle lantern to its place on a tree by the harbour, to align with the first for guidance. Her attempt to remain awake fails. She falls asleep – and wakes to an owl call. This will turn out to be a real owl rather than a human signal, and just as she has lit the second lantern along come the Amazons rather than the Swallows. Nancy and Peggy have cleverly hid their boat in the reeds at the mouth of the Amazon River, and Captain John and his crew have missed it in their trip upriver. So now the Amazons arrive to take over the Swallows' camp in an apparent victory.

> Titty did not know what to do. It was defeat, black and dreadful. Instead of the *Swallow* sailing home with the *Amazon* a captured galleon, sailed by Susan as a prize crew, everything had gone wrong. The Swallows had not captured the *Amazon*, but the Amazons had landed on Wild Cat Island, and their pirate ship was snug in harbour. If only she had not lit the lights they never could have come in till dawn, and by then the Swallows would be back.[16]

Then Titty has her idea: 'After all, it did not matter who of the Swallows captured the *Amazon*. And here was the *Amazon*, unprotected. Why not?' Titty takes the *Amazon*, paddles it quietly out through the rocks at the head of the harbour, and in the pitch black rows up the lake. When she hears the splash of water on rocks close ahead, she throws out the boat's anchor. She comes to rest near what in the morning will stand revealed as Cormorant Island, and from there hears the malefactors who have stolen Captain Flint's (the Blacketts' Uncle Jim's) sea chest from his houseboat – a chest that contains his typewriter and the manuscript he's been working on all summer, a treasure to him.

She spends the night alone on the lake in the sailing boat, cold and hungry. She finds a big hunk of chocolate left in *Amazon* and eats it on the principle: 'They always eat everything they find in a captured ship.' 'They' in this case are buccaneers and other adventurers on the high seas. Titty always succeeds in raising childhood adventure into an imaginative domain where it feels real, and when at the last she unearths Captain Flint's chest, she has realized a true story of treasure hunting. It is significant that the *Swallows and Amazons* series soon developed a true story of search for buried treasure, made horribly dangerous by real pirates after the same thing. In the second book of the series, *Swallowdale*, Titty begins imagining a character named Peter Duck, an old salt who has sailed to the Caribbees and come home with his pockets full of pirate gold. For Titty, 'she had only to think of him, when there he was, ready for any adventure in which he might be wanted.'[17] A year later, Titty's fiction has become the real adventure of *Peter Duck*, in which the make-believe of a summer holiday on the lake has morphed into life-threatening adventures in the Caribbean Sea – both unlikely and seductive. Would Uncle Jim/Captain Flint really take six children on the schooner *Wild Cat*, along with the seasoned Peter Duck, across the Atlantic in search of buried treasure? The question falls away: *Peter Duck* is a rousing tale that almost does

Treasure Island one better, a story in which the reader completely believes even if it appears to be well over the line toward romance rather than realism.

I recently discovered Arthur Ransome's posthumously published autobiography.[18] I had always assumed that he spent most of his life in a cosy cottage in the Lake District where the *Swallows and Amazons* stories are largely set, writing in a kind of avuncular mode to children. In fact, his was an enviably adventurous life, spent largely as a bohemian journalist, at home in Montparnasse, then fleeing a wife he did not like to Russia, at first to collect its folklore then as a foreign correspondent just as the Russian Revolution burst upon the scene. He seems to have understood better than the Foreign Office what was going on in the Kremlin, and have known well most of the Bolsheviks, including Trotsky and Lenin. He tried, unsuccessfully, to keep Britain from going to war with the revolutionary government. He became the lover of a woman who worked in Trotsky's ministry, later married her, made daring trips back and forth from Russia to England via Sweden and Estonia, often in danger of arrest or summary execution at border posts. Settling down to write children's books only came late in his life. I mention his adventurous existence because I think one can sense that the well-modulated adventures of the Walker, Blackett and later the Callum children are infused with a deep understanding of what perilous adventure might really entail. It's as if the children's adventures are sublimated versions of adult adventure, with just enough danger to be exhilarating. In fact, when you reach *Peter Duck* and *Missee Lee* (the latter based on Ransome's time in China as correspondent for the *Manchester Guardian*) the dangers seem quite clear and present.

The *Swallows and Amazons* books raise a question that can be asked of all the great English children's books of the nineteenth and twentieth centuries, those by E. Nesbit and C. S. Lewis, for instance: how old are these children? In Ransome's series, they seem to age a bit from book to book – their schoolwork becomes more demanding, for instance. I have seen estimates that John, eldest of the Walkers, is fourteen years old, and Nancy must be about his age. Yet no one seems to have hit puberty. Or, if they have, the bodily changes of puberty have been carefully hidden from view. If *Treasure Island* is fiction without woman, from the moment the voyage begins, *Swallows and Amazons*, like *The Lion, the Witch, and the Wardrobe* and *The Railway Children*, contains young people of both sexes who are essentially sexless. I think it is possible to detect a certain eros created between John and Nancy in *Swallows and Amazons* as they compete in seamanship and daring but it is never mentioned overtly. When the six children bathe together on the deck of the *Wild Cat*, dousing themselves with buckets of water, they seem always to be wearing swimsuits.

It's of course a postulate of children's fiction that it should be, like children themselves, innocent. The very notion of children's summer adventures must be Arcadian, Edenic, before the serpent has entered the garden. Yet as post-Freudians we cannot be quite so convinced of childhood innocence. We may be ready to find a fallen world everywhere, and all sorts of intimations of childhood sexual knowledge in however distorted a form. I do wonder in rereading *Swallows and Amazons* at what a twenty-first-century rewrite of it might give – whether a more knowing allusion to hormonal changes and embarrassments and longings might not enrich the text. The Blackett sisters' Uncle Jim, aka Captain Flint, would have been classed in 1930 as a 'bachelor', one who seems to take his greatest pleasure in games with the children – he allows himself to be made to walk the plank from his houseboat, blindfolded and fully dressed – and then will take them to halfway round the globe on the *Wild Cat*. It is hard for us today to read Captain Flint without a certain unease at his paedophilic implications. It's only by rigorously banning the serpent from the garden that we can accept a grown man living among children to his entire satisfaction.

I give up the puzzle of 'the sexual enlightenment of children', as Freud called it, in Victorian and Edwardian children's literature: it is too rich and deep a subject. One has only to think of J. M. Barrie's *Peter Pan* to begin to imagine where the puzzle might lead you. Or, more interestingly, in Lewis Carroll's *Alice's Adventures in Wonderland* and *Through the Looking-Glass*, which do in a covert way seem to want to explore what children are learning about adulthood. See, for instance, the Mock Turtle's report on his schooling, where he learned 'Reeling and Writhing . . . then the different branches of Arithmetic – Ambition, Distraction, Uglification, and Derision.' And then:

> 'Well, there was Mystery,' the Mock Turtle replied, count-
> ing off the subjects on his flippers, 'Mystery, ancient
> and modern, with Seaography: then Drawling – the
> Drawling-master was an old conger-eel, that used to
> come once a week: *he* taught us Drawling, Stretching,
> and Fainting in Coils.'[19]

Carroll's puns, like his portmanteau words, suggest that children's schooling includes learning adult social behaviour, including 'fainting in coils'. His wonderland is, as often has been recognized, a dark mirror of the real world, and as such it suggests obliquely the world of adult sexuality.

But like Jim Hawkins in the womanless world of *Treasure Island*, the children of *Swallows and Amazons* live out adventures that are glorious because they are untainted, in any acknowledged form at least, by sexuality. 'The true paradises are the paradises we have lost,' writes Proust, suggesting that the very definition of paradise is inseparable from that of its loss. The great children's books resurrect a paradise that we know to be threatened by loss – by growing up – and that is part and parcel of their seduction. We know we can't go back again. We have learned the riddle of the sphinx, to our enduring sadness. And in the end they reassure us. The final line of *Swallows and Amazons* records the return to land, and to the reappearance of the mother, along with Vicky, the baby of the family, too young to go adventuring. It's Roger who speaks: 'Hullo, there's mother and Vicky coming down the field.'

Adventure in children's books is a loop, a voyage out with many dangers and sudden changes of fortune, challenging the young to respond, to overcome adversity, to learn both self-reliance and teamwork, to return with a greater sense of integrated selfhood. At the end of the adventure there is a reconstituted family. I think of the very moving end of Nesbit's *The Railway Children*, when the father who has been absent throughout because in prison – a daring move on the writer's part, attenuated by his having been mistakenly convicted – is restored to his long-suffering wife and, especially, to the children. Such stories work – and the classic instances I have cited clearly do work, and have continued to do so over decades – because the dangers of adventure are made real enough to be convincing yet reassurance lies around the corner. The melodramatic nightmare is one you awake from, as when Alice can say: 'You're nothing but a pack of cards!' I ask myself why it is Britain that seems over the years to have produced the greatest writers of children's fiction. A quick answer might be that it has to do with the imaginings of Empire – see the great tales of India by Rudyard Kipling, see the 'adult' adventure stories of H. Rider Haggard, and so many others – and the English class structure, which once, at least, offered reassurance to those of the upper ranks that society would take care of them in the end. (Not to probe too deeply issues of English upper-class sexuality in such as Sir Richard Burton, translator of *The Arabian Nights*.)

It would probably require a psychoanalysis to say fully how my childhood reading experience has been determinative of what I write and who I am. I suspect that an analyst might find in the sense of adventure that I have been attempting to describe a characteristic of the 'latency period' that Freud thought lay between the resolution of the Oedipus complex and the onset of puberty. Adventure is a form of arousal that takes the place of a sublimated sexuality. These are for many children years of learning and mental expansion that require absorbing fictions. When in adolescence sexuality, however frustrated, becomes overt, something more than voyages and pirates may become necessary. Though as Jean-Jacques Rousseau so forcefully demonstrates in his *Confessions*, eros can itself become amalgamated to the fictions learned in childhood. When he has exhausted the meagre local lending library, Rousseau describes how he compensated his growing sexuality by his imagination, placing himself into the fictions he has read, 'appropriating' them to his own uses, creating 'the love of imaginary objects' that would be part of his character for the rest of his life.[20] I suppose that all of us who have spent our adult life teaching and writing about literature may have undergone the same determinative process as Rousseau.

I come back to Henry James in his Preface to *The American*. He has run through the traditional definitions of 'romance', as 'a matter indispensably of boats, or of caravans, or of tigers, or of "historical characters", or of ghosts, or of forgers, or of detectives, or of beautiful, wicked women, or of pistols and knives' – all reducible to the idea of facing danger. Such definitions fail; they don't take us to the true essence of romance. James goes on:

> The panting pursuit of danger is the pursuit of life itself, in which danger awaits us possibly at every step and faces us at every turn; so that the dream of an intenser experience easily becomes rather some vision of a sublime security like that enjoyed on the flowery plains of heaven, where we may conceive ourselves proceeding in ecstasy from one prodigious phase and form of it to another.[21]

It's that 'dream of an intenser experience' that I find, buried but still discernible, in my childhood reading. Does anything later in life quite live up to it? Or is it something we have to keep on recreating for ourselves?

4

Reading à deux

LINDA HUTCHEON *and* MICHAEL HUTCHEON

We are not siblings but a couple, married for over fifty years and writing together for thirty of those. One of us (Michael) is a respiratory physician (pulmonologist) and professor of medicine; the other (Linda) is a professor of comparative literature and English, both now retired.

Our lifetimes, as you might guess from our having had long academic careers, have been ones full of reading, listening and writing, both professionally and privately. Together we write on the cultural history of opera. We do recognize that the choice of this particular collaborative research focus is not self-evident for a physician and a literary theorist, but it's a sign of our shared passion for the art form. And this act of writing together has taught us a lot about how we read.

That said, it might come as a surprise to know that neither of us recalls being read to by parents as a child, though we both quickly became avid readers. Here are some of our early memories of self-immersion:

MICHAEL: I have no strong memories of being read to as a child. That may reflect the imperfect recollections of childhood or the differences in parenting styles or perhaps just the realities of life at that time, for I grew up in the immediate post-Second World War period in Canada. My very young, very shy mother was a war bride from England with a small child, living in a new country with my father's family – a situation she recalled later as hostile, particularly for a Catholic woman in a Salvation Army household. I doubt there was time or energy to think about reading stories to me when there was so much more for her to navigate alone. My father, in the Royal Canadian Air Force stationed in England, was only demobilized later to return to Canada, and he remained more or less absent through my early years. There were high school courses for him to complete before he could begin training in the expanded Engineering School established some 40 miles from where we lived in Toronto.

At age four I accompanied my homesick mother to England. Here again, while my memories of this time are clearer, reading is not a part of them – and not surprisingly. My working-class grandmother, with whom we lived at the time, was illiterate. The only stories I heard were of family happenings, never from books. Indeed, storytelling was not a family art.

On our return to Canada, however, everything changed. My parents rented their own apartment in a newly developing suburb in the north end of the city. Evenings now were spent playing or listening to the radio, while my parents read. Watching them, I was impatient to learn to read myself, but that didn't happen until I began grade school. As is often the case for an only child in a quiet and adult home, my world was an imaginative one of unstructured play, radio stories (my imagination unhampered by the 'colonizing' control of television visuals), and . . . reading.

———

LINDA: My reading memories are both similar and different from Michael's. This is an early one.

Excited as only a hyper-competitive nine-year-old who has entered her local library's reading contest can be, I recall sitting – well, actually, I suspect I was visibly vibrating on a chair – waiting impatiently for the librarian to arrive. The contest (as I understood it at the time, at least) involved reading a book and then relating what you learned from or enjoyed about the book to a librarian – who would then award you a star to be displayed on the library wall next to your name. I already had two red stars, one silver and now I wanted a gold, but wasn't quite sure about what it took to get one.

My favourite librarian, Miss Robinson, arrived just in time to prevent me from bouncing totally off my chair, and asked me what book I was going to tell her about today. I handed her a smallish red book. She opened it and asked why I had picked it and where had I found it. I pointed to the large reading table across the room. It seems I had picked up a translation of the Domesday Book for Wiltshire. It likely goes without saying that she knew that I had no idea what or where Wiltshire was. With an indulgent smile on her face, she asked me to tell her about the book. 'Well, there's this place that has land that is owned by a king, I think, and there are knights (and I'm sure, dragons for them to kill) and there are sheep and there's an abbey – I think an abbey is a church, right? But mostly there are lists, which I kind of raced through. There wasn't much of a story, and you know I really like stories.' Miss Robinson then informed me that what I had read was an eleventh-century survey of a county in England. It wasn't quite what children usually chose to read, she said. I corrected her: 'I didn't really choose it, though. It was just there. Do I get a gold star?'

To say I read indiscriminately as a child would be an understatement. To say I read voraciously would be totally accurate. I guess I was making up for lost time, but obviously with little guidance. I hadn't been read to as a child, in part because in my Italian immigrant household there were both no books and no time to read them. But when I went to school, discovered books and learned to read, the library became my escape. When I brought books back home, I read them in private, in secret almost. My mother's repeated lament still echoes in my ears: 'Where is she *now*? She knows it's time to do the dishes.' Of course, I knew. That's why I was hiding in the bathroom reading. I secretly think I became a literature professor just to make my reading habit into legitimate labour that my parents might recognize.

———

MICHAEL: And what did I read? My English relatives sent books at Christmas – probably the first that I ever owned: *Just William* stories, the *Rupert Annual* (a kind of comic or proto-graphic novel of the adventures of a young bear and his chums, such as Bill Badger). However, my family didn't buy books as a rule, but rather borrowed them from the library. I would accompany my father on a Saturday and, while he chose books for himself and my mother, I would sit with the others in the Children's Section while a librarian read aloud – usually swash-buckling stories of childhood adventure. Afterwards, with my father's help, I would pick out books to take home to read. For a Canadian boy, I suspect I had a very English reading list, though that was likely not unusual at the time: Enid Blyton; *Swallows and Amazons*; later, G. A. Henty.

For me, books became not only outlets for the imagination but also sources of information and knowledge as I progressed through school and observed my father's own ongoing post-war studies and education. And libraries were the repositories of this written world. I learned something that would serve me well through-out my life: when faced with a problem or a question, find a book!

——

LINDA: People who grew up with books surrounding them, listening to stories being read to them, might not recall the first books they ever owned, but I sure do – vividly. With my mother's permission and my allow-ance money, at age ten I joined a paperback book club, and received the first three books free! This miracu-lous bounty arrived in the mail a few weeks later. As

I reverentially unwrapped each book, I was totally unaware (though my mother was not) of my continuing knack for seeking out utterly inappropriate books for someone my age: one particularly treasured volume was John Hersey's *Hiroshima*. Since I spent so much time in libraries, I knew that I too had to label each of my books so that they would be easily identifiable. I therefore affixed to the spine of each of the three my own version of a call number and carefully (and oh so proudly) lined them up on my bedstead.

———

MICHAEL: My more or less successful turning to books to solve problems or answer questions occasionally had unintended consequences. When I was in middle school/junior high school, I was required to submit a longish essay on any topic I wished. I had an idea about a subject about which I didn't know much, but I was curious and wanted to know more. So, of course, I went to the library. I scoured the shelves looking for books that I reckoned must be somewhere there. As hard as I tried, looking under whatever categories seemed possible, I could find nothing. So, I approached the front desk where sat the librarian who looked old (to me), indeed middle-aged. 'Excuse me,' said I, 'I have to do this essay for school and I can't find any books by the Marquis de Sade.' My memories include a somewhat awkward moment as the librarian sought to regain her composure, a careful diversion away from the subject at hand, and a very strong suggestion to consider another topic for my essay. I never did find out whether the library actually had these books, hidden away under lock and key, for adults only. Or, perhaps more likely, they were censored. It was still the late fifties, after all.

———

LINDA: Less embarrassing, but also less scholarly, another of my reading memories was recently triggered by my cousin Barb: the two of us at twelve, sprawled across the floor reading Harlequin Romances, stolen from her mother's desk. Alternately enraptured by the love stories and giggling at what adults apparently did when 'in love', we were being initiated into the narrative world of popular fiction. We somehow knew our teachers wouldn't approve, though we weren't sure either why or how we knew that. In school we read 'serious' literature, which we adored too, but the illicit nature of this romance reading was its appeal. Today I often wonder whether reading detective fiction as an adult has the same appeal for me.

———

LINDA AND MICHAEL: Both of us, as you can see, have stories of childhood drives to read that were, in a way, life-shaping. One of us (Michael) trained to be a physician – and thus became a reader of symptoms, a diagnostician. The other (Linda) eventually taught literature, specializing in reading narrative, and became intrigued, early on, with what was called 'reader-response theory'. Our attraction to these very different disciplines, not surprisingly, also reflected our different personalities. We realized, as soon as we began to work together, that our disciplines of choice had reinforced personality differences to create what the French call *déformations professionelles*, which affected how we actually read.

Through his medical training, Michael was taught to read (and remember) every line. He worked slowly, methodically, with care and attention, recording each point made (and in sequential and logical order) in any book he was studying. Linda, on the other hand, had always tackled broad-based research projects and was used to starting by reading through vast amounts of materials and only then zeroing in on relevant works on which to begin close reading.

Imagine the two of us the first time we ventured into the music library stacks together to begin research into Giacomo Puccini's opera *La bohème*. In the first hour or so, Michael had reached page twenty of his first book, taking careful, detailed, very orderly notes. Linda had read a good part of a library shelf already and had a set of bizarre diagrammatic notes outlining general themes we should explore as we read further. Stunned at the contrast, we stopped and talked about the massive differences in how we read: our different paces, our different perspectives and foci. Part of the reason for the startling diversity in reading habits was professional; part was personal. We came to learn that, between us, we possess one (shared) obsessive-compulsive personality: Michael obsesses, Linda compulses. It turns out to be a productive division of labour – in reading and in writing.

For three decades, we have written together on opera and its cultural/medical history. Neither of us is a musicologist, though we both are musically trained. But we always read (both operas and their critical literature) not as music specialists but through the lenses of our other disciplines, those other systems of knowledge that have shaped our interpretative strategies – and tactics. We continue to read differently, but we now share a research history of reading operas (music and text) and reading about opera that has shaped anew our manner of interpreting what we read. Shared background, shared skills have come with time, with expanded intellectual perspectives, with broader scholarly horizons. But the challenges and pleasures of reading and writing together continue to be what we treasure. To paraphrase Dr Johnson: 'Sir, when a man [or woman] is tired of reading, he [or she] is tired of life; for there is in reading all that life can afford.'

5

A Life in Literature

PHILIP DAVIS

I don't think my parents read to me much after I could read on my own. I had found it hard to learn to read in the first place. It was at school because in those days, in the austere low-expectation England of the 1950s, parents in ordinary families didn't usually think of teaching their children – it felt like forcing them – in advance of their formal education.

One of the great heart-cries of childhood I remember was my saying in despair to my mother and father, 'I will *never* be able to read.' I hated it that what before I could naturally hear or say with ease was now an act of impatient laboriousness in an unfriendly medium, spelling it out phonetically, pointing with a finger at what hardly made for an immediate word, such was the double work involved in recalling the syllables and then trying to force them together. I could not bear the way it felt so childishly retrograde.

The school primers were called *Janet and John* books. They were boring and frustrating and humiliating. They had no story interest or pull forwards, they were baby-like books, and with their orange and yellow plastic covers they felt resistant and smelt false. My parents bought me copies so I could practise at home where I was happier, rather than have to feel exposed at school. For the first six weeks at Seeley Primary School in Nottingham I had refused to try to speak or read or write, to pick up a pencil or chalk, or move a muscle save to stand up or sit down. It was a protest about not being able to stay at home, though I also felt unhappy because the slate I was meant to chalk upon would not fit easily inside the slot of my desk and so stuck into my stomach a little – and I could not ask for help when everything seemed beyond it.

I was shocked when after the first unhappy morning my dad had insisted I had to go back again in the afternoon, and so on day after day. It was the law, he said, something I had not known was beyond my parents' control. I had thought they were in charge of everything in my life, not that there was a world out there that could constrain them even in relation to me. I was unprepared for the change: that is the word that now emotionally sticks with me for the shorthand of its double prefix: 'un', 'pre', never easily ready. They for their part were very worried by my stubborn school-strike, and went for help to see the headmistress, Miss Smith, a heavy, aged woman who looked like scary Margaret Rutherford. She simply told them, to their surprise, that holding out for six weeks was actually rather impressive, and predicted I would certainly do well in the years to come, pass the eleven-plus examination, and go to grammar school and then perhaps university. They hadn't known I was clever, not through scepticism or lack of love, but lack of confidence and experience. Shortly after they told me they had been to see Miss Smith, I ended my Do-Nothing stoppage when my mother in desperation begged me one day to do anything, chalk my hands, *'Anything'*, and I felt for her distress as worse than mine.

So, I think reading became associated with the outside world and its demands and strangenesses, with having to learn and having to find somehow my own resources there. At home, to manage the transition, we continued with our supplementary work on the *Janet and John* books, and though sitting on my dad's knee, I made progress with the reading of simple subject-verb-object sentences – 'Janet sees John', 'John sees Janet' – I was shocked at the next big development in the never-ending series. I loathed that sequence, book 1, book 2, book 3, with their change of colours also marking what level you were 'on'. And I can't remember at what level it was when it got worse; but suddenly the sentence was more than three words long and went on not just to the reassuring end of the line but across the line onto another, so that you had to keep going forward with the end no longer clearly in sight. It was like the fear of falling or gasping in the midst of swimming a mere width of the pool, reaching ahead for the elusive safety bar. I think now that was my first experience of what later I came to value in poetry: the invention – whoever inconceivably first thought of it – of the movement across the line, 'enjambment' a mumbling technical word I have always disliked: the running-on of a sentence where the turn across the line-ending was itself a form of mental punctuation. But at first these difficulties were very far from appreciated.

I was the only child of fiercely protective Jewish parents who did not formally practise their religion, going to synagogue only once or twice a year for the Day of Atonement and New Year, and marking the Feast of the Passover. They were very committed to assimilation, England being the country of their birth, and they had no allegiance to Israel except at times when its existence was threatened. They were not much involved with the small Jewish community in Nottingham, but then they were not really social beings at all, the little nuclear family being the key relation and safehold. But I think they were much affected by the Second World War and the Holocaust, and especially by the insecurity and austerity that followed. My education in this household, on the boundary between respectable working class and lower middle, was at any rate in English, not Hebrew. Much later I recognized in myself Philip Roth's account of what it meant to be a Jew among Gentiles, a Gentile among Jews, and I think I have mostly enjoyed that compound of assimilation and separateness. There were not very many books in our house but one – the only one I recall as related to that ancient foreign faith, as it then seemed to me – was a sort of Ladybird book of Old Testament stories, with colour pictures on one page and the story opposite. It was the account of the early life of Samuel that stuck with me as a thing mysterious, from the age when I began to read alone. I think I may have been six or seven. Here is the King James version it paraphrased, with all the different referents 'he' – the boy Samuel, belated only son of Ephraim and Hannah who have gratefully placed him in the care of the high priest Eli, to whom one night it happened:

That the Lord called Samuel: and he answered, Here am I.
   And he ran unto Eli, and said, Here am I; for thou calledst me. And he said, I called not; lie down again. And he went and lay down.
   And the Lord called yet again, Samuel. And Samuel arose and went to Eli, and said, Here am I; for thou didst call me. And he answered, I called not, my son; lie down again.

Now Samuel did not yet know the Lord, neither was the word of the Lord yet revealed unto him.

And the Lord called Samuel again the third time. And he arose and went to Eli, and said, Here am I; for thou didst call me. And Eli perceived that the Lord had called the child.

Therefore Eli said unto Samuel, Go, lie down: and it shall be, if he call thee, that thou shalt say, Speak, Lord; for thy servant heareth. So Samuel went and lay down in his place.

And the Lord came, and stood, and called as at other times, Samuel, Samuel. Then Samuel answered, Speak; for thy servant heareth. (1 Samuel 3:4–10)

Samuel, Samuel, Samuel. Three times that mistake as to who was calling. But I did not know about that ritual rhythm of three, and I did not really know about repetition and trial-and-error, rather than knowing what was happening all at once. As with reading, I was a somewhat scared learner of new things; but I saw that that was what it took, three sets of to-ing and fro-ing, before the thing was rightly placed and understood. I did know the feeling of vulnerable obedience in Samuel, and the being benignly sent back to bed, as if it was only a nightmare. But it was that insistent fourth call I loved: the way that Eli, an alternative adult father-figure, suddenly used his authority and power of reassurance against himself, to point to a lord or father more than both the child and the grown-up, and gently hand over to Him. It felt like a *rite de passage*, I now think, a kind of early bar-mitzvah, to know the closeness of a father and a god, and then the final difference and separation between them. The message had come disguised in human form but was from somewhere else than normal. It was the first story, I now believe, that itself called to me: to be heard, read and interpreted, and somehow then responded to and acted upon. That's what reading was when it was no longer stumbling word by word, syllable by syllable: finding something call to you surprisingly, finding something in you that was called out by it which otherwise might not be known. Reading felt natural suddenly, like the animal-like action of hunting for clues, or scenting food, or following tracks, only the food here was a sense of meaning.

There were less solemn versions of reading. Mr Martin had replaced Miss Smith as the head of the primary school and insisted with typical masculinity on greater time for sports. I was not any good at football but found I wanted to be, was excited to feel what it would be like to have heroic skill in winning the day for your team. It meant I had to imagine by reading about it instead. I did not like the library in school or town because I never knew what to choose. But I did like the title of a novel for kids, *The Young Footballer* by Robert Bateman, which came out when I was eight. What I remember was a rather useless team of schoolboy footballers who, always beaten, came upon a touchline spectator their same age who told them what they were doing wrong. What is more, he could show them. The honourable Joe was of an aristocratic family and looked weedily academic, but for all his thin legs and lofty background, he was a natural genius who could perform miracles with the ball. At the heart of the team, this disguised football-superman took them on a winning run – until just before a vital match he got injured. Then he had to try to teach all he knew to the best learner left in the team, a bespectacled youth called Stevie. I was weedy and

I wore glasses, but what struck me about the move from the genius to Stevie was something to do with replacing a wonderful fantasy, the effortless god-given talent, with something lesser and secondary but hard-won. It was here, I think, that I came upon a phrase I did not understand but wanted to: 'peripheral vision' was what Stevie was taught. This led me to the dictionary. As I got more confident, I got more attracted to phrases I couldn't immediately understand. In *Macbeth*, it was to do with blood that would 'the multitudinous seas incarnadine', so many syllables. Another was from Suetonius' *The Twelve Caesars*, in translation. It was about the emperor Tiberius who, it was said, would 'depilate his concubines'. I didn't know either of those main words but was sexually inquisitive, and would sing them to myself long afterwards to the tune of 'Gaudeamus Igitur'. This was in my early teens, after watching a TV serial production of Robert Graves's *I, Claudius*. I was fascinated by both the power struggles and the struggles for survival, especially the transformation of Claudius himself from neglected idiot-status to emperor. I loved the way the TV serial led to the book, and then the book to a sequence of other kindred books: this was no longer random choice but a sort of rhythm and career. And I was getting more interested in how one word led to another too. In tests of comprehension at school we were often asked to read a passage and then give our own definition of key words or difficult phrases within it. What I noticed was that I could never do this at one shot: I would have a first go that was in the approximate area of the word, then another go and another to refine it, to get closer to the feel of it, until there was a final word I underlined as nearest to it. This was an exciting process: that words and their meanings came out of discovery and feeling; that often somewhere, somehow, inside oneself one already dimly knew them without looking them up.

But back in my childhood I never really liked the unknown or the abnormal. Children's adventure stories felt beyond my league, and I didn't like the gangs, Famous Five or Secret Seven. I was more into some struggling loner, trying (I now think) to become individual. There was another book like *The Young Footballer*, a previously spurned gift that I found in a cupboard, about Carlos, a young racing driver, while I was suffering from a cold and feeling at a loose end. I was surprised to find myself enthralled by the ups and downs involved in simply mastering a discipline, it hardly mattered which – getting some luck, taking the opportunities and the kicks. It wasn't to do with cars: I liked playing with little models, but never wanted to drive and never learned. It was to do with what I was to recognize, twenty years later, in Chekhov's saying about the need to squeeze the slave out of oneself.

Reading as interpretation. Reading as a way to learn growing up. Reading on how to deal with the relation of the inner and the outer realms, or the difference between home-world and the world outside. There was something in all this about hiddenness and disguise, and a need to read so as to find the inside of appearances. My parents were not fussy about what I read as long as I was reading and relishing, and for a long time I trawled a local newsagent for DC comics imported from glamorous America: especially Superman and the way he was hidden within mild-mannered bespectacled reporter Clark Kent, just as Zorro the masked avenger was the secret identity of Don Diego, an apparently timid young nobleman. They hid their talents, they protected their specialness. Theirs was to me like another version of the story of Joseph which I had read in that book of Old Testament stories. Joseph had been sold away by his elder brothers, jealous of the coat their father gave him, only to re-form his life as an Egyptian official. In time of famine, the brothers then come to this overseer in need of grain, not knowing that it is their brother. I loved the double vision in it, the hidden boy within the powerful man. That turn of knowledge and power were sufficient in themselves, there was no need then for revenge. I guess a story like that of Joseph prepared me for relishing the rise of Claudius, the second chance for misfits and rejects. Again, years later, still thinking through the medium of sport, I loved it when Muhammad Ali adopted his rope-a-dope strategy against George Foreman in Zaire. He just lay back on the ropes and invited the frightening Foreman to punch himself out, before launching a quick offensive comeback. It was like Superman imagining he had lost his superpowers, and how he would cope without them as a common mortal. But Ali wasn't just pretending he had lost his powers, in a sort of existential experiment; he had to some extent really lost his gift during his enforced absence from the boxing ring in protest against Vietnam; and the two things overlapped so that he could also half-pretend to himself he was only pretending he was a lesser thing. What he had still though was a super resilience defying the reduction to ordinariness, an intelligent and defiant mentality. I relished that better than his powers, I loved a second life won out of the losses of a first one.

But, on the other side of that thought of the hidden, there was also in my youth a television serial I used to watch with my dad which must have been somewhat based on John Wyndham's science fiction novel *The Day of the Triffids*. My mother would not watch it because it was so frightening but my dad said it would be okay for me. It was about a form of plant life taking over life on earth – but doing so by inhabiting human forms. You thought it was your friend or your relation, but actually it was an alien life-form incarnate within their familiar bodies and voices, to take you over in turn. It might reassuringly seem to be your own father: it wasn't really. It took a strange kind of nerve and belief to see through the false comfort and unreal reassurance, to dare infer the alien within the human. I didn't tell my father how much this takeover terrified me, because I also somehow needed to keep watching.

I had never liked childhood stories about non-human things, but in those early years around six I was equivocally attracted to the fairy tale 'Beauty and the Beast'. The simplified comic-book version I had read had three powerfully disturbing components for me. One was to do with the plucking of a rose that wasn't one's own property, and the forfeit that had to be paid for it: a father surrendering his daughter to a beast. The second was that within the appearance of a repulsive beast a prince was trapped. The third was that a kiss from the beautiful girl, reduced from princess to a Cinderella-existence by her older sisters, could turn him back into a prince again. It felt even then deeply erotic. I could understand that she would want to kiss a handsome prince, but to kiss the ugly beast even in the deeply hidden hope of making him handsome again: that was a huge risk. And yet the sexuality, which I know I felt, was transformative.

But the other main element in my early reading was my assuming the character of the work's protagonist afterwards. The errant schoolboy, Richmal Crompton's William Brown; Nottingham's own Robin Hood; cowboys in print or on screen:

these were the various wilder characters I liked to carry over into my often solitary play by turning down my socks and making liquorice water, wearing a green cap and carrying a bow, or riding horseback on the arm of the settee. I didn't just want to be them, I wanted to make them last longer, extend them into my own life, and re-create them. Once I secretly added some grains of salt to the parents' sugar bowl, and when my mother asked me about it following an unhappy experience with their cup of tea, I told her I was being William. I didn't seem to feel guilty; I hadn't quite registered the transfer from book to real life. But my mother seemed satisfied and there were no consequences. It is clear to me now that all this was like a form of rewriting of the books and programmes, to give them more life and to give me their life. For I recall that if something went wrong in my acting out, and I suddenly felt it had become silly and unreal, I would want to close the episode by saying out loud 'More next week!' and start again before the point at which I had lost the emotional atmosphere it was meant to perpetuate.

I always felt instinctively that you had to do something with the reading after the reading had stopped, to carry it on emotionally. The culmination of this sense of always being *moved* to do something with it was in school rather than home. A teacher got us eight-year-olds, I think, to read Erich Kästner's *Emil and the Detectives* and helped us turn it into a play. Miss Bignall liked me but God help a poor typecast boy, she chose me to play the Professor, a youth with horn-rimmed glasses who liked to take them off and polish them, like his father, when he was going to say something important and organize the others. I could do that on stage, as if I was indeed in some ways too old for my age; but really inside it was Emil I had felt for when reading the book: the boy packed off to journey alone by train to his relatives in Berlin, with his mother's precious banknotes in an envelope in his inside breast pocket. I read this to my grandson the other day and had the same anxious feeling again in the places of transition:

> 'And for heaven's sake, don't lose that money.' At her last words Emil clutched his pocket in sudden panic then gave a sigh of relief . . .
>
> Emil felt his right-hand pocket, and was not satisfied until he heard the envelope crackle, though the other passengers looked honest enough, and not in the least like thieves or murderers.
>
> Emil would have liked to check his money again . . . so as soon as the train moved off he went into the adjoining toilet and took the envelope out of his pocket. The money was still there and he counted it. Then he wondered what he could do to make it safer, and had a good idea. He remembered he had a pin . . .

Always trying to make it safer, counting it again, never leaving it be. And then the boy falls asleep, only awakening of course to put his hand again into that inner pocket on the right-hand side . . . and find 'the pocket was empty, the money had gone'. I think I weirdly sensed that beneath any literal detective story that would follow was the secret psychological detection that if you fear something long enough, it *will* happen; it is already happening in the very effort to safeguard against it; you will somehow have made the disaster occur despite yourself. And naturally the loss would occur in the midst of sleep not just because Emil was simply off his guard in the outer world but because of the strange workings of (what I could not then call) the unconscious in the inner one. If this seems a disturbing insight, I have to report that I also experienced it behind my own back, so to speak, with an implicit sense of excitement, of recognition and discovery. It was as if there was something privately as important as the sheer explicit content, something that came out of being able to begin to think of it and explore it and bear it and be it, however unhappy or disturbing 'it' might be. It was like a private adventure and a second skin.

I also began to assume there was some relation between being a reader and being an actor. But I gave up play-acting one precise moment in the first year of secondary school at High Pavement Grammar. In rehearsal of a Roman crowd scene, I knew I could and should take a lead in spontaneously baying for blood, and indeed I wanted to impress the director from upper school. But like everyone else, I stayed shyly, stupidly, passively silent. I missed the call, I couldn't find a place for myself out there, among them all, and acting was gone.

Instead, with the help and support of my parents, I found I was a good student and I disappeared into my books, until no one could tell who I was but that. It did not matter what the subject was. While my mother trudged round Nottingham picking up books I needed, my sole concern at this point was to do well, to forge an identity through being more successful in tests and exams than I had ever imagined being. I hadn't known I was clever. I came across a book on how to study and was gratified to find that I was already doing much of what was suggested. It made me feel like a home-made professional, someone who had found for himself from within his practice a method of note-taking and memorialization, without being taught it. But the mechanism, though passionately adopted, was itself pretty near regardless of interest or natural skill. It was so thorough and consuming as almost to make success foolproof, though nervously I would never have dared assume so. To go back to my football stories, I was like a player so well drilled as never to trust to taking any creative risk.

There were moments when something else took over, though. I remember being told to read aloud in class the great rhetorical passage from *Julius Caesar* where Marc Antony gives his funeral oration, 'Friends, Romans, countrymen'. I had never read it before, but suddenly got taken up in hearing myself assume its voice:

> You all did see that on the Lupercal
> I thrice presented him a kingly crown,
> Which he did thrice refuse. Was this ambition?
> Yet Brutus says he was ambitious,
> And Brutus is an honourable man. (III.2)

I was really enjoying its mastery when the teacher stopped me dead. All he could hear was my enjoyment. I hadn't a clue that it didn't sound deadly serious, outside me: it felt excitingly serious inside. But the hidden subsidiary within reading – the secondary thing which is the relish of the rhetorical question, or the excitement at Emil's anxiety, or the good won in being able to think even of the discreditable – had shown through for once. He made me read it again, more soberly, and, embarrassed and deflated, I didn't enjoy it any more. Usually this teacher was very encouraging of me. But during a period when I was doing badly with my essay writing, I asked him to show me what was wrong with it. I suppose what I felt was helplessness must have come over as aggression and challenge. Feeling cornered, I now think, he said to me what I never forgot, 'The trouble with you, Davis, is that you are not as good as you think you are.'

The pressure of trying to do well came from me, not from my parents. They would have been relieved if I had been happier and less driven. But despite setbacks the strain was long sustainable because of the intrinsic reward of the status achieved. It may seem as though this was no more and no less than ambition. But it was more vulnerable than that. Though from a more mature external perspective the essays and the exams were routine, for me they were a life, an identity and a genuinely threatening test of nerve and stamina. Many years later, I suddenly remembered it in the light of reading Frederic Manning's *Her Privates We*, an account of soldiers in the First World War in which it was not the fighting but the waiting to go over the top that was most terrible to them. This can only be ridiculously embarrassing, to compare a schoolboy's nerves in the face of tests to a soldier's fear of death in the mud fields. But in truth I was undergoing large experiences within a small one, a content larger than the mundane little form in which it was both released and constrained.[1]

But increasingly it was literature that became different from the study of chemistry or history and was not just a means to an end. And this began not in school but in reading done at home. The first adult fictional book that really mattered to me came at a point of early adolescence, maybe about thirteen. It was certainly at a time when I kept feeling I was making mistakes. It was as though I was repeatedly offending or upsetting or annoying people outside, friends and family, while inside having no such intention. I felt like an innocent blunderer, no better but humiliatingly worse for feeling innocent when it also meant being ignorant. It kept on happening in a variety of settings with a different range of people, so I knew back-to-front, by inference, that it must be down to me. I had been trying to read some of the classic authors in a rather routine fashion but then came upon Thomas Hardy's *Mayor of Casterbridge*. And if now I had to re-imagine and explain its sudden explosive effect on me, it would be from a passage like the following. The mayor, Michael Henchard, gradually loses everything, bit by bit, including his girlfriend to the man, Donald Farfrae, who had once been his second-in-command in business and now was besting him. Henchard had once tried crudely to engage clever Farfrae in a bare fist fight, in the old fashion. Now he learns that the woman Farfrae has taken from him is dangerously ill, that Farfrae has gone off without knowing it, and only he, Henchard, knows where he has gone, to fetch him back. In one scene he had been the attacker; now only a little later but on a better impulse he is the urgent messenger. There is no simple continuity to it. But Farfrae still regards him suspiciously as the attacker:

> 'Come back to Casterbridge at once!' Henchard said. 'There's something wrong at your house – requiring your return. I've run all the way here on purpose to tell ye.'
>
> Farfrae was silent, and at his silence Henchard's soul sank within him. Why had he not, before this, thought of what was only too obvious? He who, four hours earlier, had enticed Farfrae into a deadly wrestle stood now in the darkness of late night-time on a lonely road, inviting him to come a particular way, where an assailant might have

confederates, instead of going his purposed way, where
there might be a better opportunity of guarding himself
from attack. Henchard could almost feel this view of
things in course of passage through Farfrae's mind.[2]

This was the blundering of a misfit now writ large in the
form of an old, hasty, physical type of man, at once brutal
and sensitive, suddenly turned outside-in, into a terrible self-
consciousness. His soul sank within him, it says. Why had he
not thought in advance of how Farfrae would be bound to see
it? He could almost feel it now from Farfrae's point of view.
These things take the life from inside Henchard; they begin to
diminish and kill him. This passage then was secretly to do with
me, my getting it wrong in life, not able to live easily from within
outwards. It was a relief to see it in another: if more humiliating,
then less embarrassing. But being to do with an old type of man,
it was also at the same time to do with my father. I didn't realize
the same thing could serve almost simultaneously two purposes.
I had begun to see, with some pain, that my father was not some
god as I had sort of assumed before; that as himself a vulnerable
and awkward man he too made gaffes, offered repetitive defensive
bluster, and showed the weaknesses of any man. Our family had
been built upon the maximum of verbal communication: you
were meant to share your worries, to be honest and never lie, to
seek help in the very security of something always being able to
be said straight, named, discussed, motivated, advised upon. My
mother was the one who was good at opening it up. 'What's the
matter? You can tell me. How can I help?' But now I had secrets
and reservations and separate thoughts. That meant from now
on I turned slowly but ever increasingly to reading instead of

speaking, to literature instead of my parents. And this because in literature, unlike my other school subjects, the facts were never real facts unless they were also emotional. It was what I found, many years later in George Eliot's *Daniel Deronda*, another of those texts that were to release from childhood and adolescence long-held but inchoate blockages and dilemmas:

> He was ceasing to care for knowledge – he had no ambition for practice – unless they could both be gathered up into one current with his emotions; and he dreaded, as if it were a dwelling-place of lost souls, that dead anatomy of culture which turns the universe into a mere ceaseless answer to queries, and knows, not everything, but everything else about everything – as if one should be ignorant of nothing concerning the scent of violets except the scent itself for which one had no nostril.[3]

That is why after all the success of answers to the exam questions, I took both what I had and what I hadn't into the reading of literature: emotional knowledge in the excitement of finding thoughts and ideas, and ways of phrasing them, that seem to ring an instinctive emotional bell of semi-recognition. And in that endeavour I wanted, and ever increasingly so at university, not to think by theories and agendas, out of imposed professionalism, or the old ambition to do well academically. Instead, I unashamedly and sometimes desperately sought to *use* literature as a form of mental expression and inquiry, as my alternative to religion: in shorthand after Deronda, not to do thinking 'about', but to do thinking 'within'. It meant having thoughts and ideas as if always for the first time, felt afresh like an almost personal revelation from the book working within oneself. It may have been naive to go to literature seeking answers and solutions to life, but that is what I couldn't help stubbornly wanting as a core belief in the background – however subsequently thwarted and chastened, refined or modified, that core quest for verbal insight and relief was to become. Tell me what you know, I asked story or poem that really seemed to matter, and what you help me find in myself.

A few years later, in that inner assembling of moments of help from different books and times and authors, I associated that passage from *The Mayor of Casterbridge*, and the feelings and resonances it gave me, with this from a father in D. H. Lawrence's *The Rainbow*. It was a link that was part of my personal anthology, my felt repertoire of touchstones and lifesavers in extended mind or alternative memory – scattered things that amid my minor version of diaspora still did good and held true. Will Brangwen roughly turns on his little daughter Ursula when a charwoman complains to him of her playing carelessly in the church, only to be challenged by his wife on their child's behalf:

> His voice was harsh and cat-like, he was blind to the child. She shrank away in childish anguish and dread. What was it, what awful thing was it?
>
> The mother turned with her calm, almost superb manner.
>
> 'What has she done, then?'
>
> 'Done? She shall go in the church no more, pulling and littering and destroying.'
>
> The wife slowly rolled her eyes and lowered her eyelids.
>
> 'What has she destroyed, then?'

He did not know.

'I've just had Mrs. Wilkinson at me,' he cried, 'with a list of things she's done.'

Ursula withered under the contempt and anger of the 'she', as he spoke of her.

'Send Mrs. Wilkinson here to me with a list of the things she's done,' said Anna. 'I am the one to hear that.'

'It's not the things the child has done,' continued the mother, 'that have put you out so much, it's because you can't bear being spoken to by that old woman. But you haven't the courage to turn on her when she attacks you, you bring your rage here.'

He relapsed into silence. Ursula knew that he was wrong. In the outside, upper world, he was wrong. Already came over the child the cold sense of the impersonal world. There she knew her mother was right. But still her heart clamoured after her father, for him to be right, in his dark, sensuous underworld. But he was angry, and went his way in blackness and brutal silence again.[4]

What got me was that turn from the child hurt ('under the contempt and anger of the "she"') to the child nonetheless still feeling for the father who stupidly hurt her, caught out as he was by the cleverer mother in all his ungainliness. I thought of my own father and mother, and the pain of criticism made, understandably enough, in the midst of a crisis for my unlucky parents in financial difficulties. I thought above all about this other world, an underworld referred to in the final paragraph, beneath the clear conventional everyday world in which he was wrong. That everyday world was really not sufficient.

So, the odd thing is that though reading had started as a demand from the outside world, from school, increasingly it became a form of movement into the inner one. It is what D. H. Lawrence in *Fantasia of the Unconscious* called a 'retreat to the centre' – retreat not in the sense of defeat but the withdrawal that is also a refuge in thinking and a place of recharging, from which to begin again to come back out. 'To be still . . . to turn away . . . Not to rush around on the periphery, like a rabbit in a ring, trying to break through. But to retreat to the very centre, and there to be filled with a new strange stability.'⁵ It meant a licking of one's wounds but more than that, a release of something potentially creative out of the pain, a hidden exhilaration that things not going right could still be found useful.

The end of this phase of my story comes with the experience of my having a teacher who was also a novelist. Hidden away in the provinces, working away as a schoolmaster in the school in which he himself had been taught, Stanley Middleton shared the Booker Prize in 1974. The more he taught me, in his rather quiet and reserved way, the more I wanted to know what was the relation between the man, the teacher and the novelist. In primary school I had had a secret trick I used against teachers I disliked. I employed my spectacles to reflect light from the ceiling lamps to make what I imagined was a death ray going into the head of the instructor in front of me. I thought it was a malign version of Superman's X-ray vision that I could see through my glasses but no one else could. To the teacher, if noted at all, it must have seemed an odd nodding twitch, more like something out of Claudius. In secondary school, this had changed. I looked at Middleton telling us that this line of poetry was a treat, a marvel –

If I did love you in my master's flame,
With such a suff'ring, such a deadly life,
In your denial I would find no sense,
I would not understand it.

I wanted instead to flip a switch, to get into my head whatever this meant to him in his mind, in his experience of literature. It was from *Twelfth Night*, Act I scene 5, where Viola, disguised as the boy messenger Cesario, tells Olivia of the love borne her by the Duke Orsino. Later I read Middleton's novel *Cold Gradations* in which a retired schoolmaster hears those words from his youthful education in a final performance. In the box in a London theatre, 'as he revelled in this bursting language of spring, he had suddenly thought that he would probably never hear these words, fresh and familiar, again . . . Ice of death. A blank, my lord. She never told her love. That. That.' Middleton in the classroom and Middleton at the writing desk were suddenly connected.

And I remember a couple of the lads were complaining to me in his class that I, the cleverly efficient exam-topping one, could never really understand literature if I did not try to write it myself. I said I wouldn't do that, wouldn't try to write poetry, and just stubbornly shook my head when they pressed me. We all knew Stanley Middleton was a writer himself, a novelist. I fully expected him to disapprove. He said nothing in class about my refusal, but later in the year recalled the incident to my father and mother at parents' evening and surprisingly praised me for knowing my mind and being resolute even in seeming negative.

He also said to me, about some writing I had done on Michael Henchard, 'You have imagination.' I was astonished: I thought that was where I was sorely lacking and inartistic. I never could bring myself to dare to invent novel situations, fantastic stories or unfamiliar settings, beyond my ken or outside the reality I clung to. But he meant I could imagine other people's feelings through my own, and I had not realized that that too was imagination.

So, I come to the close here, leaving my teens, and thinking about the questions put to me by the editors of this collection as a writer about reading and the relations of books to individuals' existence. We shall ask academic critics, they said – and I winced at that professionalized description – 'How has reading shaped them as persons and as authors? In what way has reading impacted their choice of profession and their research?'

I feel a little sceptical about neat chronological causation and clearly routed developmental answers. In this essay I have been reading my life in literature backwards and then reading it forwards again. There is in that a danger of tautology or circularity: that I have recalled and selected only what in retrospect I think the past contributed to what I was to become. But really I cannot tell how much the past created that future, or the future has created that past, and expect only an inextricable mixture of the two if I have managed to write well enough to escape the too obvious themes and trajectories, and overflow the easy categories and summaries as literature itself does. But I do trust it when a passage such as that on Michael Henchard recalls for me another, about Will Brangwen: these sudden re-formed links seem to have their *own* memory within me, independent of control, resonantly emotional, a life in literature. What I trust are things made distressingly or hearteningly clear and salient by dint of undeniable feelings – including perhaps above all the not very dignified and often ineffectual struggle to grow up, using literature instead of God and in place of parents. And if 'grow up' is not the right term either, at least there is Yeats in his 'Dialogue of Self and Soul' and the meaning of line after line, like stage after stage, in a stumbling life:

> What matter if I live it all once more?
> Endure that toil of growing up;
> The ignominy of boyhood; the distress
> Of boyhood changing into man;
> The unfinished man and his pain
> Brought face to face with his own clumsiness;
>
> The finished man among his enemies? –

I do still feel the presence of such enemies within the over-professionalism of academic literary studies during my time, when I think instead of emotional knowledge and the raw individual need for help and expression in a life; of the relation of reading and personal psychology; of the power of realism in the novel and in the lives of ordinary readers; and of the hidden biographies of writers within their writings. What have I done? I have written books about readers and reading – about thought and questioning, feeling and memory, mental life and mental trauma and mental flourishing through literature – always concentrating on key passages that seemed to kick a hole through walls of silence or convention. I have published works on Victorian realism and the secularization of purpose; biographies of writers to try to see how they worked and lived; articles on brain-imaging to try to reach the pre-conceptual force of a dramatically shifting word or vital sentence-shape in an important situation. And I believe I can see some of the psychological origins for that in what I have written here.

But though I have loved talking and teaching, and have needed to write about what I thought, I never set out to be a lecturer, researcher or professor as such – that was incidental albeit necessitated, as compared to what from youth remained raw and personal within. For sure I made compromises as well as efforts in order to assimilate to some degree within the institution, to be employed and published and somewhat recognized. But really the university descriptors were just the external terms and conditions for carrying on doing what I wanted to do, more aggressively, in the chinks of freedom within the set routines, and in the unmarked area in between literature and life. I say 'in between' because at best I never knew *where* I was, whatever it was called externally: it was a hybrid form, a holding-place for reading and feeling and thinking, nominally called 'literary criticism', and aided also by elements of 'philosophy' and 'psychology' within the makeshift amalgam that insistently related fictional and real. And the commitment was always hedged around with threatening warnings and demeaning negatives – that literature was not as good as life and should not take its place; that my kind of middle-man writing was never as primary as being a poet, or novelist or dramatist.

So it is that when I try to reach a conclusion on what reading literature has been for me, and not just for my 'profession' or my 'research', I first have to adapt four quietly private words wrung out of a poem by Stanley Middleton in the selection I edited for him after his death – protectively understated words that fight their way through the twist and the turn of life's negatives. They are these: 'I am not ungrateful.'

And then, in inner truth, something more is needed than that 'not un'. For shorthand, this juxtaposition. Once more, my mother in my childhood: even just chalk your hands, don't do nothing, do something, anything, how can I help you. And with it, this from Hopkins in 'Carrion Comfort', against the despairing cry of 'I can no more': 'I can' – the poet then struggling to spell it out across the line, like a raw child still, within the human sentence 'Can something, hope, wish day come, not choose not to be.' That is what it has meant to me, stronger in shorthand without proper name or title: Not choose not to; Can something.

6

Reading (in) My Father's Shadow

HETA PYRHÖNEN

The table lamp casts light on my dad who lies on the floor. He is reading Aleksis Kivi's *Seven Brothers* to us three girls. I am on the upper bunk of the bunk bed. I love this book, it is exciting, humorous, its language is rich and beautiful. My father's reading is highly associative, for events and details in the text make him go off and interlace his reading with his own stories about his childhood and youth. As his family's stories are braided with that of the seven brothers, I think the brothers are my kin. Illustrations of them look like my father's relatives: thick unruly hair, beady eyes, rustic.

My father's stories briefly enumerated: When four years old, he woke up, but could not get up, because his own father had died in the night and his arm lay heavy over his son. After the loss of his father, he never saw his mother again, because she had tuberculosis and was sent to a sanatorium. Father was sent to his grandparents' farm and returned home only for his mother's funeral two years later. His young cousin died in an accident when a workbench, fastened on a wall, fell on her head, crushing it. Was there a cracking sound when her skull broke? I wondered, but never asked. His grandfather suffered a stroke when they were working in the woods. The men cut saplings and, using their coats, made a stretcher to carry him. The grandfather was placed on the ground every now and then so that hymns could be sung. Someone had run ahead to fetch the doctor who was 30 kilometres away. 'Run, don't pray,' I shouted in my mind. The grandfather died shortly after. Aunt Olga took my father's two sisters to live with her, but not him, because she was afraid of the unruliness of boys. Father was sent to his aunt Selma's house, yet Selma had just died in childbirth, and so her husband took father in. The motherless baby was fed cream, milk and butter with a spoon; Dad would have liked to have received the same fare. Frightened by Selma's fate, the rest of Dad's eight aunts resolved to remain brides of Jesus. While in gymnasium, all the members of the family with whom my father lodged died when Russians bombed their house during the Continuation War against the Soviet Union. His other sister died of cancer when he was a young adult.

When my father was sixteen, he joined the army and was first stationed in Eastern Finland and then Lapland. The war stories were chapters in themselves. They were too much for me and I actively closed my ears whenever he started recounting them. Not listening felt, however, like a betrayal. My Uncle Topi had lost his leg when he stepped onto a landmine, and when I said that his leg ought to be revenged, Father took it as a sign of my capacity for ethical thinking. I disagreed, recognizing it for a crude wish for revenge. Whenever Uncle Topi with his prosthetic leg visited us, there would be much talk of politics with the uncle smoking cigarillos and the sound of cognac being poured into snifters. When the rapid conversation changed into laughter, I knew that, despite everything, Finland had somehow actually won the war.

These first contacts with being read to left me convinced that in literature someone must always die, and that death comes in many forms, not only as physical demise but as the extinguishing of hopes, wishes, security and love. Father's own stories were sad, but his telling of them was humorous. He never complained or expressed self-pity. My mother disliked reading aloud, so only my father read to us. He read all kinds of books, the *Kanteletar* (Finnish folk poetry), *Shock-Headed Peter*, Donald Duck comics and Wilhelm Busch. His favourites were *Hookeybeak the Raven* and *Max and Moritz*, and we all laughed when the boys were ground to grains. This association of books with death was strengthened by the fact that, whenever my parents travelled together without us children, my mother would go through what we should do in case they died. Father's remaining sister would take us, it had already been agreed. (Mother was nine years old when the Winter War started and had her own anxiety-filled stories of the war.) All their documents and bankbooks were hidden in the hollow underneath the lowest shelf of our grey bookcase. One time she cleared the shelf and went through the papers with me. It was a solemn moment.

I learned to read at school. One of my favourite books was a huge black Bible with Gustave Doré's impressive illustrations. This Bible was a real tome, so heavy that you had to carry it with both hands, and I loved the way it heavily weighed on my legs when I opened it. One had to be careful, as the pages were super thin. Bible stories were strange, exciting and frightful. I liked most the story of Samuel when God quietly calls him. As in fairy tales, the call is repeated three times. Did Samuel hear

God's voice or his own inner voice? Having wilfully closed my ears to Father's war stories, that voice impressed on me the idea of being directly spoken to, of being accosted by a narrative. It was a real discovery to notice that books are filled with all kinds of sounds, noises and voices and, more still, that I could hear them, and they could address me directly. But I was distressed to read in the New Testament these words: 'Therefore I speak to them in parables: because seeing they do not see, and hearing they do not hear, nor do they understand.'[1] It was this link between the senses and understanding that proved to be personally significant for me.

In my dad's stories about his childhood and adolescence I did hear what I thought of as reams and reams of sorrow. I sensed that in him were, as it were, neatly folded layers of sorrow, tears and fragility and if one cut an opening, they would cascade out. It was only later when studying literature that I realized the bedtime reading trained us to hear beneath the voice and decipher between words. Indeed, when my father was in his fifties his telling of childhood stories got more sombre. The suppressed emotions took hold, and he sank into a deep depression that incapacitated him for almost three years.

I became a voracious reader. I loved all kinds of adventure stories. The sound of hoofs on the pampas, the struggle against howling wind, and the lashing of Zorro's whip. I particularly enjoyed *Robinson Crusoe*. Crusoe reverberated with another book I liked, *Every Woman's How To: A Practical Guide*. That book was a veritable treasure trove: you had a practical problem, and then you solved it with skill. For me, Crusoe was the epitome of a resourceful, in fact, a feminine, person. Here is Robinson, after finding a fruitful valley: 'I saw here abundance of cocoa trees, orange, and lemon, and citron trees; but all wild ... I mixed their juice afterwards with water, which made it very wholesome, and very cool and refreshing.' How Crusoe not only organized and managed his world but reflected on and sorted out his feelings and occasional despair was enjoyable. Also, I liked the sense that I could stow away Crusoe's survival tactics in my mind for potential future reference.

I devoured books by Montgomery, Alcott, Anni Swan, Maria Gripe and Austen, the Brontës. Of course, I dreamt of having talent with words. Yet what most drew me to these books was that the protagonists had to learn to navigate socially in their families and communities. Although I enjoyed adventure, these books had wholly different survival challenges than adventures. They necessitated different types of skills, a wider range of emotions and finer qualities of self-reflection from the female protagonists. With my best friend, we acted out these books, donning suitable clothes. Many of these games lasted for months.

My most memorable childhood reading experience was Charlotte Brontë's *Jane Eyre*. A novel about an orphan child, misunderstood, suffering loss after loss, it spoke directly to my whole being. Jane's thoughts, feelings and her very passionate way of being in the world felt intimately familiar. Again, there are voices – Bertha's anxious sounds, Miss Ingram's hostile, cold voice, Mr Rochester's mellifluous singing voice – and, of course, his desperate shouting plea to Jane sounding across vast distances. But the most significant sound is Jane's inner voice that she hears when Rochester tries to bully her into living with him out of wedlock. His fervent, loud badgering stands in stark contrast to her quiet, measured and firm, declaration of independence and separateness: 'I care for myself.'[2]

We tend to think of the books we read as children with nostalgia and fondness. But what about books that have left a lasting negative mark on us? In hindsight, *Every Woman's How To* has been the most damaging book I have read. It made me feel personally addressed by vexing things I encountered. I tried so hard to distil them into clear-cut problems so that they could be solved. It took a long time to realize this was a mindset and shed it.

Father had heart issues and was every now and then taken to hospital. I feared he would die. *Every Woman's How To* does not supply advice on situations such as these. Lacking other resources, I remembered mother's story of her tactic during wartime. She recounted that her father and eldest sister refused to take shelter during bombings, remaining in their home on the fifth floor. On her way to school, Mother took care not to step on cracks on the pavement. That was her way of trying to ensure that a bomb would not hit their building. Hence, whenever I went cycling, I guided the wheel of my bike over pebbles in such a way that they made a small ping. That meant my father was given one extra day of life. I gathered days for him, and those days turned into weeks and months. Record-keeping, however, was very difficult; by and by I lost count. Frustrated, I eventually decided that one ping equalled a week, but that was cheating! Finally, I could not but concede that I was resorting to magic and superstition: I gave up.

Before I started school and learned to read, my father told me that I should study hard so that one day I could become a psychoanalyst, but I knew I would not, because then I would always have to keep my ears open. I was in third grade when my father gifted me the Finnish translation of Robert F. Kennedy's

13 Days: A Memoir of the Cuban Missile Crisis for Christmas.
I started reading it but did not understand it, which greatly
frustrated me. I understood most words but could not make
sense of them together. Next year the gift was a book about
Yugoslavian partisans, and then an autobiography by Aino
Kuusinen, *Jumala syöksee enkelinsä* (God Topples Down His
Angels). Aino Kuusinen was the wife of Otto Wille Kuusinen,
a Finnish communist who fled to Russia and became a member
of the Kremlin inner circle: in 1938 he did nothing to save
his now-estranged wife from being sent to a gulag. After
Christmas, the process was always the same: a week or two
later, my father would ask me if I had read the book (I had
really tried, but failed); then he would look surprised and say
he could read it. So, the book passed from my hands to his.

I knew these gifts were well-meaning, he wanted to share
things that interested him and talk about them. For me,
however, they created a sense that things simply were beyond
my understanding: I was blind, deaf and did not understand.
It was this expectation of a lively conversation in which both
express their views and assessments that crushed me. Later,
when I was in high school, he started giving me books on
psychoanalysis, for example, Alice Miller's *For Your Own Good*
and *The Tragedy of the Gifted Child*. As I was then older, these
books made sense and were even stimulating.

Father died in 2004. The night before he died, I visited him
in the hospital. He was reading the newspaper, but pushed
it aside and began eagerly explaining to me how he planned
to have some trees cut so that he could buy a red convertible.
He had not had a driver's licence in ten years and the land
he was planning on harvesting was the graveyard where most

of his family were buried. This was an amusingly wonderful vision, and I could see him in a bright red car, speeding from the graveyard where now stood only gravestones. I marvelled at the compactness of this fantasy – what payback at the persons who had left him alone far too soon. The next night we were called in to say goodbye. His last words were 'I will pull through.'

I have tried to capture the perspective of the child I once was to convey that which characterized my early listening and reading. The early bedtime stories meant, of course, the passing on of traumatic memories. In the words of Galit Atlas: 'The people we love and those who raised us live inside us, we experience their emotional pain, we dream their memories, we know what was not explicitly conveyed to us, and these things shape our lives in ways that we don't always understand.'[3]

Surely, many painful emotions were passed on, but those evenings under the yellow lamplight also passed on a love for language, form, cadence and narrative. Although I at times closed my ears, I did understand much and hear the humorous slant in most things. I learnt to trust the serendipity of reading: I know that the books, phrases or words that I need eventually reach me. I know I will hear, understand and cherish them.

Today, I think of reading as *being with* a dialogic other. Is it ironic or a secret blessing that what Thomas H. Ogden says about psychoanalysis describes reading for me? In conversation with a book a reader is 'free to engage in an unimpeded stream of consciousness, a type of consciousness generated by means of a relatively unencumbered interplay of the conscious and unconscious aspects of their two minds working/dreaming separately and together'.[4]

7

Reading in Times of War

NATALYA BEKHTA

This essay was very different before 24 February 2022, when I opened my usual news website at about 7 a.m. to read the following titles: 'Five fighter jets and two helicopters of the Russian armed forces were shot down'; 'the enemy has breached the border in Chernihiv, Sumy, Luhansk and Kharkiv oblasts' and 'President Zelenskiy has issued an order to inflict maximum losses on the invading army'. The feeling of reading this in the morning news was utterly surreal. I still have no words to describe exactly how this felt and, for some reason, an urgent need to do so. I have always thought that speaking of my personal experience was not particularly interesting – what can *I* say that would be of interest to others that has not been said so many times before in human history. I guess this is a consequence of being an avid reader: human literary history has such an abundance of accounts of our horrible and wonderful life. And yet, the need to communicate, joined by an inability to do so, remains, nine months since February 2022.

Having coped with the initial grip of shock, I started ringing up my family in Ukraine, to discover they had been up since 5 a.m., notified by another phone call about the invasion and bracing for an impact of the unknown. This would arrive in the form of Russian bombs at a small airfield next to my parents' village, which sent them on the move as refugees. Except, at that point language offered an alternative, shielding us from the horrible reality for a little longer: my parents were not 'refugees' (a horrible fate) but simply 'temporarily displaced persons'. And not even that, they just left their house to stay with family elsewhere for a moment.

Since those early days of the full-scale Russian-Ukrainian war I have had a chance to *see* language at work in material reality – to see a materialization of language – on multiple occasions. And reading became a very necessary search for ways of expression for the reality that was shattered on 24 February, a search for words that would rebuild that reality. As I write this essay in the middle of that search, it will take me a while to arrive at the topic of childhood reading, central to this collection. First I must consider the language itself, the way literary texts record it and the way reading changes its meaning in times of war.

Sofia Andrukhovych's short diary-like essay was the first thing I read when I was struggling with my own inadequacy during the first days and weeks of the large-scale war (what can I do to help? How can I be of use, living abroad? Can I at least write, tweet, post something, spread the word, appeal to the world, to my Russian colleagues? Anything?).[1] I also discovered that language, when used incorrectly in that raw situation, had a very physical impact: certain words, questions and comments physically hurt, or caused disgust, or rage. ('How horrible, I hope your family is all right,' many friends would text. But what kind of selfish sentiment is that, for me to worry only for my family when all of my people are under attack?) Andrukhovych, as she was fleeing Kyïv with her children, put these unarticulated reactions into words:

> Before the war, I was a writer. Today, on the ninth day, I feel unable to string two words together. It's hard to believe that just over a week ago we were living a normal life. I have to try very hard to remember what that life was like.
>
> Those who survive will be able to reflect on it all. For the time being, our words are exalted, exaggerated; our shock, rage and hatred are best expressed in obscene language. We talk about our love for one another as we never have done before, as though our lives depended on it.[2]

Re-reading what she wrote on the ninth month of the war I catch myself thinking how these paragraphs are both ordinary and over-the-top sentimental. It is striking how context, in which a text was read, can become distant so quickly. But I remember how her words felt exactly at the time of their writing and my first reading. As time passes by, impulsive, raw texts start to seem exaggerated or naive, but in times of war, as I discovered, these texts are exactly right. Shock, rage, obscene language and love. And, above all, it is a relief to find someone able to say this out loud, to use language to say basic, ordinary things and able to discern, name and order the overwhelming emotions.

Another writer, Kateryna Kalytko, records this same observation:

> На сьомий день прямих спостережень
> за нищівною потужністю зброї

я знову почала дивуватися мові.

. . .

Посеред пожежі
людина, яка говорить, спершу здається дивною –
русалкою, що припливла
подивитися на кораблетрощу.
Але потім – гостро і чисто видно
простоту і шляхетністю чуда:
рухаються вуста.
Людина говорить.
Мова у неї – твоя.[3]

To offer my very rough translation:

On the seventh day of direct observations
of the destructive force of weapons
I started to marvel at language again.
. . .
In the middle of fire,
a person who speaks seems strange at first –
a mermaid who swam here
to watch the shipwreck.
But then – you see acute and clear
the simplicity and valour of the miracle:
the lips are moving.
The person is speaking.
Her language is yours.

Kalytko's poetry collection *Liudy z dieslovamy* (People with
Verbs), from which I quote this excerpt, was already submitted

to the publisher at the time when the large-scale war broke out. The publication was halted, and when the volume finally did come out later that year it was redesigned and Kalytko included new poems written in the darkest of days of this war. This book is thus a record both of an old language, which has had time for reflection, and of a new one that only just starts to emerge in the midst of raging fire. I think that from now on these (stylistic?) tensions will be visible for a long time in any text a Ukrainian would write, be it a poem, a piece for a literary magazine or an essay for a collection on reading.

In an interview when touring Ukraine with her new book – yes, touring with poetry during wartime – Kalytko said that to write during war the poet needs courage, if only to admit that she is at a loss, that she is coming up with language on the spot, as if during a live broadcast. That same autumn, when receiving the prestigious German Book Trade Peace Prize at the Frankfurt Book Fair, Serhiy Zhadan said the exact same thing: 'For a writer the situation with language during war is unbearable.'[4] A writer is used to relying on a vast field of possibilities of language. These possibilities used to seem endless and now it turns out that they are quite limited, that the familiar, pre-war words and structures do not really 'convey your current state, do not explain your anger, pain and hope'.[5] Precisely in this order: anger, pain and hope. Recall how Andrukhovych put it, just a few days into the war: shock, rage and hatred and love. There's another text registering the progression of feeling from death to love, written in times of what we now call the small-scale 2014–22 Russian-Ukrainian war: Volodymyr Rafeyenko's *Mondegreen: Songs about Death and Love* (2019). I shall return to it below.

Of course, there's also fear. But it does not compare to the overwhelming anger at the injustice and suffering that the Russians have caused with this war. Nor does it compare to the overwhelming sense of tenderness, care and love for your closest ones as well as for the whole nation, which, suddenly, materialized into a concrete, not imagined community. In Benedict Anderson's well-known observation, modern nations have been made tangible as nations, as communities united on the basis of this one feature of identification, through the written word: the novel and newspaper. This role of literature in a society is fast forgotten, when there is no threat to the national community, when the very idea of a nation recedes into the background as an outdated identity category. But it is starkly activated when a foreign army attacks your country. And the literature then again assumes, to borrow a phrase from Pascale Casanova, a 'combative role'.[6]

Being a literary scholar myself, I couldn't help but notice how many other, previously abstract categories assume lived concreteness in times of war. And (re-)reading, for me, became a concrete instrument for grounding myself in a certain stability of language, fixed on a page, that would offer a countermeasure to the unfolding chaos. People who've been through the beginning of this war back in 2014, like Rafeyenko, have already been able to start processing, so I can rely on their words – and on those by Andrukhovych, Kalytko, Zhadan and others – to try and process this new catastrophe.

Reading (through) anger, pain and hope

Volodymyr Rafeyenko, in his *Mondegreen*, adds another crucial modality to the three I highlighted in the subtitle above: laughter. Laughter in the face of an existential threat. Laughter at the hapless enemy, at the frail dictator Putin, who would like to project an opposite image. This laughter is also an inflection of language: international media insist on referring to Putin as 'President', as if that title means the same thing in Russia as in the countries with democratic elections. Academics continue to write countless useless books on 'understanding' his mind, his evil genius and the like. What the production of such discourse does is a *construction* of a certain invincible image, of a mastermind that ought better not be messed with. This discourse formats reality in tangible ways, by developing international politics, for example, based on an idea that Russia is a great superpower and that engaging with it militarily is a sure Third World War, and so on and so forth. But laughter intervenes and exposes a completely different side of this reality, at least for a Ukrainian. Once it was possible to start reflecting again, after the first Russian invasion in 2014, I observed a revival of satire in Ukrainian fiction. Ironic, sarcastic, flamboyant and angry, texts like Ivan Semesiuk's *Farshrutka* (2016), Oleh Shunkarenko's *Pershi ukraïnski roboty* (The First Ukrainian Robots, 2016) and his *Bandera Distortion*, (2019), Vladyslav Ivchenko's *Tretii front* (The Third Front Line, 2016), as well as Rafeyenko's works, would reveal an effective mode of talking about Ukraine's war-torn present and a potential format for devising a better future.

Reading anger and pain thus surprisingly easily combines with comic relief. And that is where one can find hope these days.

Rafeyenko, a native of Donetsk and a well-established Russian-language Ukrainian writer with a degree in Russian philology, had to flee in 2014, when the Russian-backed militants took control of his native town. He moved to Kyïv and decided to start learning Ukrainian in order to write his first book in what used to be the language of his grandmother. *Mondegreen* is the result of these efforts. In an interview, Rafeyenko reflects on the reasons for his choice:

> People came to my city to protect the speakers of the Russian language. But I, a Russian-speaking person, worked as a scholar of Russian philology, wrote in Russian, received honorariums. I didn't need any protection. This slogan – protection of the Russian speakers – has simultaneously made me a victim and a cause of this war. People, who came to my city, made the war my personal business.[7]

This biographical context and Rafeyenko's sudden geographical and linguistic displacement is important for the understanding of the language that *Mondegreen* offers for those who, like me in the spring of 2022, turned to re-reading in order to find in familiar books narrative structures for making sense of the new reality.

'Mondegreen' means a misunderstood or misinterpreted word or phrase resulting from a mishearing of the lyrics of a song. This is one of the major themes of the text, the inability to hear each other, to forge mutual understanding in a community torn by political contradictions and difficult history. The title also foreshadows the logic of the text that follows. There's a clear setting: the text is held together by its protagonist, Habriel 'Haba' Habinsky, who flees the war in Donetsk in 2014 and moves to Kyïv, where he studies Ukrainian and works in a grocery shop ('Beautiful and Useful'), located in a huge, maze-like shopping mall ('Karmatown'), since his journalistic writing and tutoring are not enough to sustain himself in the very expensive capital of Ukraine. The rest of the details are not so clear. There is no coherent plot – in fact, the plot is only a rudimentary pretext for an exploration of Haba's/Rafeyenko's/Ukraine's present, past and future. It is a setting for Haba's hallucinatory travels through layers of Kyïv's topography and history. These travels, in turn, are an occasion to meet strange people, animals and characters straight from folk tales and the meetings also offer an opportunity to explore parody, travesty, multiplicity of styles and languages.

All this may be described, in a nutshell, as 'excessiveness of language', to borrow the phrase from *Mondegreen* itself:

> Through the memories of a non-existent past, through folk tales and dreams, the refugee, and even more so this rarified version of him – the refugee-polyglot – finally comes face to face with being . . . And only later, this excessiveness of language, of course, finds very concrete, although not always comfortable or understood, representations. For example, already in those very first months after he began studying the language, this neo-Kyivite began to receive rather regular visits from the mare's head.[8]

The Mare's Head is a figure from a bizarre Ukrainian fairy tale in which the head visits a girl who is in exile in the forest, having been thrown out of the house by her evil stepmother.[9] It is yet another hint at the refugee fate of Haba/Rafeyenko, although it seems that the Mare's Head is here because of the sheer joy of working with this incredible image and the linguistic fun it implies: 'Haba could not fathom where the Ukrainian people got this figure. Why a head? Why the head of a mare? What happened, and why, that made it, alone and concerned, tumble across Europe? And when will it stop tumbling? And what will it do then?'[10] Some versions of the tale include verses and alliterations that accompany the tumble of the arrival of the Mare's Head. It is, furthermore, Haba's tutor in Ukrainian, a materialization of a forgotten, ignored language (in contemporary Donetsk), as it were, that pops up in the least comfortable moments to lecture him on the rules of word usage.

In an extended interview about the book, Rafeyenko mentioned that the tale about the Mare's Head came back to him during writing, decades after he'd heard it from his grandmother. And so 'in these encounters with the Mare's Head ... there is a feeling of coming back to one's roots'.[11] 'Linguistic memory', in other words, seems to be connected to childhood reading, as well as to the songs he heard his grandmother sing.[12] As was usual during the Soviet era, his grandmother, an engineer, stopped using native Ukrainian when she moved from the village to the big city.[13] Her own children and grandchildren then grew up with Russian as their first language. But what happens if one decides to excavate the family linguistic past, as an adult? It would seem that the stories one heard or read as a child reappear in forceful ways and suddenly reveal just how much of one's self has been shaped by memories, experiences and reading that one doesn't even remember having had. According to Haba from *Mondegreen*, one's honest desire to 're-settle' to the language one was exposed to as a child calls forth 'characters from folk stories' and 'various mythological figures, giving birth to ruinous protuberances[14] of memory. And this, my friends, is truly terrifying.'[15]

Haba returns to this memory of childhood stories time and again throughout the book:

> The mare's head is a familiar character for Haba. His grandma, whose Eastern *Surzhyk*-laden Ukrainian was her native language, would tell him that folk tale about it countless times during the terrifying years of his childhood . . . Haba forgot neither the nightingale nor the insidious coalminer worm, who, in one of the tales (*as it was recalled now*) would seek out lazy kids at night and eat their ears.[16]

Imagine a child dozing off in bed, peacefully, when suddenly an ear-eating worm appears!

> The worm, with a long moustache (*usually named Laurentius*), in old-fashioned glasses and sorrowful blue eyes, and with a smoking cigarette held by tweezers, sits on a boy's chest and ponderingly gnaws the child's ears, periodically spitting out bright blood on the floor, inhales, and goes back to gnawing . . . The crystal chandelier above the bed, all damp and pink, clinks, chinks, dings, and pings . . . A bloodied dad and mom don't know what to do, or how to act.

'It's your fault,' the father yells, 'You let him watch Soviet cartoons after 9 pm when he should have been studying the Ukrainian alphabet.'[17]

The sinister scene thus momentously changes into a cheeky poke at the Soviet cartoon aesthetics and the whole thing ends with both parents singing The Beatles' 'Yesterday', accompanied by dad playing the guitar, which expels the worm and calms down the child – yet another poke at the Soviet pop scene and an allusion to how coveted foreign vinyls were behind the Iron Curtain. There's much more to unpack in the above quote, as is the case with nearly every scene and sentence of *Mondegreen*'s ceaseless play with linguistic and cultural artefacts, but my interest here is in the way this text thematizes adult memory of childhood reading (and being read to). In a significant parenthesis, Rafeyenko/Haba inserts a disclaimer, 'in one of the tales (*as it was recalled now*)', reminding his readers that memory is notoriously unreliable. Moreover, an adult reader cannot but project his current reading experience and his learned abilities to interpret, over-interpret, infer and speculate on the books he read as a child (and the memories about them). The adult reader sets early mythological imagery into a wholly new life context.

I opened this essay with a brief reflection on Sofia Andrukhovych's diary-like piece, which tried to put into words the experience of one week of living under the Russian attack. In less than a year my attitude towards that text changed dramatically – from marvelling at its painfully precise language to reading it with the detachment of an observer ('I could easily write the same thing, what's the marvel in that!'). Only the memory of the effect of that first reading still survives, propped by Sofia's sentence, 'Today, on the ninth day, I feel unable to string two words together.' I remember being in that state, lost for words without which one could also find no meaning in what was happening. A truly unbearable state, as the proverbial fog of war was descending onto my country and no pre-existing sense-making instruments could offer any help.[18] That is why coming across people who could start speaking (writing) at that point is akin to witnessing a miracle, as Kalytko observed too.

Andrukhovych's text is a recent one and, given its circumstances, it carries a big affective weight for me. Even so, it can no longer be re-read in the same conditions as those provided by the original setting. How, then, do the books read decades ago change upon new re-reading? It seems impossible to read again as one did as a child. And when Haba Habinsky hypothesizes about a boy's nightmares, caused by a fairy tale, how much of it is his adult projection? More generally, Rafeyenko's attention to fairy tales in *Mondegreen* is striking, if connected to the theme of the present collection of essays. As the editors write in the introduction, certain childhood books may become 'transitional objects for life', providing consolation and safety in moments of crisis. Thus, one may speculate, in addition to providing a record of language and bizarre ancient imagery for the new, bizarre reality of life during war, the Mare's Head, along with other childhood tales, returns to provide – even if unconsciously – safety images for a mind in distress.

But what kind of safety do the childhood tales offer? Theirs is definitely not the rosy escapist world without drama, conflict or pain. I read a lot as a child and teenager. Among all those piles of books, two immediately come to mind: Astrid Lindgren's *Brothers Lionheart* (1973) and Hans Christian Andersen's *Wild*

Swans and Other Tales. Both are extremely tragic stories, when re-read from my adult perspective, so why were they so fascinating to me as a child? In *The Brothers Lionheart* a ten-year-old Karl is dying. But his thirteen-year-old brother Jonatan reassures him that it's not scary because he'll live in another world after the body dies. Except a fire breaks out in their house and Jonatan dies himself, saving Karl. In a few months Karl dies from his disease and joins his brother for adventures in Nangijala. Nangijala turns out to be a place with its own problems and evil forces, where Jonatan is lethally wounded again. There's a promise of yet another land, with only happy adventures, but the reader doesn't get to see if that promise is true.

A Ukrainian edition of Hans Christian Andersen's collection of tales, beautifully illustrated by the Italian painter Libico Maraja, was my most prized book. Its imaginative worlds fascinated me: flowers that come to life, people that turn into swans, toy figurines that talk. But looking back at these tales now what strikes me is how tragic most of them are, too. Even those with a happy ending, like 'The Wild Swans', are stories of a long road of hardship and suffering. The Steadfast Tin Soldier falls in love with the Paper Ballerina but they both burn to ashes in the fireplace. The wonderful flowers, who come alive and dance during the night, are dead by the morning and the little girl has to bury them in the garden.

So, what kind of transitional objects can such tales be? I think there's a complex layering of memory at play when we talk about childhood books. To come back to *Mondegreen*: on the one hand, the Mare's Head is scary – to an *adult* Haba, which registers the way an adult would (re)read such a story. But this magical figure is also curious, witty and even comical at times, revealing a simultaneous presence of that early childhood encounter with the Mare's Head as something much more fascinating than scary. In my own recollections of the favourite childhood tales I remember how they offered imaginative story worlds and 'workable' ideas for my own play of make-believe. I remember the satisfaction coming from the act of reading and of looking at the particularly felicitous illustrations, of devising games involving characters from stories, even full mental models of Pippi Longstocking's house and my own recurrent adventures for Karl and Jonatan, visualized with the help of illustrations from Hans Christian Andersen's tales.

I do not have an answer to the above question, only a speculation. While scary images in children's stories create affective weight and may thus be a rhetorically effective way of getting the lesson of the story to sink in, these images are not necessarily scary in themselves.[19] There is nothing inherently scary about a head of a horse. It is perhaps when this image is taken out of its imaginative plane and literalized, collapsed into the everyday reality – that is, read with an adult mind so preoccupied with everyday drudgery, with the fear of dying, and all the other fears – that the Mare's Head becomes first and foremost creepy. These tales also open up a whole different plane of thinking about the world. As the linguistic experiment of *Mondegreen* reveals, children's stories and folk tales carry almost a utopian duality in themselves: a fairy tale can be both a soothing and a horrifying thing.[20] The Mare's Head is both scary and curious. It helps Haba with learning the language and embarrasses him with its presence; it is a reference to fond childhood memories and childhood traumas; it can make you cry or laugh. Books and tales, read during childhood, may thus be what discovers for the young reader and later makes bearable the inseparable pain and joy of human life.

8

Reading as a
Rambunctious Boy-Girl

LAURA OTIS

'When you were a baby,' my mother used to tell me, 'I would read *Madame Bovary* in French to keep my mind from *rotting*.' I cried all the time, she said, and taking care of me left little time for reading. The way she said that word, '*rotting*', showed me that a mind that didn't read turned to stinking slime like a potato pushed to the back of the cabinet.

When she and her younger sister went to New York, she bragged, she would keep the money their mother gave them for the day. She would allow them only one small meal: three English muffin halves and coffee at Schrafft's. The rest she would spend on books at Brentano's, which wasn't her sister's idea.

I grew up in a house where books covered most of each wall. I would lean my head back and study their patterns, dark and light, thick and thin, books with names like *The Magic Mountain* and *For Whom the Bell Tolls*. I heard a lot about Mann and Hemingway and Dostoevsky, whom my father loved. Television was regarded with disgust, and its snow-filled screen sliced by lightning zig-zags offered no temptation. I saw only one movie before I was ten, which imprinted itself on my consciousness. I couldn't watch all of *The Sound of Music*, though, because towards the end I got scared of the Nazis and cried, and my mother had to take me out. 'It's all right. They get away,' she said, but frustration tightened her voice. Like television, crying disgusted her, and I always seemed to be crying.

My favourite bookcase stood in the living room, the one with the darkest hardcover books. When I was learning to read and write, I copied sentences from *The Yale Shakespeare* and proudly showed them to my parents. I had no idea what they meant but reproducing them made me feel important. In elementary school, we got Scholastic flyers each month from which we could order books. With my mother's approval, I bought most of them, and once when my stack came in, a boy said to his friends, 'Well, that ought to keep her busy for a weekend.' I didn't need to pretend to love reading. When I read, I felt alive. I liked very little of the life around me, but books showed me other ways of being and ways of loving the world.

When I was in high school I told my mother something I had seen in *The Sun Also Rises*: the bulls in the bullfight were mirroring the relationships among the characters. She stopped what she was doing and stared at me. 'Go tell your father what you just told me,' she said. When I did, he seemed as embarrassed as I was, but neither of us could oppose anything she asked. One day when I was reading and she was vacuuming, she raised the roaring mouth of the vacuum and held it inches from my face. I screamed with terror, and she laughed. 'If you're just reading for *pleasure*,' she said, 'you can help me clean.' I wasn't supposed to read for fun. She was coaching me to do something with literature, but not something I wanted to do. Like so many suburban women at that time, she was using her child as an avatar in a cut-throat video game against the other mothers.

My childhood reading years ran from 1967 to 1974, so that anything I read swam into me in the stream that was washing women's minds. My mother had earned an advanced degree in psychology, and she wanted to do research and discuss literature with witty people. She ended up in a Long Island development where, as my ex-husband put it, you had to grab the car even to go take a piss. She liked swimming, hiking, birdwatching, gardening, anything you could do outdoors. She loved travelling and, above all, she loved learning. The caregiving tasks culturally assigned to her (shopping, cooking, cleaning, washing, ironing, sewing) crushed her mind like stones. She associated this work with women, and I don't think Jack the Ripper hated women as much as my mother did. A sadistic god (and my father, who provided the other x chromosome) had given her a daughter.

My mother dressed me in blue and kept my blonde hair cropped short. In third grade a girl taunted me, 'Hey, kid, yuh wearin' yuh bruhthuh's socks!' I can't say whether focused training or inner instincts turned me into a boy. When I wasn't reading, I wanted to be in the woods, chopping down trees and building teepees and forts. I led kids on Lost Walks, where we would walk for miles until we were sure we were lost, then find our way back home again. On one of them, a friend and I got trapped in the middle of a creek because the ice along the edges had melted. I couldn't understand why the kids who went with me always got in trouble. I didn't. What was wrong with exploring the world?

In a fourth-grade assignment where we were asked to describe ourselves, I wrote, 'I consider myself a boy, and anyone who calls me a girl, I'll kill.' Kids chased after me yelling, 'Girl! Girl!' and I tried to kill them without success. I often spoke of killing people, and my mother laughed her approval. My father quietly disagreed. 'There's a book called *Crime and Punishment*,' he said. 'It's about a man who wants to kill someone and does. Things don't turn out the way he wants.'

If my mother or I had been ten in 2024, we would have transitioned ourselves the hell out of womanhood. In 1970 we had books. I relished stories of action, adventure and survival, which usually featured boys. 'Girls are dumb,' I thought, 'like Liesl, who almost gets her whole family killed when she gasps because her stupid boyfriend has become a Nazi. I am not like that. I am not a girl.' My favourite book, *Powder Keg*, told of a boy who fought in the Battle of Bunker Hill. The Americans lost the battle because they ran out of gunpowder, so the boy went with a commando team to raid the British powder stash in Barbados. I also loved tales of aggressive girls who worked, played and fought with boys. The books I liked best showed children without parents. Who needed these incompetent, nay-saying creatures? The Australian book *To the Wild Sky* depicts children who survive a plane crash and wander until they find a town. In *From the Mixed-Up Files of Mrs Basil E. Frankweiler*, a girl and her little brother move into the Metropolitan Museum of Art – until the story falls apart when the girl becomes obsessed with some stupid statue, I recall thinking. My role model was Pippi Longstocking, with her thick braids, irreverence and thing-finding. Pippi was happy, I sensed, because she didn't have a mother, something that no one needed.

I didn't want to read about people like myself, although I wasn't drawn to science fiction or fantasy. I disdained anything supernatural. I wanted gritty realism, books about people in different places, especially poor people in my own time and in the past. I read the Laura Ingalls Wilder books so many times, I almost learned them by heart. I liked *The Witch of Blackbird Pond*, about a girl from Barbados who is forced to live with New England Puritans and gets caught up in their witch trials. Lois Lenski's books about poor children resonated most powerfully. There was *Blue Ridge Billy* about Appalachia and *Strawberry Girl* and *Judy's Journey* about migrant farm workers. I loved Judy because she fought the people who mocked her. 'Judy hit the big girl hard,' is a sentence that has forever stuck in my head.

Almost all the books I read described white children. At the time, I didn't notice anything missing. Of the thousands of books in my house, I can recall only one by someone who wasn't white: *The Fire Next Time* by James Baldwin. I don't know how I knew he was Black. How was this possible in 1972? On the yellow school bus, kids chanted, 'Nixon now, McGovern's a cow!' At the bus stop a boy I didn't like said, 'Some people around here are Black, but they're not n*****s.' His father worked as a cop in New York City. In the Long Island suburbs, children read about revolutionary and frontier heroes while people were marching for Civil Rights.

Some children's books took me beyond the white world, especially a biography of Harriet Tubman. She was my kind of person, leading people out of slavery. I cared about what people did, not what colour they were, and like Pippi, she became a role model. For the same reason I loved *The Island of the Blue Dolphins*, in which an Indigenous girl survives alone on an island. She was living my dream – to survive alone, and as she built a shelter and sought food, I followed her with fascination. I also loved *Children in Hiding*, now known as *Tomás Takes Charge*. In it, two city kids, Tomás and Fernanda, set up house in an abandoned building after their father disappears. Something was mentally wrong with Fernanda, who didn't dare leave her house. I identified with Tomás and admired his resourcefulness as he kept himself and Fernanda going. He would have been better off without his stupid sister, but he cared more about her than about himself. Action, movement, freedom, self-sufficiency: that was what I wanted, and I found it in books about all kinds of people.

My parents liked to see me reading, but they watched with horror as I showed signs of an inherited disease. Even before I could read or write, I used to make up stories. Once I asked my father to write one down, and I never got over my disappointment when he couldn't read his writing and it was lost. My parents had met when my father, who had studied physics, was enrolled in the Iowa Writers' Workshop. He had wanted to live as a freelance writer but didn't succeed and became an engineer instead. One of his older sisters had wanted to write, too. As I followed the lead of another hero, Harriet the Spy, my parents did everything they could to discourage me. Writers lived in poverty, chaos and pain, draining the people around them. I wrote anyway. I couldn't *not* write. I needed to write as I needed to breathe.

Consuming books at the rate I did, I had to create my own stories. I developed an imaginary world of Woodsgirls, led by Jenny with a thick blonde braid. In the absence of superfluous adults, Jenny organized a band of girls who thrived in the woods. Jenny could climb any tree, tame any animal. Jenny fought with boys. As I learned to write for myself, the Jenny stories grew from a few pages to hundreds. I wrote them all in my head first, saying them out loud, rocking alone on a swing for hours.

Adolescence hit me like a bulldozer that smashed everything flat. Like a mental illness, it turned me into another person. I became stupid. I became a girl. I painted my fingernails pale blue, lime green and yellow. It was 1974. I cared about nothing but whether boys wanted me, and of course, none of them did. I took a bath only once a week, as people in Laura Ingalls Wilder's books did. My mother didn't indicate otherwise, except to hold a strand of my oily hair to her nose and wince. 'Wash yuh heah!' ordered one fat girl. Kids kicked me, threatened me, threw me against walls. They spat on me and pulled my hair. A boy I didn't know followed me part way home, saying over and over, 'You're really a dog, you know that? You are such a dog.' I still read, but now I wanted books about sex. I fell in love with D. H. Lawrence. I discovered the literary love of my life, Emile Zola, through a review on the back of an orange D. H. Lawrence book: 'Horrible, disgusting writer!' it said. 'Even worse than Zola!' Next trip to Brentano's, I hit the Z section and found gritty realist bliss.

The hormonally induced madness lasted forty years. My time of fertility was mercifully short, but sexual stupidity filled the middle of my life with humiliation, terror and abuse. I caused untold pain to others besides suffering grief myself. Pippi, Judy and Harriet didn't seem relevant when I got hit and worse. In more than one language, I was threatened and called a bitch and a whore. Men caught on, generally before I did, that reading and writing meant more to me than satisfying their desires. The kindest men rejected me straight out; the sadists kept me around longer. I am grateful to the men who realized, decades before I did, that I had no interest in a partnership, family or parenthood.

In my early fifties I awoke as though from a forty-year nightmare. When the sexual longing died, the madness went with it, and I started feeling like Jenny again. One day in a French bookstore I realized I had stopped reading. I was working non-stop and I had ceased to explore bookshops and get excited when I found an unread Zola novel. That day, I stayed in the bookstore, scanned every shelf and left with an enticing stack. Biology had bulldozed the middle of my life, but my life wasn't over. I might still have forty years left to become the person I wanted to be.

At sixty, I am a teacher and scholar of literature, especially in relation to science. I teach Mann, Dostoevsky and sometimes Zola, but not Hemingway, whom I don't like. I write gritty realist novels in which women sometimes fight with men. I live and travel alone, staying on the move as much as I can. Four times I've driven around the United States for a month or more with a large teddy bear for company. In the happiest moments of my life, I've been exploring the world alone. In one of them, I was rocketing at 80 miles per hour across Wyoming in purple dusk. Rod Stewart's 'I'm Losin' You' was twanging from the tape deck. As I shot across Crazy Woman Creek, I didn't yet know where I was going to stay the night. I felt alive, and I know that Pippi would have approved.

When my mother was in her early sixties, she developed early-onset dementia. She panted with fear when she got lost in the house among her thousands of dusty books. 'I've lost my book!' she would cry to me. 'Someone stole my book! I can't find my book!' My father explained that she could no longer read. Still, each morning she would clutch a book and carry it around with her everywhere. I was fighting to free myself from my husband (Tomás, who was trying to Take Charge) and struggling to survive in my first tenure-track job. Even so, I read to her. I recorded whole Jane Austen novels on tape. I visited her and read books in French. In one of her last winters, two feet of snow fell on the small Pennsylvania town where she was living. In my motel room I took the only book I could find (the Bible) and hiked out to her nursing home, kicking my way through three-foot drifts. Though crushed by madness, my mind was re-emerging. I had never felt more like Laura Ingalls Wilder.

9

Figuring Stories,
and Jumping Off the Page

PAJTIM STATOVCI

I grew up in a home that had no books. I was two years old when my family, forced to flee the Yugoslav Wars, found refuge in Finland. Unfortunately, because we couldn't really take anything with us from our home in Kosovo, I did not have books in my family's language, Albanian. Maybe – or partly – because I didn't have access to books in my own language, I don't remember ever even being encouraged to pick up a book.

My reading journey is anything but typical. My family is working class, both of my parents were from the rural heart of Kosovo and didn't read. We didn't go to the theatre. We didn't discuss politics. We didn't talk about music, art, architecture or literature, we didn't go to the library, we didn't buy books or concert tickets. I didn't learn to read until I was in school, at the age of seven or eight.

Once I had learned how to read in Finnish, I was introduced to the small school library, to a few shelves containing a modest selection of children's books, a few classics and some schoolbooks. I remember instantly being drawn to the library, although books were somewhat foreign objects to me. Still, I quickly became a frequent sight there.

After school I went in to flip through pages, look at the mesmerizing pictures, slowly figuring out the connection between text and stories. This took quite a long while, months and years of trying to read without really being able to keep up with the plot. I did, however, from the earliest stages of my journey as a reader, know how to appreciate expressive language, the beauty and rhythm of certain words.

Before I was introduced to books, stories had only existed in oral form. Every now and then my mother or father would tell me a story from Albanian folklore. One followed a mother of four children who was buried inside a wall, another told a story about a snake that transformed into a dragon, yet another was about a chimera that could vanish in the blink of an eye. These stories were rather chaotic and brief, and always cut too short. After the story came to its end, I remember feeling rather dissatisfied, and I kept asking my parents for more details. I craved for more events, more excitement, more drama.

I memorized the stories I was told, and then I picked up a tendency to tell them to my siblings and friends, to other kids who lived in the same residential complex, editing and adding to the original story, trying to make them better, captivating, thrilling. Much to my joy and satisfaction, I succeeded and even gained a kind of reputation for being a storyteller.

As I kept growing up, my hunger for books and stories only grew. My family had settled in Porvoo, a small, picturesque city around 50 kilometres from Helsinki. When I was ten the new building of the main library of Porvoo opened its doors to the public, and when I visited the library for the first time, I cried. It was the most beautiful thing I had ever seen. I was floored by endless shelves carrying tens of thousands of books, records, films, magazines and newspapers. And the best part was that everything was up for grabs, all the films, the books, the stories, free of charge.

Then one day, it all clicked, my reading got better, almost as if overnight, and the new library became a place I considered better than home. I still remember how excited I was about books like *Alice's Adventures in Wonderland, James and the Giant Peach* and *Robinson Crusoe*, and how touched I was by *The Diary of a Young Girl, Holes* and *To Kill a Mockingbird*. Some of these childhood favourites I read repeatedly, over the course of many years. I sat for hours in a bean bag chair, reading, occupied, annoyed if I needed to take a bathroom break.

I rarely, however, borrowed a book, and if I did, I kept it hidden from my family and even friends. For some reason, taking a book out felt scary, out of place, wrong even. I was extremely uncomfortable when the librarians kept telling me that I am more than welcome to take the books home with me too. But I was too ashamed to do so, maybe because I thought that books weren't meant for someone like myself, or maybe I thought that the books wouldn't belong in our home, they wouldn't be 'at home' there.

In retrospect, I think I needed to keep books to myself, a secret of some kind, my own universe, since I clearly didn't want to share that with others. In fact, I was very protective of them. So, I would go pick up a book from the shelf, sit down, read until I couldn't read anymore, then return the book to its place and continue the next day from where I'd left off. And I would get jealous, even angry, if someone had taken out every copy of a book I hadn't finished yet. Because then I had to wait for weeks to be able to continue.

During the 1990s the war in my home country made the entire world feel scary, gruesome and unsafe to me. Everything became unpredictable. Anything could happen in the real world, lives ended in the snap of your fingers, nothing was certain. Films, books and reading became an escape from it. Unlike the real world, I was rarely distressed by stories. I could read and watch and read and watched everything.

As time went by I noticed that I had developed a taste for what I liked to read. I wanted to be challenged and surprised by a good plot, I wanted to be shaken, questioned, made to think about what I consider right and wrong. I wanted to understand evil, and people that scared me, to travel through time and space with someone I didn't necessarily care for. Through reading, I could do that, string along like a ghost, an outsider, get to see places and meet people I knew nothing about.

I was a very sensitive child and did not have many friends. But in my imagination, I wasn't like that at all. Reading made me feel more confident and secure. It was almost as if I got to exist as someone else in another plane. The power and strength that reading gave me was available to me even when I wasn't reading. At any time, my body could be in one place, and my mind in another. I could create anything out of nothing, and find refuge there, paint a picture of a valley and build a kingdom, tell myself stories after stories, re-narrate actual events.

I closed my eyes and got to be anything I wanted: a dragon and a whale, a king and a queen, a wizard and an assassin, a barbarian and a druid, a soldier with supernatural powers who could end an entire war, or a castle that housed a million cats. My world of fantasy became a game of chess that I played against myself, always changing figure, form and position. I started my writing career by closing my eyes. Like always, I soon started seeing interesting characters and their voices. However, this time, I wrote what they looked like and what they said on a single Word file, and began reading, writing, the story like I would read as a child in the library, one chapter at a time.

A year later I had sent out a manuscript and had signed a publishing contract, and a few years later my first book was published. In the first interviews I gave it says that I – a student of literature in his early twenties who simultaneously works in a grocery store to cover living expenses – have succeeded in my first attempt to write a novel. I, however, disagree with this claim because, in many ways, I feel like I have always been doing this.

I can't explain how and why, but from the first time I held a book in my hands I have known that one day I will get to slide my own book between the shelves, among the stories that have rescued and inspired me, to become not only a reader but a writer.

As an author, I am constantly asked why I write. It is a difficult question because I write for so many reasons. Lately, however, I've taken the liberty to change the question: to whom do I write? Because the answer to that is simple: to myself, and to everyone like myself.

10

Reading from the Spine

LAURA OULANNE

There is a fascinating randomness to what sticks in our memory after the experience of reading a work of fiction. Instead of names or traits of characters, the order of events, intriguing twists or surprising endings, it often seems to be ephemeral things like singular images, moods that are difficult to verbalize, a detail of the material world or a stray phrase. It could also be the place where you read the book or how the book felt in your hands. For me, such bits and pieces evoke bodily associations that make them undeniably present and affective. Once recalled, they might help recover the more 'knowledgeable' content of the work, such as events, contexts and ideas, but the bodily memories will usually demand to be considered first.

From my childhood I can recall many enchanting and stimulating experiences of engaging with stories that I read or that were read to me. However, somehow the childhood memory that always emerges as the most repeated and most intensely felt is not one of reading stories at all. It's reading the spines of books. Lying in a speck of sun on the living room floor, my eyes scanning and rescanning the towering presence of the big bookshelves; exploring the shelf in a friend's room for new reading material;

being mesmerized by the abundance of spines and the promising mystery of unread books at the city library. Grabbing the book, starting the adventure – I recall this with feeling, but what I don't necessarily remember is where each adventure took me. The spines of books had the power to move me, concretely, from one book, one shelf to the next, and to direct my hands towards gestures of choosing, picking up, opening. Often the book titles were incomprehensible to me, just floating words, and the same goes for the contents of the books I selected. Still, each spine and book was significant *as* the call to enter, move and be moved, even if it simultaneously banned entry and understanding.

The quite literally marginal elements of fiction, including spine and cover texts and art as well as the materiality of the book object, have received some attention in literary studies. Yet something remains to be said about the interplay between understanding and not understanding, being intrigued and remaining puzzled, being called to enter and banned from it, that characterizes my early experiences of interacting with books. What happens between a reader and a book when very little information or knowledge is transmitted, but still some sense and feeling is generated, possibly enough to lead to more and more reading and even to choices that determine the course of one's life?

Being moved

Of course, looking at book spines sometimes also led me to pick up my own spine from the floor and pick up a book from the shelf. Some I read, some I just looked at. The covers of the popular mystery series that filled half my parents' bookshelf fascinated but also scared me with their terrified female faces or still-life arrangements of jewellery and cut-glass tumblers speckled with blood, whereas the world literature classics and Finnish modernists sitting beside them often displayed abstract surfaces that made me no wiser about their content. As a small child, of course, I would prefer books with pictures, including children's books, but also a 1950s *World Atlas*, whose illustrations of mysterious deep-sea fish or the solar system I was mesmerized by. I cannot remember the content of most of the books I picked up, however, but I remember how the spines and covers directed my attention and affected the concrete positioning of my body in the space of the living room.

It makes sense that my repeated actions solicited by books would result in vivid memories. To me it is counterintuitive to see memory as a storage of past events and knowledge located somewhere inside our brain; it is rather a shifting structure that is inscribed and layered onto our bodies and their habitual routes in the world, old experiences being constantly reanimated in the present. Phenomenologists call this 'body memory', meaning the implicit know-how and skills formed by habit, which cannot be recalled as knowledge but is enacted in the present efforts and experience of my lived body. Our body memory is active when dancing or riding a bicycle, doing activities that fall somewhere between automatic repetition and conscious steering. It is also enacted in painful experiences and trauma.

The relationship between reading and body memory is curious: reading is often seen as a rather intellectual and disembodied activity, but in fact it requires and affects the body in multiple ways. What I am recalling from my childhood is a know-how for being-with-literature that was formed before I had much knowledge about the art form. I knew how to pick up a book and pick up the words from its pages, and this activity gave me bodily metaphors to work with: when thinking and writing, I experience a tingle in my hands, as if they are ready to pick and mould the matter of words and ideas. Holding a book in my lap became a dear experience to me, associated with both a safe sense of privacy and a promise of getting in touch with something new and unknown. I also learned that reading had an effect on my body, and that it was possible to be both here and there at the same time: sitting on a chair or on the ground or lying in my bed, occasionally looking up and getting distracted, while experiencing thrills of adventure or new ideas, or weeping over heartaches and losses.

But first there were the spines. Tilting my head to read book titles became a learned bodily trait that I still almost involuntarily repeat any time there is a bookshelf in sight. Libraries, of course, are the most intensely activating places for such memories. They are spaces designed for succumbing one's body to the attraction and guidance of books, skipping or shuffling from one spine to another. The city library of my childhood promised warmth and safely structured excitement in the dark winter afternoons of my hometown. Its tingle is hard to define: the sense of being invited to move forward, not just towards new stories but towards possible real future lives. I was drawn from the children's and young adult section over to the other side of the building, housing the more impressively voluminous rows of endlessly intriguing books. I would make excursions to pick a random book with closed eyes, then become haunted by the long row of Prousts or the equally long one of Catherine Cooksons and add one of both to the eclectic pile that was handed to the clerk for checking out. I seem to have mostly picked books that were way above my skill level: big and heavy ones, ones with intimidating grown-up names, ones in foreign languages. When I first explored the university library of my hometown at fourteen, by coincidence, I marched over to the philosophy shelf and carried off some heavy phenomenology to pass time with me in an armchair. My knowledge of phenomenology was limited or non-existent and did not increase much during that sitting, but I was convinced it was the coolest thing. I understood very few of the words in the book I was reading, but the experience of picking it up and cradling it was, in retrospective phenomenological terminology, sedimented onto my body memory.

If anything was precocious in these interactions it was my aspirational interest and the intentionality of my lived body, not my level of comprehension. The fine-grained analysis of perception in Merleau-Ponty was completely beyond me, as was the linguistic extravagance of *Finnegans Wake* that I had similar romantic library encounters with. I also rarely read these exciting books from start to finish. Yet when I was sitting down with them, and even when I was opening them for the first time, picking them up from the shelf, something happened: I spent time with the words, I wandered within the books from one word to the next, like I wandered in the library from one spine to the next. I was intrigued and affected. I grasped nuances, perhaps more and more each time – and then again less, as I became distracted and more focused on the performance of reading than on what I was reading.

Still, the books kept calling and I kept wandering from book to book. While repeating the small movements from one book to the next at the university library of my hometown I was also moved on a slower and wider scale, as I ended up studying at the same university, then another, being drawn towards the ideas and topics that intrigued me. This involved some understanding of what was between the covers of the books that moved me, of course. Yet the original experience of being moved by their mere surfaces was never too far away. It was re-enacted in each instance of reading, and still is.

Similarly, I still fail to feel like I have learned or understood much through reading. Or rather, I feel like the understanding is happening in the present continuous and cannot be separated from the bodily act of reading. One rarely reads such confessions from professional authors; however, author Siri Hustvedt for one has expressed similar memories in an interview for *The Guardian*, where she explains among other things that Simone de Beauvoir's *The Second Sex* affected her 'viscerally' and defined her intellectual development even though it was too difficult for her:

> Rereading it later, I wonder exactly what I understood
> at the time. It is not an easy book. I suspect that, despite
> my struggles with the text, I gleaned its essential message
> – that women were treated as outsiders to history as the
> eternal feminine, had always been other to man, and that
> these injustices ran deep. I became a feminist.[1]

According to the same interview, Hustvedt has read for knowledge and information as well, and so have I. I have enjoyed plots, identified strongly with characters and parsed texts closely for obscure meanings and contextual intricacies. Furthermore, I have been lucky to end up doing all this for my work. However,

I want to explore the intriguing interaction, be it a clash or a collaboration, between two styles of reading, which I venture are recognizable for most readers, professional or not, as I see them before me and feel them in my body when I think about my early reading experiences. Why is it important to stare at books, fondle them and be moved by them physically, in space? Why was it significant that I stared excitedly at Joyce and Merleau-Ponty as a young person even though I didn't internalize a thing? With these questions I turn to the company of some modernists now in my bookshelf.

Reading as dusting

My childhood reading recollections are defined by two things: encountering books as foreign, intriguing things that have the power to move me by their mere presence, and the experience of reading something that is too difficult to comprehend while still being moved by it. Maybe these books intrigued me because they safely enforced just this barrier of worlds. I could see something on the other side and sense that it was magical and new, but was not 'sucked' in or toyed with completely. In contrast, I remember the experience of very overtly being toyed with at the cinema, where a well-meaning grown-up took me to see Disney classics such as *Bambi* and *Beauty and the Beast*. I felt shocked and almost physically violated for days afterwards, after riding the well-calculated affective rollercoasters of the animations on the big screen. This was and remains a question of personal sensitivity and I know this experience is not shared by all children or adults – I was not that fond of actual rollercoasters either. However, this memory seems informative because while being physically repulsed, pushed away by supposedly immersive fiction, I was able to find some kind of 'deep' enjoyment in exactly the kind of reading that forbade any emotional or intellectual deep-sea diving.

This has been the effect of many of the modernist texts that I have ended up reading and writing about from the position of a literary scholar. As a young person I was drawn to the masculine spines of Camus, Fitzgerald and Joyce, because they were available and had a recognizable aura about them. However, it is modernist women like Djuna Barnes, Jane Bowles, Katherine Mansfield and Gertrude Stein whose prose and poetry have most affected what I now think about reading. Their work also expresses ideas about reading that resonate with my early experiences of being moved by books.

For instance, Gertrude Stein's early experimental collection *Tender Buttons* (1914) presents an array of everyday, homely things. 'Presents' seems accurate, because the text does not really describe its objects. The titles of short poem-like entries in the book often denote material, everyday objects or food: umbrellas, cups, vegetables, roast beef. They are marched onto the page and then played with, as things and as words. The text produces and experiments with recognizable associations around the things but remains so obscure to the extent that it can be compared to the foreign-language volumes or complex subjects that I was drawn to as a child. In Stein's work, the materiality of language itself often becomes the moving force of the text: how the words look and sound and what they do moves the text forward and creates associations, instead of or besides the referents they may evoke. Like my remembered child-self in front of a bookshelf, the reader is invited to hop from word to word, perhaps making sense of them, perhaps just encountering them. Stein has also written what can be interpreted as reading instructions in the same work: 'any time there is a surface there is a surface'.[2]

Similarly, in her more accessible work *The Autobiography of Alice B. Toklas* (1933), Stein uses the voice of a fictionalized version of her partner to provide some practical guidelines for reading:

> I always say that you can not tell what a picture really is or what an object really is until you dust it every day and you cannot tell what a book is until you type it or proof-read it. It then does something to you that only reading never can do.[3]

Dusting and proofreading are defined as comparable practices, which enable one to 'tell' what something 'really is' and allow the text to 'do something to you'. This remark can easily be tied to the biographical knowledge we have of the couple's life and their roles in it: Alice appears as the pragmatic one, the typist and hostess who took care of the things in the house while Stein talked about art with other geniuses. Yet it also resonates with Stein's own method of writing, and the styles of reading invited by her texts. In this dusterly way of being with objects of art, static contemplation is replaced by a recurring practical interaction that has to do with the material of the work – be it its concrete surface or the stuff of language it is made of. This surface becomes present-at-hand, to use Heideggerian terminology, instead of quietly remaining the equipment or basis that produces the effect of the work. The purpose of a work of art *is* to be present as a surface, in comparison to a tool whose aesthetical being disappears when it is time to use it. Even further, if we follow Alva Noë, a work of art is a kind of 'strange tool' that exhibits its own tool-being and thereby makes visible and creates something new out of a practice that might be lost in our everyday experience, be it dancing, writing or looking.

Dusting, to expand Stein's metaphor a bit, is interesting to think about in relation to the experiences and practices of childhood reading I recall: repeated, rhythmic and bodily interactions with text-bodies and the absence of immediate comprehension, knowledge or identification. A child may pick up a book several times, play with it, taste the words, paying attention to different material and formal features each time, then abandon the book to pick up another one and so on. Some texts, like Stein's, may benefit from a dusterly attitude even from a grown reader who aims to write and think with them. The tone of *Tender Buttons* is warm and humoristic, even though the work keeps its emotional distance. It can also offer philosophical insights for a reader so inclined, but it is not hammered in. You can perhaps never become quite familiar with the text, know it or indeed master it, but it may still befriend you. On the other hand, you can also grasp some interesting nuances of an emotionally immersive work of fiction if you start paying attention to its surface.

I did not discover Stein as a child, but these days engaging with her work always rekindles pleasure and excitement similar to the one I felt as a child, when approaching tempting spines on a shelf. This seems to be another experience shared by Hustvedt: 'I didn't "get" Gertrude Stein as a teenager. I had to grow into an adult to feel the music, humour and rigour of her work,' she states in the interview. Music and humour are characteristics likely to be appreciated by children in any literature (including nursery rhymes and wordplay), or anyone not reading for propositional meaning. As an adult reader and even a literary scholar, one might occasionally ask oneself, what about the 'childish' ways of reading could be retained in research practices – and what might already be there but escape our adult attention. That modernist texts invite and even promote a childish or dusterly reading attitude goes slightly against the received ideas of modernism as the clever art of subjectivity, interiority and encrypted meaning.

Virginia Woolf's novel *To the Lighthouse* is another fascinating case. In this novel, a work of art (Lily Briscoe's abstract painting) features as both a surface and an organizing element, people seem often opaque but also meaningful to one another, material things experience and manifest time passing indifferent to the grand events and emotions that structure human lives – and words float around, available to the senses like material things but refusing penetrating inquiries or attributions of meaning. An example I am thinking of are the excerpts of 'A Garden Song' by Charles Isaac Elton (1899), recited by Mr Ramsay. The recurring line 'Luriana Lurilee' sounds like Latin to Mrs Ramsay, who muses:

> The words (she was looking at the window) sounded as if they were floating like flowers on water out there, cut off from them all, as if no one had said them, but they had come into existence of themselves . . . She did not know what they meant, but, like music, the words seemed to be spoken by her own voice, outside her self, saying quite easily and naturally what had been in her mind the whole evening while she said different things.[4]

Mrs Ramsay does not consider the words in their original context of publication. Like an occasionally absent-minded or 'unskilled' reader of literary texts, she does not 'know what they meant', and attaches their meaning to her own life. However, this process of signification does not rely on the meaning of the words but on a sense of connection that reaches beyond the individual and the boundaries of the senses, expanding into images of the natural world and musical associations.

This passage offers a vision of reading related to Stein's dusting. Mrs Ramsay as a model reader engages with the matter of sounds and letters without necessarily 'knowing what they mean' but still arriving, as if through collaboration with the matter of language, to a sense of an understanding. Indisputably, she is touched and moved by the stray pieces of poetry. Perhaps some of the connections made by the words might remain obscure to a critical mind educated in the humanist tradition, but they 'make sense' to her on a pre-reflective level that involves the body and its embeddedness in the world of flowers, water and music. This goes against the grain of what we are accustomed to think of as an intelligent or learned reading, but it demonstrates the power and peculiarity of literary language and art, the same power that called me to literature as a child.

Katherine Mansfield's short story 'Miss Brill' (1920) contains another fascinating instance of not knowing, and still somehow understanding. The eponymous character experiences a moment of ecstasy while listening to a band playing in the park. She feels an inexplicable, universal connection to the environment, the tone of the music and the other people listening to the band: 'Yes, we understand, we understand, she thought – though what they understood she didn't know.'⁵ The moment is soon negated, as is typical of Mansfield's stories, when Miss Brill overhears someone insult her and her dear fur collar, and quietly returns to her small home. Thereby also the inspired expression of her vision easily reads ironically as a demonstration of the impossible human aspiration to know or empathize with others. However, I claim that the sense of expansion and inexplicable understanding from the moment of the character's epiphany is prone to be left lingering in the reader, and thus remain an experience as real as the disappointment that ensues.

Miss Brill's unknowing understanding also seems like a guideline to possible ways of reading the story and another sneaky demonstration of the power of literature to move us. The character cannot express what she and the others in her imaginary community of park-goers understand or know, but she is clearly having an experience of being moved and changed. This moment is rendered successfully into words by Mansfield, to be felt, even if not known, by the reader. We will never know the actual thoughts of Miss Brill – she is made of paper and ink – nor any one or true meaning of the story. Nevertheless, when the reader finishes the story, however distractedly, they have gone through some version of the epiphanic moment with the character, felt some of it in their reading body. Their experience has shifted at least a tiny bit. So, while on one level declaring empathy, communication and community among strangers impossible, the story manages to communicate, create a community and involve the reader in it.⁶ To 'understand' this, the reader does not need to 'know' if this is what Mansfield intended, or apply a sophisticated apparatus of analytical concepts. Reading, even absent-mindedly, is enough.

Mansfield's epiphany, like Stein's word-things and Woolf's floating phrases, can help address some myths about reading. Even people trained to analyse, explain and discuss texts don't always know, 'get' or remember what a text is about, or have much privilege of understanding over any other reader of that same text. We spend time with words, worlds and spaces, fictional and material, and interact with them as the material beings that we are, eyes and fingers and all. Here we come back to the insufficiency of the container metaphor for the mind. If I try to conceptualize the human minds as a container where information is stored and can be drawn on at will, I can only see myself as a leaking one. I never feel like I possess or have internalized the entirety of a text, be it fictional or theoretical, so that I could access its contents like an inner library. I need the actual library, the actual books, and my own writing as it slowly takes material form and interacts with the writing I am quoting, to think and create meanings. To me it seems like the work of reading and thinking happens somewhere between my body and the texts that are read and written – much like dusting happens between the dusty surface and the duster, even if initiated by the mind and body of Alice B. Toklas.

Perhaps I was drawn to some modernists, even as a reader too young to 'get' them, not only because they happened to be there on the shelf, but because something in them is actually the opposite of what we tend to understand as difficult. They present us with words and images and leave it to us to do something with them, be it 'dusting' and lingering with repeated, nonsensical words and phrases, listening to the ring of an incomprehensible line of poetry, or grasping at an understanding that will never quite reach the threshold of everyday words. Even as they depict failures of internalizing or understanding, they communicate something crucial about what literature can do. Indeed, much of fiction, or even theory, might be beyond our efforts at internalizing; we can only come into contact with part of it, tugging a corner, caressing a surface, looking at the play of a field of colour. Still, we are moved and shifted, and some understanding is created, even if we cannot quite place it in the mythical brainy interiority of a humanist subject. And our bodies in front of bookshelves may be moved to pick up yet another volume.

Moving forward

As I was drafting this essay I was waiting for a very delayed shipment of my property, including my books, to make its way across the Atlantic into my new home in the North. During months without an apartment or furniture, I had almost forgotten what it's like to have a bookshelf of one's own to rest one's eyes on, wandering and making associations while writing, always open for the possibility of being called, to move myself over to the shelf and grab the book spine of a relevant title volume. As a result of this temporary lack I resorted to libraries and the Internet, appreciating both but also noting how the latter does not offer the same kind of aid for a thinking process as a physical bookshelf. At the library I experienced the relief of wandering the stacks and finding my own books again, after a period of only picking up orders from a tiny reservation shelf due to the global pandemic.

When finishing the text, I have regained my books and shelves, and every day I watch my one-year-old daughter being drawn by its gravity. First it was only her gaze, as looking at book spines was what most often calmed her as a small baby. Now she furiously interacts with her own little shelf of baby books but is also at least as enthusiastic about Willa Cather (she likes the picture of the writer on the spine of her collected letters), Lydia Davis and other grown-up books that happen to be at the right height for her to pull off the shelf. In addition to piling books on the floor and using them as chairs, she has understood how to hold them for reading and loves repeating this gesture, even if the text occasionally is upside down.

Based on the early and more recent experiences with books and their spines I have recounted here, I will not attempt to say anything about the future of reading, the book-object or the library. They have, however, taught me to understand the connection, or rather the inseparability, between a moving body and a thinking mind. Even as a researcher, one needs bodily engagement with things and words. Looking at personally recalled experiences of reading-as-not-quite-reading or reading-while not understanding has led me to new metaphors for reading and understanding. Our minds might be more like dusters than like containers, and our bodies might actually do much of the thinking.

This should not come across as a devaluation of learned readership and thus contribute to the current plight of the discipline of literary studies. What literary scholars do is indeed a skilled practice and directly relevant to life as embodied beings in the world. I hope this kind of reading can reside in peaceful cohabitation with critical aesthetics and deep-rooted knowledge of symbolism. If we occasionally get in touch with the child-like reader we all might be carrying within us, and dwell for a moment on the excitement in front of the pure matter of words and pages, we might understand more about the call of literary art. Most importantly, I hope my reading of reading here adds a voice to the small but persistent choir suggesting that literature is not there for a purpose, of making us better people or teaching us about the world. This kind of thinking easily leads to demanding calculable benefits for the world driven by unsustainable economies. Rather, it might be an ethical move to let books be, even a little distant and quiet on the shelf, yet powerful enough to move other things in the world.

11

The American Boy

DANIEL MENDELSOHN

One spring day in 1976, when I was fifteen years old and couldn't keep my secret any longer, I went into the bedroom I shared with my older brother, sat down at the little oak desk we did our homework on and began an anguished letter to a total stranger who lived on the other side of the world. We lived on Long Island, in one of twelve identical 'splanches' – split-ranch houses – that lined a street in a suburb that had, until relatively recently, been a potato farm. It was very flat. The stranger to whom I wrote that day lived in South Africa, a fact that I had gleaned from the brief bio under the author photograph on her book jackets, which showed a middle-aged woman with a pleasant face and tightly coiled grey hair, her eyes narrowed and crinkling at the corners: perhaps humorously, perhaps simply against the sun. I had got her street address from the *Who's Who* in our school library, where I often spent recess, bent over an encyclopedia entry that I particularly liked, about the Parthenon. Over a grainy black-and-white photo of the ruin as it appears today you could flip a colour transparency of how the building had looked in ancient times, gaudy with red and blue paint and gilding. I would sit there, day after day, contentedly toggling between the drab present and the richly hued past.

For the letter I wrote that day I used the 'good' onionskin paper, anxiously feeding each sheet between the rollers of a black cast-iron Underwood typewriter that had been salvaged from my grandfather's braid-and-trimmings factory in the city. I used it to type up school reports and term papers and, when nobody was around, short stories and poems and novels that I never showed to anyone – single-spaced pages so shaming to me that even when I hid them in the secret compartment under a drawer in the oak cabinet across from my bed (where I also hid certain other things: a real ancient Egyptian amulet I'd got as a bar-mitzvah gift from a shrewd godparent, a half-completed sketch I'd made of a boy who sat in front of me in English class). I imagined that they gave off some kind of radiation, a telltale glow that might betray the nature of the feelings I was writing about.

Now I was putting those feelings onto these translucent sheets, which protested with a faint crackle every time I advanced the carriage. When I was finished, I put the letter into the lightweight airmail envelope on which I'd typed the address: Delos, Glen Beach, Camps Bay, Cape 8001 South Africa. I didn't make a copy of what I wrote that day, but I must have confided a fear that my correspondent would reply to my effusions with a form letter, because when her answer came, a few weeks later, typed on a pale-blue aerogram – the first of many that would find me over the next eight years – it began, 'I wonder whoever told you I'd send you a "form letter" if you wrote to me. Are there really writers who do that?'

It was a question I didn't know how to answer, since she was the only writer I'd ever tried to contact. Who else would I write to? In those days, I had two obsessions – ancient Greece and other boys – and she was, I felt, responsible for both.

The author to whom I wrote that day, Mary Renault, had two discrete and enthusiastic audiences; although I didn't know it at the time, they neatly mirrored my twin obsessions. The first, and larger, consisted of admirers of her historical fiction. The second consisted of gay men.

Between 1956 and 1981 Renault published a number of critically acclaimed and best-selling fictional evocations of Greek antiquity. Like the works of Marguerite Yourcenar (*Memoirs of Hadrian*) and Robert Graves (*I, Claudius*), authors to whom she was compared, Renault's novels were often cast as first-person narratives of real or invented figures from myth and history – a technique that efficiently drew modern readers into exotic ancient milieus. The best-known and most commercially successful were *The Last of the Wine* (1956), which takes the form of a memoir by a young member of Socrates' circle, through whose eyes we witness the decline of Athens in the last part of the Peloponnesian War; *The King Must Die* (1958), a novelization of the early life of Theseus, the legendary Athenian king who defeated the Minotaur; and a trilogy of novels about Alexander the Great – *Fire from Heaven* (1969), *The Persian Boy* (1972) and *Funeral Games* (1981).

Renault, who was born in London in 1905 – she emigrated to South Africa after the Second World War – had published a number of crisply intelligent contemporary love stories between the late 1930s and the early '50s; to her meticulously researched re-creations of the past in the later, Greek-themed books she was able to bring the emotional insight and moral seriousness you expect from any good novelist. Many reviewers appreciated the way she reanimated both myth and history by means of ingenious psychological touches. (She once said that the Theseus book didn't jell until she had the idea of making the mythical overachiever diminutive in stature: he's a legendary hero, but also just a boy with something to prove.) Patrick O'Brian, the author of *Master and Commander*, was an admirer: he dedicated the fourth Aubrey-Maturin book to her, with the inscription 'An owl to Athens', the ancient Greek version of 'coals to Newcastle'. Academic classicists were also enthusiastic. One eminent Oxford don told an eager amateur that to get a sense of what ancient Greece was really like one had only to read Renault – 'Renault every time.' ('That really bucks me up,' she exclaimed, when this remark was reported to her during her final illness.) The combination of historical precision, literary texture and epic sweep won Renault a large public, particularly in the United States; her books, which have been translated into some twenty languages, have sold millions of copies in English alone.

One of those copies was a thick Eagle Books paperback of *Fire from Heaven* that was stuffed into a bookcase in our downstairs playroom, next to the black leather recliner. I read it when I was twelve, and I was hooked. Alexander the Great was my first serious crush.

It was my father who put the book in my hands. A mathematician who worked for an aerospace corporation, he had been a Latin whizz in high school and sometimes enjoyed thinking of himself as a lapsed classicist. When he gave me the paperback I looked at the cover and frowned. The illustration, of a blond young Greek holding a shield aloft, wasn't very convincing; I thought he looked a lot like the boy who lived across the street, who had once taken a bunch of us waterskiing for his birthday.

My dad said, 'I think you should give this a try,' averting his eyes slightly, in the way he had. Forty years later, I wonder how much he'd already guessed, and just what he was trying to accomplish.

Fire from Heaven traces Alexander's childhood and youth, ending with his accession to the throne, at the age of twenty. I finished it in a couple of days. The next weekend, I went to the public library and checked out the sequel, *The Persian Boy*, which had just been published. It views Alexander's conquest of Persia and his nascent dream of forming a vast Eurasian empire from an unexpected angle: the book is narrated by a historical figure called Bagoas, a beautiful eunuch who had been the pleasure boy of the defeated Persian emperor Darius and who later became Alexander's lover, too. I read *The Persian Boy* in a day and a half. Then I reread both books. Then, after taking my dad's copy of *Fire from Heaven* upstairs and placing it inside the oak cabinet, I got my mother to take me to the B. Daltons bookstore in the Walt Whitman Mall, in Huntington, where, for $1.95 I bought my own Bantam paperback of *The Persian Boy*. Its cover featured, in miniature, the haunting image that appeared on the hardback edition from the library: a Michelangelo drawing, in dusty-red chalk, of an epicene Oriental youth in three-quarter profile, wearing a headdress and earrings. Whenever someone mentions '1973', or 'junior high school', this small, delicate, reddish face is what I see in my mind's eye.

My fascination with these books had little to do with their canny evocations of Greek history, the persuasiveness of which I couldn't appreciate until years later. An important narrative thread in each novel is a story of awakening young love – homosexual love. In *Fire from Heaven*, Renault sympathetically imagines the awkward beginnings of the relationship between

Alexander and Hephaistion, a Macedonian of high birth who, the evidence strongly suggests, was the former's lover. In *The Persian Boy*, Bagoas, sold into slavery at ten, already world-weary at sixteen, finds himself drawn to Alexander, who has suddenly become his master as well as the master of the known world. In both novels, arduously achieved seductions give the narratives a sexy charge: Renault makes Alexander the aloof object of the longings of the other, more highly sexed characters, Hephaistion and Bagoas, who must figure out how to seduce him.

Most seductive of all to me was the young characters' yearning to love and be loved totally. 'Say that you love me best,' Bagoas dreams in *The Persian Boy*; 'I love you . . . You mean more to me than anything,' Hephaistion exclaims in *Fire from Heaven*; 'Do you love me best?' Alexander asks in the latter novel's opening scene. (These expressions of deep emotional need run like a refrain through Renault's contemporary novels, too.) As it happens, 'longing' (in Greek, *pothos*) has, since ancient times, been a key word in the Alexander narrative. In a history of Alexander's campaigns written by the historian Arrian (second century AD), *pothos* recurs to describe the inchoate craving that drove Alexander, far more insistently than any mere lust for conquest or renown. Renault clearly felt the pull of all this longing, too: in addition to the three Alexander novels, she wrote a psychologically oriented biography, *The Nature of Alexander*.

Reading Renault's books, I felt a shock of recognition. The silent watching of other boys, the endless strategizing about how to get their attention, the fantasies of finding a boy to love, and be loved by, 'best': all this was agonizingly familiar. I knew something about *pothos*, and thought of the humiliating lengths to which it could drive me – the memorizing of certain boys' class schedules or bus routes, the covert shuffling of locker assignments. I was astonished, halfway through *Fire from Heaven*, to find that this kind of thing had always been happening. Until that moment I had never seen my secret feelings reflected anywhere. Pop music meant nothing to me, since all the songs were about boys wanting girls or girls wanting boys; neither did the YA novels I'd read, for the same reason. Television was a desert. (*Will and Grace* was 25 years in the future.) Now, in a novel about people from another place and time, it was as if I had found a picture of myself.

There's a scene in *The Persian Boy* in which Bagoas realizes that he's in love with Alexander; in the slightly high style Renault developed as a vehicle to convey Bagoas' oriental provenance, she describes this moment as (I now realize) a kind of internal coming out – a moment when, for the first time, a young person understands the nature of his own feelings:

The living chick in the shell has known no other world. Through the wall comes a whiteness, but he does not know it is light. Yet he taps at the white wall, not knowing why. Lightning strikes his heart; the shell breaks open.

Reading *Fire from Heaven* and *The Persian Boy* was such a moment for me. Lightning had struck, the shell lay broken open. I had begun to understand what I was and what I wanted; and I knew that I wasn't alone.

Renault was herself a lesbian, the elder daughter of a doctor and a primly conventional housewife. It was not a happy home. Both the contemporary and the Greek novels feature unsettling depictions of bad marriages and, particularly, of nightmarishly passive-aggressive wives and mothers. Renault's mother had clearly hoped for a 'nice' girl instead of the unruly tomboy she got, and preferred Mary's younger sister. (Decades after I first encountered Renault's books, it occurred to me that all this could well be the source of the 'love me best' motif that recurs so often in her work.) In later life the author made no bones about having wished she'd been born a boy. Her first-person narrators are always men.

Indeed, it's possible to see in her lifelong fascination with dashing male heroes, Alexander the Great above all, an unusually intense authorial projection. In a letter to a friend, Renault recalled admiring the head of a statue of the Macedonian conqueror, which had given her an 'almost physical sense of the presence of Alexander like a blazing sun below the horizon, not yet quenching the stars but already paling them . . . His face has haunted me for years.' David Sweetman, in his *Mary Renault: A Biography* (1993), referred to *Fire from Heaven* as 'a love letter to the boy hero'. It's no accident that her very first book, written when she was eight, was a cowboy novel. From the start she seems to have been searching for an ideal boy protagonist, a fictional reflection of an inner identity. In all her work, boyishness is an unequivocally positive quality – even, or perhaps especially, in women.

Although Renault was entranced by the Greeks from an early age – by the time she finished high school, she had devoured all of Plato – at St Hugh's, a women's college at Oxford, she studied English. After taking her degree, she decided against teaching, one conventional route for unmarried, educated middle-class women, and instead trained as a nurse; her first three novels, published during the war years, were written during her off-hours from clinics and hospitals. In 1934 she met Julie Mullard, a vivacious young nurse who became her life partner for nearly fifty years, until Renault's death. In a 1982 BBC documentary, the two come off as unpretentious and suspicious of self-dramatizing fuss.

The couple stayed in England during the war, but after Renault won the $150,000 MGM prize for *Return to Night*, a 1947 novel about a woman doctor in love with a handsome, troubled, much younger actor, she became financially independent. ('You're the best of all . . . I love you. Better than anyone,' the doctor tells her lover in the novel's final pages.) They emigrated to South Africa almost on a whim, after reading travel advertisements following a particularly grim post-war winter in England. It was in Africa that Renault wrote the last of her contemporary novels. Soon after, she turned to the Greeks.

As she later told the story, the decision to start setting her novels in ancient Greece began with a question rooted in her early reading of Plato. During a pleasure cruise that she and Mullard took up the east coast of Africa, Renault recalled, she got to thinking about the Greek historian Xenophon, a stolid, less intellectually adventurous fellow-student of Plato's in Socrates' circle, who later became famous for the military exploits he recounted in his *Anabasis*, and began to wonder what the members of that circle might actually have been like, as people. The product of her inspiration was *The Last of the Wine*.

Towards the end of her life Renault wrote that the novel was 'the best thing I had ever done'. It's not hard to see why she thought so. A shrewdly unsentimental historical portrait of Athens at the beginning of its moral and political decline, it is enlivened by a love story between two of Socrates' students and deepened by a surprisingly vivid re-creation of Socrates' philosophical dialogues as, well, dialogue. There are rich and nuanced cameos of historical characters (not least, Socrates himself) and grand set pieces, all rendered with exacting fidelity to the original sources. Renault fans like to cite her stirring description of the great Athenian fleet's departure for its invasion of Sicily, a misguided campaign that ended in disaster.

And, perhaps better than any other of the Greek novels, *The Last of the Wine* demonstrates how Renault used subtle but telling touches to persuade you of the Greekness of her characters and settings. Classical Greek tends to be loaded with participles and relative clauses; Renault reproduced these tics. ('He, hearing that a youth called Philon, with whom he was in love, had been taken sick, went at once to him; meeting, I have been told, not only the slaves but the boy's own sister, running the other way.') She also used 'k' rather than the more usual Latin 'c' in her transliterations of proper names (Kleopatra, Sokrates), which gives her pages just the right, spiky Greek look. As a result of this minute attention to stylistic detail, the novels can give the impression of having been translated from some lost Greek original.

It's possible to see Renault's shift from the present to the past as motivated by something other than intellectual curiosity. Setting a novel in fifth-century BC Athens allowed her to write about homosexuality as natural. In *The Last of the Wine* the narrator muses on the abnormality of Xenophon's apparently exclusive heterosexuality: 'Sometimes indeed I asked myself whether he lacked the capacity for loving men at all; but I liked him too well to offend him by such a question.'

The hinge that connects her earlier works, love stories in which intelligent people – doctors, nurses, writers, actors – struggle with various emotional conundrums, and the later, historical fiction, in which the fact of love between men, at least, is no conundrum at all, is a novel called *The Charioteer*. Published in 1953, it is set, despite its classical-sounding title, during the Second World War and wrestles with the issue of 'Greek love'. Older gay men can recall that, in the 1950s and '60s, to walk into a bar with a copy of this book was a way of signalling that you were gay. Today, the book is referred to as a 'gay classic'.

I finished reading *The Charioteer* for the first time on 28 December 1974, when I was fourteen. I know the date because I recorded it in my diary. The man who placed it in my hands was a music teacher, around my parents' age, whom we knew to be gay: he had a 'roommate' with whom he shared a house in a nearby suburb. My mother and father were open-minded, and they saw nothing wrong in letting their four sons hang out with this civilized man, who took us to concerts and restaurants, and who let me sing with the church choir he directed.

What my parents didn't know was that the music teacher sometimes left copies of *Playgirl* lying around when I visited his house. I was both curious and embarrassed. Curious because of course I wanted to look at pictures of naked men, having spent hours pretending to be interested in the *Playboy* centrefolds the kids on my block would steal out of a neighbour's garage; and embarrassed because I perceived that it wasn't appropriate for this middle-aged man to be making porn available to a four-teen-year-old. Curiosity prevailed. Two years had passed since I'd read the Alexander books – paperback copies of which were now stacked, along with Renault's other books, into a neat little ziggurat in my bedroom cabinet – and there were things I wondered about, specific things, that weren't described in the Mary Renault books. I would wait for my teacher to go into another room, to start dinner or put on a recording of Thomas Tallis, and would snatch the magazine up and look at the photographs, which both titillated and repelled me. It was exciting to see the nude male bodies, however patently silly the cowboy boots or policeman hats might be; but it was hard to connect those images to the ideas of love that I had taken away from *Fire from Heaven* and *The Persian Boy.*

I remember the day that this teacher handed me the jacketless hardback of *The Charioteer*, with its dark-grey buckram boards. We were downstairs in his den, and he'd been playing me a rare LP of ancient Greek music. I was feeling very grown-up and was trying to impress him with my passion for all things Greek – a subject that led me, soon enough, to Renault's novels. He said, 'If you like Mary Renault, there's another one I think you'll be interested in.' He motioned me to follow him upstairs to his bedroom. He searched in a bookcase for a moment until he found what he was looking for. I took it home and started reading it. At first the Second World War setting disappointed me; I had no interest in modern history.

The title of *The Charioteer* alludes to Renault's beloved Plato. In the dialogue called 'Phaedrus' the soul is likened to a charioteer who must reconcile two horses, one white and well behaved (the rational and moral impulses), the other scruffy and ill-bred (the passions). Renault's book recasts the Platonic conflict as a human drama. Laurie Odell, a wounded young soldier who is recovering at a rural hospital – his given name is Laurence, but Renault pointedly used ambiguous names and nicknames whenever she could – finds himself torn between a secret love for an idealistic Quaker youth, Andrew (who seems drawn to Laurie in an innocent, non-sexual way), and a more complex, physical relationship with a slightly older naval officer, Ralph. The plot pushes Laurie towards a culminating choice between the two men. That choice implies another: whether to remain a loner or to enjoy the solidarity afforded by the local gay set, whose members Renault paints in campy colours: they're named Bunny and Binky and Bim, and wear Cartier bracelets. Laurie, by contrast, is a kind of holy fool: 'His loneliness had preserved in him a good deal of inadvertent innocence; there was much of life for which he had no formula.'

I, too, was an innocent. By a kind of literary osmosis that is possible only when you're young, I absorbed without question Renault's idealization of severe, undemonstrative men; I wasn't yet able to recognize, in the author's clichés of gay effeminacy, certain unexamined prejudices of her own. Nor did it occur to me to question a central element of the text: the rather dated assumption that it would be better for Andrew were he never to be made aware of his sexuality. (It 'would scatter his whole capital of belief in himself,' Laurie thinks. 'He must never know.')

Now, of course, I can read the book as it ought to be read, as a coming-of-age story: Laurie abandons the inchoate but potent ideals of adolescence, symbolized by the pure and curiously sexless Andrew, in favour of an adult relationship, one that is physical as well as emotional, with complicated and compromised Ralph, who, like Laurie, bears physical as well as emotional scars. But, because I was so young when I read the novel for the first time, I saw the arc from the ideal to the real, from youth to maturity, as a tragic one. To me, Andrew and Ralph were figures in a vast allegorical conflict. Under the white banner of Andrew there was Renault, and true love, and the ancient Greeks, with their lofty rhetoric and marmoreal beauty; under the black banner of Ralph there was *Playgirl*, and sex, and thoughts about naked men – the messy and confusing present.

Although there was much of life for which I had no 'formula', either, I thought I knew enough to decide that, if being gay meant marching under the black banner – aligning myself with my music teacher, or the few characters you saw on TV who, you somehow knew, were gay: the limp wrists and the effete, the spineless Dr Smith on *Lost in Space* and the queeny Paul Lynde character on *Bewitched* – then it would be better to remain alone.

Unlike Renault's Greek novels, which portrayed desire beneath the scrim of a historical setting, *The Charioteer*, whose characters used words like 'queer', allowed for no evasions. 'I know what I am,' I wrote in my diary the day I finished reading it for the first time. By then I was obsessively in love with a yellow-haired swimmer who put up with my dogged stalking for three years before he turned around one day early in our senior year and, planting himself in front of his locker, which I had gone to some lengths to ensure was next to mine, told me quite calmly that he didn't want to talk to me anymore, and didn't. But I had never thought of my feelings for him as 'gay' or 'queer': it simply was how I felt. 'I know what I am,' I wrote. 'Now I must think what to do with it.'

'What you are ... what to do with it' is a paraphrase of a line from *The Charioteer*. Someone utters it during a climactic scene at a birthday party that's being given for a young gay doctor. At the party, the characters start arguing about what would now be called identity politics: about whether the thing that sets you apart ought, in some fundamental way, to define you. As lonely as he is, Laurie finds himself resisting the temptation of joining this group – of 'making a career' of his 'limitations', as he puts it to himself. It's in response to this debate about identity that Ralph articulates the liberating formula: 'It's not what one is, it's what one does with it.'

Renault grew up in an era in which it was difficult to think of homosexuality as anything but a limitation; to her credit, she was independent-minded enough to try to resist that prejudice. Later in the book, the doctor rejects the premises that make blackmail possible:

> I don't admit that I'm a social menace ... I'm not prepared to accept a standard which puts the whole of my emotional life on the plane of immorality. I've never involved a normal person or a minor or anyone who wasn't in a position to exercise free choice . . . Criminals are blackmailed. I'm not a criminal. I'm prepared to go to some degree of trouble, if necessary, to make that point.

Renault later wrote that this passage of dialogue 'gave the starting-point to my first historical novel' – *The Last of the Wine*, in other words, the novel in which homosexuality wasn't considered a limitation.

When I was fourteen, the characterization of homosexuality as a 'limitation' seemed reasonable enough. How could it not be a handicap, when it left you with freakish feelings that no one else you knew seemed to share, apart from middle-aged men who left dirty magazines around for you to pick up, feelings that you knew, more instinctually than consciously, you had to hide? What I did with it, after a few anxious months of trying and failing to picture the vast, nearly featureless landscape of the future, one in which the only road sign now, brand-new, freshly painted, bore the word 'queer', was to try to be good – to try to be like Laurie Odell. 'I must make some good resolutions for the new year,' I had written in my diary. 'I will try to do better next year.'

The next year, I turned fifteen, and still didn't really know what 'better' might mean. Finally, I decided to write to Mary Renault and ask her.

In my first letter to Renault, I poured out my story: ancient Greece, discovering her books, discovering that I was gay through her books. In her reply, which arrived in mid-April, just after my sixteenth birthday, she deftly deflected my adolescent effusions while putting to rest my anxieties about form letters:

> Are there really writers who do that? I knew film stars do. You can't blame them, really; apart from the fact that about half the people who write to them must be morons who think they really are Cleopatra or whoever, they get such thousands that if they attempted answering themselves they'd never get to the set.
>
> Writers, though, write to communicate; and when someone to whom one has got through takes the trouble to write and tell one so, it would be pretty ungrateful to respond with something off a duplicator. I think so, anyway.

This, as she had intended, pleased me. And yet of my fervent confessions there was only the briefest acknowledgement, which segued immediately and harmlessly into a charming compliment and a gentle dismissal:

I am truly glad the books have meant all this to you; especially as you write very good English yourself . . . Greek history, or something, has certainly given you a clean and simple style. I wish you the very best of luck with your work, and a happy fulfilled career.

I read and reread the letter. I was a gay adolescent; I was accustomed to overinterpreting. Just as I wasn't what I pretended to be, so everyone and everything else, I thought, concealed secret meanings, communicated in hidden codes. (I had to think a moment before I realized that 'a duplicator' was a copying machine.) But there was nothing else, apart from the scrawled signature and, below it, printed instructions about how to fold the aerogram. 'Verseël Eers Die Twee Syklappe, Dan Hierdie Een – Seal The Two Side Flaps First, Then This One.'

'Meant all this to you'? Maybe I hadn't been clear enough. I sat down and started another letter.

This time, I enclosed a few pages of one of the short stories I had secretly written. Like nearly everything I wrote then, it was about an intense friendship between two fourteen-year-old boys, one of whom was, inevitably, serious and dark-haired and creative, while the other was, just as inevitably, carefree and blond and athletic. This story, which was more ambitious than the others – it had a prologue set in a kind of classical limbo – was, like the others, a slavish pastiche of Renault: her diction, with its faint aura of prewar England ('Phaedo, whatever do you want?'), her settings ('Under the ancient olive tree, the two young men were talking'), her characters ('Speaking of Sokrates, have you seen him lately?'), even her punctuation. (Renault, according to her biographer, had a particular fondness for the semicolon. I still remember the thrill I felt when one of my college professors wrote, in the margin of an undergraduate essay, 'You have semicolonitis!') I was convinced that this lofty effort would persuade her that I would be a worthy correspondent. Feeling very much the author, I was emboldened to ask her whether she, too, had a kind of compulsion to write, although I secretly doubted whether hers had the same source as mine. For me, writing was a kind of sympathetic magic, a way of conjuring the swimmer boy and keeping him close.

She wrote back within a couple of weeks, at the end of April. I know she must have read the story because of her tactful allusion to it:

> Your nice letter came this morning. Something tells me you are going to have a future as a writer. Keep at it; very few people get published at 16 or even 20, but don't worry . . . There is only one way to learn to write and that is by reading. Don't read for duty, try all the good stuff though, sample it, then devour what stimulates and enriches you. This will seep in to your own work, which may be derivative at first but this does not matter. Your own style will develop later.

Now that I am a writer who has received mail from young readers, I appreciate the patience and gentleness of this paragraph. I doubt that, at the time, I registered the implications of 'which may be derivative'; it was enough that she thought I had a future as a writer. This show of confidence dulled the disappointing force of her equally graceful but firm leave-taking:

Yes, you are right, I do have a compulsion to write and am very frustrated and unhappy if I am kept from doing it ... And this is the reason I can't go on writing to you. Not that it is too much trouble; writing a book is very much more trouble; but if I wrote more than one thank-you letter to all the people who are kind enough to write to me, I would never write another novel again. Or I would have to take to those 'form letters' – rather than which I wouldn't answer at all.

So this really is goodbye – but the very best of luck to you all the same.

This time, I felt no great disappointment. Over the next months, as my stalking of the blond swimmer became more abject, as more and more meals ended with me bursting into tears and locking myself in my room as my parents clumped helplessly down the hallway after me, the sentence 'Something tells me you are going to have a future as a writer' served as a charm. I knew I had no right to expect anything else from her.

Then, that December, she sent me a Christmas card.

I will never know why she changed her mind and wrote again, eight months after she said that she couldn't go on corresponding; at the time, I was so excited by her overture that I didn't dare ask. But I can speculate now. When I read Sweetman's biography, ten years after Renault's death, I learned that the mid-1970s had been a particularly trying period for her. In the autumn of 1974 she fell and injured her leg, necessitating an irritatingly lengthy recovery. Soon afterward, Mullard, who was highly strung, suffered a minor breakdown and had to be briefly institutionalized. At just about the time that Renault and

I exchanged our first letters, she had decided to put her affairs in order and make provisions for her estate. Perhaps she thought that a letter from an American teenager every now and then might provide some distraction, despite (or perhaps because of) the adolescent turmoil it contained.

Something else has occurred to me. Like all writers, Renault spent much of her time alone; a good many of her friends, as I also learned later, were gay men, often ballet dancers and actors and theatre people. What she did not have in her life, as far as I know, was children – or students. I wonder whether she wished for some. (In *The Charioteer*, Laurie is described as someone who 'usually got on with strong-minded old maids'; was that how she saw herself?) Shrewdly drawn scenes of apprenticeships, of actors or princes or poets learning their craft, figure in a number of the novels. In *The Last of the Wine*, Socrates, faced with an earnest, if pretentious, student, resorts to 'teasing him out of his pomposities' – as canny a characterization of what it's like to teach freshmen as any I know of.

Renault's special feeling for the relationship between a teacher and a student imbues the poignant finale of *The Mask of Apollo*, her 1966 novel about an Athenian actor who gets mixed up in Plato's disastrous scheme, in the mid-360s BC, to turn a corrupt Sicilian tyrant into a philosopher-king. Years after the fiasco, the actor meets the teenaged Alexander, already charismatic and alive with curiosity about the world, and realizes, wrenchingly, that this youth would have been the ideal student for Plato, now dead:

All tragedies deal with fated meetings; how else could there be a play? Fate deals its stroke; sorrow is purged, or turned to rejoicing; there is death, or triumph; there has been a meeting, and a change. No one will ever make a tragedy – and that is as well, for one could not bear it – whose grief is that the principals never met.

I wonder whether something like this was in Mary Renault's mind that day in December when she decided to write back to me after all. Maybe she liked the thought of having a student – someone to tease out of his pomposities. Maybe, with all that grief around her just then, she thought she could at least avoid the grief that comes of never making contact.

We corresponded for the next eight years. I always addressed her as 'Miss Renault' or 'Mary Renault'; I still can't think of her as 'Mary'. She only ever addressed me as 'Daniel Mendelsohn' and, once I was in college, 'Mr. Mendelsohn'. During that time I finished high school, went to college, graduated and got my first job. She published her biography of Alexander and two more novels. We didn't write often – a few exchanges a year – but knowing that she was out there, interested in my progress, was like a secret talisman.

During the first few years, when I was still in high school, I tried not to be too familiar or too earnest – the mistake that I had made in my first couple of letters. (Recalling a lesbian novel she disliked, Renault wrote of its 'impermissible allowance of self-pity' and 'earnest humourlessness'.) Instead, I would tell her about what I was reading, some of which, of course, was chosen with an eye to pleasing her. 'I am delighted you've been reading the Phaedrus,' she wrote to me early in 1978, when I was a senior in high school. 'It's good furniture for any mind.' Sometimes she would make suggestions. 'Have you ever tried

Malory's *Morte d'Arthur*? It is very beautiful. On no account read a version pulped down into modern English, it ruins the flavour.' A year earlier, I and the other eleventh graders had been made to memorize the opening lines of *The Canterbury Tales* in the original Middle English, an exercise that we both feared and derided; reading her letter, I began to wonder, as I hadn't done before, what it might mean for language to have 'flavour'.

Occasionally there would be an item about her or one of her books in the news; it gave me a thrilling sense of privilege to be able to write to the author herself to learn more. When I was a junior in high school, the teacher who had given me *The Charioteer* showed me an issue of a magazine called *After Dark*, which I only later realized was a gay magazine. It featured an ambitious photo spread about the upcoming movie adaptation of *The Persian Boy*, and referred to young dancers and actors who were hoping to be cast as Bagoas. Excited, I wrote to Renault asking for details. 'I certainly wish they had not raised the hopes of so many actors in this way,' she replied, explaining that the movie rights hadn't even been sold yet, 'and I wish too that so many actors didn't imagine that the book author has any say in the casting! They could as fruitfully approach the office cleaner.' (Sweetman, in his biography, relates how a young actor had written to her, offering to have 'the operation' if it meant getting the part. 'That,' she wrote back to him, 'would be gelding the lily.')

I continued to send her the stories I was writing. As I reached the end of high school, these were getting darker: the beginning of my senior year, in the autumn of 1977, had been scarred by the confrontation with the blond swimmer. Later that day I ran out of my house and walked around the blandly identical neighbourhoods for hours. At one point I climbed to the top of an overpass and looked down – not serious, but serious enough. Then I burst out laughing, amused by my own theatrics; it was a beautiful autumn afternoon, and in a year I'd be in college, where I'd be able to study Greek and Latin and find new, like-minded friends; where, I secretly hoped, there might be a Laurie Odell for me. I wrote about this incident to Mary Renault, aware, as I did so, of wanting her to perceive that I was learning from her – that I wasn't giving in to adolescent foolishness. I was, after all, someone who had a future as a writer.

She read these later stories, too. By this point, one (or sometimes both) of the two inseparable friends who were always at the centre of my fiction, the brunet and the blond, the writer and the athlete, would die of a rare disease, or meet with a terrible accident. As she had done before, and would do again, Mary Renault ignored the impermissible self-pity and the earnest humourlessness, and simply encouraged me:

> Just carry on enjoying yourself with writing. Love what
> you are doing and do it as well as you can, and the tree
> will grow. Nobody ever did their best work at 17 except
> people who died at 18! You are now just getting the soil
> in your garden right – except that unlike a garden, even at
> this stage your work is producing flowers, very likely not
> yet ready for the flower-show, but giving you a lot of joy.

The stories did not, in fact, give me much joy. But knowing that she had read them did.

I wrote to Renault less frequently once I went off to the University of Virginia. (The swimmer had grown up in Virginia;

I thought there might be someone else like him there.) I started learning Greek during my first semester, and found a kind of happiness in grammar, which insisted on a level of precision not available in English: the nouns, often familiar-looking (*anthrōpos*, *historia*, *klimax*), each one of which has five different forms, depending on how it's used in a sentence; the vast spiderweb of the verb system. For me, as for many beginning classics students, learning Greek and Latin unlocked the secrets of my own language. With delight I learned that 'ephebe' consists of *epi*, 'upon', and '*hēbē*, 'youth': an ephebe is a male at the acme of his youth. And you learn, too, to sniff out a fake. The word 'homosexual', for instance, is a solecism, a hybrid of Greek (*homos*, 'alike') and Latin (*sexualis*, 'sexual'). A *homo*- word with a purer pedigree, as I learned when I started reading Homer in Greek, was *homophrosyne*, 'like-mindedness', which is the word Odysseus uses, in the *Odyssey*, to describe the ideal union of two spouses – the kind of union that he's trying to return home to.

My own quest for *homophrosyne* was proving unsuccessful. No Laurie Odell had materialized. How did you make contact? There was, I knew, a gay student union that met regularly in one of the many red-brick-and-white-stucco neoclassical buildings on campus, undistinguished knockoffs of Jeffersonian originals. But I was dismayed to see that the building was right in the middle of the campus; I was terrified that someone I knew would see me going in. So I would walk past the posters for the meetings, my eyes briefly alighting, as tentative as a fly on a peach, on the word 'gay', as I made my way each morning to Greek class, during my first year or, the next year, to Greek 201 ('Plato's *Apology*') or, the year after, to the course in which, for the first time, I read Sophocles in Greek. The text, I remember, was

Philoctetes, a play about a crippled hero who has been abandoned on a desert island for so long that it's no longer clear whether he can rejoin society.

Beneath my fear of being found out, a larger anxiety lurked. I was starting to worry that, even if I were to 'make contact', the ideal I'd found in *The Charioteer* didn't exist. There was a boy in one of my English classes, a tall, dark-haired prep with a beaked nose and a Tidewater accent, who, I now realize, was trying to make contact with *me*. He'd stop me after lectures and ask if he could borrow my notes; once, after mentioning that he was in one of the choral groups, he called to invite me to come to his dorm room to listen to his new LP of Purcell's *Come Ye Sons of Art*. But I never called him back. After a while he started asking some other kid for notes at the end of lectures.

I studied hard and absorbed my grammars and didn't confide any of this to Mary Renault. She had brought me to the Greeks, and had shown me what I was, and it was somehow shaming to let on that I was having a hard time finding anyone like the characters in her novels. Somewhere in *The Persian Boy*, when the young Bagoas is being schooled at Susa in the arts of the courtesan, the kindly master who is preparing him for service to the king reminds him of a crucial rule of life at court: 'Never be importunate, never, never.' I was no longer sixteen, and I was determined never to importune her.

She must have noticed, at any rate, that I was no longer enclosing short stories with my letters. That's because I wasn't writing anymore. How silly those stories had been! I was 21; I was going to be a scholar, not a writer. I was comforted by the incantatory rhythms of grammatical paradigms; by syntax, which was soothingly indifferent to emotion. During my senior

year, *Funeral Games* was published. I went to the local bookstore
every day to see if it had come in yet and, when it did, bought it
and read it right away. The novel begins as Alexander is dying and
proceeds to describe in grimly unsentimental detail the story of
the internecine power struggles that resulted from his premature
death. I was struck by the starkness of the narrative. Gone were
the exalted adolescent yearnings of *Fire from Heaven*, gone the
plush erotic orientalisms of *The Persian Boy*. It was as if all feeling
had been stripped away. I read it with a kind of sour enjoyment;
it matched my mood. I wrote her to tell her how much I'd liked
it. 'Your letter gave me very great pleasure,' she began her reply:

> Besides its generous appreciation of what the book is
> about, this is actually the first letter about it from an
> ordinary reader – meaning of course one who had no
> professional or personal reason to read the book. I am
> so glad that you liked it.

I knew what she meant, but I was a little hurt. I, at any rate,
thought that I had a 'personal' reason to read it.

My letters to Renault were even less frequent after I graduated from college. I was too embarrassed. For one thing, I had
decided not to go on to do a graduate degree in classics, which
she had once urged me to do, on the ground that it was always
good to have 'solid' knowledge of a subject, even if one wanted
to be a writer rather than an academic. I wrote that I was for-
going graduate school because I 'hoped to gather knowledge
of the world' – probably because I had read somewhere that
she had become a nurse in order to gain real-life experience to
write about.

I moved to New York City and found a job as an assistant to a small-time opera impresario whose obscene tirades against disloyal conductors and greedy sopranos would seep, like his cigar smoke, beneath the smoked-glass door of his inner office in the tiny 'suite' he rented, in the Steinway Building on West Fifty-Seventh Street, into the area where I was stationed. Sitting at my desk while he shrieked into the phone, I was too timid even to quit. But in my letters to Renault I swaggered and lied and pretended to be using my classical learning to gain insight into the real world. In the spring of 1983 I wrote her a letter that I ostentatiously typed on our company stationery ('DANIEL MENDELSOHN, ASSOCIATE'): 'I've found that reading Plato while one isn't actually studying intensively gives one an entirely new perspective – like being a Christian on weekdays.' (That last phrase is an almost verbatim citation from *The Charioteer*.) I went on grandiosely, 'After all, it wasn't meant to be read and discussed at cocktail parties, but lived, in a way; or so I think.'

The fact is that I wasn't spending much time on Plato. Mostly I was going out to bars: Boy Bar, down on St Marks Place, where young men, self-consciously 'over' the disco aesthetic just then, lounged in khaki shorts and Topsiders and played pool at a table under a giant stuffed fish; the Pyramid, where you'd go afterward, once your standards had started to erode; the Works, on the Upper West Side, with its aloof actor-waiters in their too carefully pressed polo shirts, lined up neatly against the black walls like empty bottles; bars that didn't last long enough for me to remember their names, while I tried, as I continued to put it to myself, to 'make contact'.

Sex rarely appears in Renault's books; it's either omitted altogether or suggested with such elegant circumlocution that

I sometimes didn't realize that certain passages were sex scenes when I first read them. This was partly because of the author's own idealized exaltation of platonic love, and partly for reasons that she identified as writerly ones. 'If characters have come to life,' she once wrote, 'one should know how they will make love; if not it doesn't matter. Inch-by-inch physical descriptions are the ketchup of the literary cuisine, only required by the insipid dish or by the diner without a palate.' As I reread her books in high school, I looked in vain for signs of what lovemaking might actually be like; what (for instance) 'a trick I learned at Susa' (as Bagoas recalls of an attempt to liven things up in bed with the Persian emperor) might be, or what 'the sufficient evidence of his senses' (the hint that Laurie and Ralph have finally slept together, in *The Charioteer*) might allude to. But in college I had finally, if fleetingly, discovered sex, and in New York it was everywhere, if you wanted it. It seemed perfectly reasonable to have sex if you couldn't find love. Occasionally, I'd bring someone home, or go to his place, and often it would be pleasurable and sometimes it would be someone I liked. But always in the back of my mind was a certain image of what I wanted, and since nobody I met quite matched it, I held back. I had come to feel that getting involved with real people was, somehow, a betrayal.

Sometimes I comforted myself with this thought: hadn't Laurie Odell also been a loner? The first summer I lived in New York, a friend told me about a gay therapist who 'did group' on the East Side, and suggested that I join; it was a great place to meet nice guys, he said. I went for about five sessions. Some of the men were in relationships with each other: one couple consisted of a tall, extraordinarily handsome young man of about my age and his 'lover', a short, quite ugly man in his forties with a gigantic nose. I thought it surprising that they would be together. Never having had a lover, and embarrassed by my lack of experience and, even more, by the secret ideal that was keeping me from experience, I rarely said anything during the sessions. Finally, one day, the others turned to me all at once and asked me to talk about myself. At some point, inevitably, I mentioned the Mary Renault books and what their vision of love meant to me. 'Oh, *Mary*,' the big-nosed lover of the beautiful ephebe said, and only after a moment did I realize that he was not referring to the author but addressing me, 'join the *real* world!' I never went back to 'group'. I recorded this incident in my journal. The entry ends with the sentence 'I ought to write Mary Renault soon.' But I didn't.

In April 1983 I wrote my last letter to her. In it I lied and concealed and sprinkled the pages with allusions to Plato. I enclosed, as I sometimes liked to do, a cartoon from the *New Yorker* having to do with the ancient world. In it, a corpulent king is getting the lowdown from his vizier on a visiting delegation: 'The Athenians are here, Sire, with an offer to back us with ships, money, arms, and men – and, of course, their usual lectures about democracy.' In early May she replied. She began by thanking me for the *New Yorker* cartoon: 'I don't know if it would have amused Thukydides; he didn't amuse easily, he had seen it all; but I bet it would have given a good laugh to Philip of Macedon, when that arch democrat Demosthenes made a pact with the Great King of Persia.' Then she went on to tease me. 'I'm glad you're enjoying Plato. Of course he meant his ideas to be lived . . . But he certainly felt happy at having them discussed at drinking parties. Look at the Symposium!' I was too mortified to reply. I thought she must be appalled by me.

That summer I decided that I wasn't cut out for 'the real world', and began to make plans to apply to graduate school in classics. Early in September 1983 I walked out of the Steinway Building just as a handsome man, blond and square-jawed, pedalled past on a bike; he grinned and rang his little bell at me. We dated for a while, but, as before, I wasn't quite sure what to *do*, now that I had a 'relationship'. Later that month I wrote in my journal, worrying that, whereas the characters in books seemed to have so much forward momentum, I didn't. I still wasn't sure how you got to be the author of your own life. The journal ends there. The only additional item is a clipping from the *New York Times*, dated Wednesday, 14 December 1983.

I had been thinking about sending Renault a Christmas card but hadn't got around to doing it. Then, that Wednesday morning, I walked into the Steinway Building, went through the lobby past the display of grand pianos, got into the elevator, scanned the front page of the *Times* and suddenly said, loudly, 'Oh, *no!*' I slumped against the back of the elevator and started crying. The only other person in the elevator was old Mr Koretz, the Holocaust survivor who rented the office next to ours.

'What happened?' he asked, stooping a little and bringing his large face close to mine, his eyes gigantically magnified by his glasses. He was tall, often wore a raincoat, and his slightly phlegmy Middle European consonants were comforting. 'Did someone die?'

I shoved the *Times* in his direction and pointed. Down below the fold, next to the contents, under the heading 'Inside', was the item that had caught my eye: 'Mary Renault Dies. The historical novelist Mary Renault, who based many of her best-selling books on the legends of ancient Greece, died in Cape Town. Page B5.'

Mr Koretz gave me a noncommittal look. 'It was someone you knew?'

'Yes.' I nodded; then I shook my head. 'No.' He gave me a look. 'It's hard to explain,' I said.

After work, I hurried home to write a condolence letter to a person whose existence I couldn't know of until I turned to page B5 and saw there, at last, the discreet proof of a suspicion I had long entertained but never dared ask about ('the writer's companion of the last 50 years, Julie Mullard'). 'Dear Miss Mullard,' I began; and then, not for the first time, poured out my heart to a stranger in South Africa.

A month later, a card arrived. On the front, the words 'IN MEMORIAM MARY RENAULT 1905–1983' were printed in black. To my surprise, the handwritten note inside suggested that this companion knew who I was. ('She was never aware of any generation gap. People were people to her.') Had Mary Renault discussed me with her companion? What else had they talked about? At that moment, I wasn't so much afraid that my confidences had been shared as I was startled to realize that Renault had existed for other people: that she wasn't only 'Mary Renault', who wrote novels and sometimes wrote to me, but was also 'Mary', which was how Mullard kept referring to her, a woman who might have casually discussed this and that with her companion – for instance, the letters she had been receiving over the past decade from a young American – the way my parents discussed this and that: work, *New Yorker* cartoons, things that had come in the mail.

I put Mullard's card in a large manila envelope that, years earlier, my mother had provided for this correspondence, labelling it, as she liked to do when she organized my things,

with my initials, in blue Magic Marker ('Mary Renault: DA.')
I'm pretty sure that, as I did so, I told myself that this was the
last letter I'd ever be receiving from Camps Bay, Cape Town,
South Africa.

For the next 25 years, this was true. Then, one morning in
December 2008, the letters started coming again.

It was because of a review of a book of mine, a collection
that contained an essay I'd written about Oliver Stone's film
Alexander. I had ended the piece by mentioning how Renault's
Alexander novels had inspired me to become a classicist and,
eventually, a writer. The reviewer mentioned the Renault
connection. Three weeks later, a handwritten letter with
colourful South African stamps was forwarded to me. 'Dear
Daniel Mendelsohn,' it began, and went on:

> G. W. Bowersock's NYRB review of your How Beautiful
> ... reveals that the Daniel Mendelsohn of whom I am an
> avid reader is no other than 'the American boy' of whom
> Mary Renault used to speak with enjoyment many years
> ago!

My correspondent identified herself as Nancy Gordon. The
handwriting was firm and clear, although she was quite elderly.
('I am 87. Old. Old. Old.') She told me that her late husband,
Gerald, a lawyer and writer, had been a member of Pen South
Africa when Mary was president, and that the two couples –
Nancy and Gerald and Mary and Julie – had spent a good deal
of time together. Nancy was the sole survivor of the little group.
'Mary, Julie and Gerald are all gone, but I feel somehow called,'
she wrote, 'as humble messenger from Mary, to salute you. She

would have been so chuffed!' At the end of the letter were her signature and e-mail address.

Then, in a P.S., she asked, 'Do you still feel for Mary?'

It was a complicated question. Of course I felt for 'Mary'. In every sense, she has accompanied me through my life. The ziggurat of books has been disassembled and reconstituted in various apartments and graduate-student lodgings over the years, but it is still there. The Eagle Books *Fire from Heaven* and the Bantam *Persian Boy* are now so fragile, the pages so brown and brittle with age, the covers so mummified in Scotch tape that long ago lost its adhesive, that you can't really read them. They're sitting on a shelf in my bedroom, as wizened and unrecognizable as relics.

And yet, as the years passed, I wondered whether I would have been recognizable to her. When Sweetman's biography of Renault came out, I read it right away; in one passage he writes about Renault's distaste for 'the worst aspects of the [gay] subculture . . . the constant search for sexual gratification without affection, the impermanence of most relationships.' Well. I'd never found a Laurie; although I'd been with some good men, the one-night stands vastly outnumbered the affectionate encounters and long-term relationships. In graduate school, I had been a leader of the Gay Alliance and been involved in a good deal of campus activism. I debated, as I did so, whether this constituted 'making a career of one's limitations', and decided that it didn't.

So yes: I still felt for Mary. But what had she felt for *me*? I knew, of course, that she had read my letters carefully – and not only because of her thoughtful replies to them. In 1978, when I was in my first year at Virginia, her penultimate novel, *The Praise Singer* about the great lyric poet Simonides, was published. On page 44 there's a scene in which Simonides, who was famously ugly, recalls how, as a youth, he had resolved to kill himself: having climbed to the parapet of a temple, he looks up at the bright sky and realizes he's being foolish. In real life, he went on to have a happy and fulfilled career. She had indeed paid attention.

But had there been anything else? Until I got Nancy's letter, I thought I would never know. This is why I said 'yes' when, after a year of writing to Nancy – a correspondence that has grown far larger, by now, than the one I shared with Renault – she invited me to come to Cape Town, to see Delos, the bungalow down by Camps Bay, the beach where Renault and Mullard had lived, where Renault had received my letters and written hers to me, and to meet some of Renault's friends, who had also wondered what had become of 'the American boy'.

We spent four days in Cape Town. 'We' because I took my father: I owed him this. We stayed in a hotel overlooking Camps Bay. It was odd, as we drove there from the airport, to see the words Camps Bay on road signs. I'd been writing the name for years, and had never thought of it as a real place.

The climax of our visit was a dinner party at which Nancy Gordon gathered a few of Mary Renault's old friends. Nancy is small and vivid; she greeted me and my father wearing a floor-length, brightly patterned cotton dress, with horn and wooden bangles going up both arms. In the distance, we could see Table Mountain's strange flat top, the mist pouring over it like dry ice off a stage. Before the others arrived, she pointed to a chair in the corner of her living room: 'Mary used to like to sit in that chair. She'd sometimes come over to our place for a drink looking out at the beach and I remember she would suddenly get up and say, "I must go write to my American boy."'

My American boy. When we had checked into our hotel, we found an envelope from Nancy containing a few handwritten sheets labelled 'Remembering Her'. One of the memories she'd jotted down was of the family who lived in the bungalow next to Renault's, 'with lots of kids, all very blond'. The boys, Nancy wrote, had all been excellent surfers, and Mary had loved watching them. Now, as we stood there in Nancy's living room next to the chair, looking out the large plate-glass windows at the surf where the neighbour boys had played, I thought: Mary Renault had turned away from the blond boys to write to me.

The other friends arrived. To each man or couple, Nancy would exclaim that I was 'the American boy' to whom Mary used to write, all those years ago. Over dinner, they all traded what were, clearly, favourite anecdotes. There were stories about Mary and her love of sports cars, stories about how Mary had found out that her gardener was growing marijuana and spent the night flushing it down the toilet, the story of how Mary and Julie insisted that the fig leaf on a bronze statue of Mercury they'd bought be replaced by an anatomically correct male member. 'As nurses,' Renault had told the workman, 'we *certainly* know what penises look like.' At one point, I mentioned that she had made me read Malory's *Le Morte d'Arthur*, and everyone laughed. 'She made *everyone* read Malory,' someone cried out. 'All of us had to!'

I sat and listened, waiting to hear something that would give me a clue to what she'd have felt about me and my writing. What would she have made of my first book, with its matter-of-fact descriptions of the way that I and so many of the gay men I know have lived – the endless talk of wanting boyfriends, of finding a 'real' relationship, and the late nights spent hooking up online?

At some point I asked Owen Murray – a former ballet dancer to whom Renault, he told me with a sly grin, had once said, 'I wish I'd been born with your body and face' – whether she knew about what really went on between men. I had visited the house he shares with his partner, which is filled with small mementos of Renault: Venetian glass paperweights that had sat on her desk and windowsill, the statue with its add-on penis. Taped to the refrigerator were photographs of Murray, shirtless, still muscular, smiling broadly, at gay parades, on gay cruises, at gay clubs; I figured that he would know what I meant when I said 'what really went on between men'. But it was hard for me to fathom his response. 'Mary wanted her men friends to live up to the Greek ideal,' he said. I was a classicist, and I knew that the ideal of 'Greek love' was itself a fantasy of Victorian 'inverts' who, as Renault had done, projected their *pothos* for an accepting society onto the distant past. The 'Greek ideal': what could this mean in real life? When I pressed Murray on this point, he said, 'She liked her friends to be coupled.' I shut up and listened to the stories.

Towards the end of the evening, the conversation turned to the many correspondents Renault had had. 'People used to write her *all* the time,' Owen said. 'Married men who were secretly gay, closeted men – there were *thousands* of letters when she died.' Someone else mentioned a prominent American politician who had come out to Renault in a letter, as I had done all those years ago; the others nodded knowingly, enjoying the expression on my face when I heard the famous name. I asked where all these letters were and what had become of them. Owen said that they had been destroyed after Mary's death, in part to protect the men who had written them. I thought of my onionskin pages, blackening and curling in the flames.

During the next couple of days, I visited some of the men who had been at Nancy's dinner. Each showed me some precious relic, and each offered me a keepsake. Owen gave me an address book, with alphabetical tabs, in which Renault had scrawled notes on various works in progress. (Under 'I' there's a page on which she wrote the word 'Ideas', and then a few lines with a sketch for a scene that ended up in *The Mask of Apollo*.) There were some copies of manuscripts ('Notes on Oedipus', 'Notes on the King Must Die'), given to me by Roy Sargeant, a theatre director who was making plans to stage a play he'd commissioned, in which the shades of Renault and Alexander meet in the Underworld. Nancy gave me the dainty porcelain cup Renault drank from as she worked.

I took them all. Then my father and I flew home. At some point, I turned to him and shared a thought I often have as I sit awake on a long-haul flight: I think, I told him, about the bags of mail in the cargo hold below, what fervour they contain, what lives they might alter.

Eventually, my father fell asleep. I remained awake, replaying in my mind the events and conversations of the previous few days. In particular, I was thinking of something that Owen had said at Nancy's house. Although I had been enjoying the anecdotes and reminiscences, I was feeling unsatisfied; there was no way of knowing, finally, what Mary Renault would have thought of the man that the American boy had become. Then, towards the end of the evening – during the conversation about all the people who wrote letters to Mary Renault – Owen, who'd been watching me react to the surfeit of new personal details about her, spoke up. He talked slowly and loudly, as if addressing the others, but I knew that he was talking to me. 'Mary used to say to people who wrote wanting to know her that they should just read her *books*.' He paused and then gave me the tiniest smile. 'But she understood why they wrote her personal letters.'

At that moment, sitting at a table 8,000 miles from home, I saw that I'd come to South Africa chasing a chimera. I had already found the Mary Renault I needed, years earlier. I thought again of the yellowing books on my shelf; I thought, too, of the relationships that had never quite worked out, edged aside by a phantom out of a novel. She had shown me a picture of what I was, when I needed to see it, and had given me a myth that justified my fears and limitations. The writers we absorb when we're young bind us to them, sometimes lightly, sometimes with iron. In time, the bonds fall away, but if you look very closely you can sometimes make out the pale white groove of a faded scar, or the telltale chalky red of old rust.

That was last year. As I write this, I'm sitting in my office. Hanging on the wall opposite my desk is a signed photograph of Mary Renault. When Nancy Gordon first wrote to me, she mentioned that she had it, and that she had been wondering to whom she might give it. ('I can't give it to just anyone.') So she sent it to me, and I framed it. It's clearly from the same sitting as the one that appeared on Renault's dust jackets, the one in which she's crinkling her eyes against the sun. On the bottom she had scrawled, 'With love from Mary'; but there's nothing at the top, no dedication. I suppose it was for Nancy and Gerald. Then again, when you're a writer, you never know who will end up reading you, or how. I never pretend, when visitors ask me about it, that it was meant for me. But she is up there, watching me as I write.

12

A Typewriter's Travels

CRISTINA SANDU

My great-grandmother used to question her grandchildren's homework. It was the 1960s in a small Romanian village. She would sit in her armchair, straight-backed and proud. She would pose questions, nod gravely and turn the pages of the history book. After every few questions her eyes would wander to the bottom of the page and she would turn to the next one. But at some point, that movement betrayed her, as she turned too early or too late, and the children eventually realized: she could not read.

Before learning to read I went through a similar ritual, though without any other audience than myself. Following with my finger the lines of a book, I would invent a story. I always felt this was very original, sort of an omen of what was to come later, but surely many children go through a similar ritual. Jean-Paul Sartre used to 'read' books before he even understood what they were, seeing them as strange objects that split like oysters.[1]

One does not need much to start creating. There is a great passage in Ingmar Bergman's autobiography, where he tells of his first films: as a child he would be punished by being closed inside a dark cupboard, where he would project the red and green light of his lantern on the wall and pretend to be at the cinema.[2] My grandmother, unlike her mother, could not only read but also use a typewriter – with Finnish letters. The machine had been brought from her son's new home country, Finland. This possession gave her a special status in the village. Neighbours would come to her and dictate 'official' letters to important people. One angry villager wanted to send a letter to 'somebody in the government' about a neighbour whose fence was encroaching on her side of the garden. My grandmother typed and typed, having retired from her job in the milk factory. For me, a child who did not yet know the alphabet, this meant one thing: writing equals dealing with important matters.

———

Life was rich in stories in that village on the outskirts of Bucharest whether one could read or not. During the years of dictatorship and well into the 1990s, people did not own much, and hence social gatherings were important. Even queuing for something – corn, bread, water – could become a social event. Despite scarcity, jokes were abundant and tinted with dark humour. During my childhood visits to the village, the anecdotes and the social life-style remained strong. Days were full of spontaneous encounters with friends and neighbours, always sharing something: a meal, a coffee, news, anecdotes.

Sometimes fairy tales were told to entertain us children. Even though some of these tales were similar in Finland and Romania – especially the ones from the Brothers Grimm and Hans Christian Andersen – the language coated them in newness. Familiar tales were rendered surprising by the phonemes absent from my mother tongue: especially the strong consonants ş and ţ, and the closed vowels î and â. Joseph Brodsky writes about the 'acoustic fascination' that a child feels, being sensitive to a strange, irregular sound. A child is attracted to new words in the same way as to stories and new characters.[3] I remember – maybe unreliably, betrayed by nostalgia – learning Romanian as a kind of doubling of everything: every single thing from bread to chicken would be shifted slightly out of place, hence begetting its double.

'Little Red Riding Hood', in Finnish a short and dynamic 'Punahilkka', became in Romanian 'Scufiţă Roşie', echoing strangely the name of my family's village, Comuna Roşu, 'Red Village'. This association makes me think of how Vladimir Nabokov would stroll as a child on the beach in Abbazia and repeat the English word 'childhood', which sounded mysterious to him, even more so as it got mixed up with Robin Hood and Little Red Riding Hood, which were read to him by his English governess.[4] A child's mind is prone to these sorts of creative associations. For me the red-hooded girl and the red village became inseparable: the characters, the excitement and the dangers of the tale leaked into reality. Moreover, the boundary between reality and the world of the fairy tales seemed to thin down as there was no book between the teller and us listeners. Instead, we had straight eye contact and lively hands that were free to accompany the story with gestures.

Somewhere in this movement between Finland and Romania I learnt to read and write. Yet Romanian remained a strongly oral language for me, despite the later discovery that the bookshelves of the house were full of Mircea Cărtărescu, Mihai Eminescu and translations of French and English authors. Every attempt to read in Romanian stopped short. Put down in writing, my fluent and quick-paced second language slowed down and stuttered. The meaning remained obscure, as if behind a veil. Romanian was for me a language full of gestures and tonal changes – everything that rendered what was being said more dramatic. I never learnt to read it with ease.

Another order seemed to reign in Finland, where storytelling was not a similarly social affair as in the Romanian village. Also, the *way* people narrated stories was different, including intonation and gestures. Stories were read instead of being told; they were a more private experience. Children had their own library cards and stories had their dedicated time slot. This does not mean, of course, that stories did not give as much pleasure in Finland as in Romania, but the pleasure was different. The same book – a novel by Roald Dahl, Louisa May Alcott or Anni Swan – could be read out by an adult for weeks, giving a slow and prolonged experience of suspense.

———

I have not invented much for my two novels, but simply gathered what I've heard during my visits to Romania, because nothing I could imagine would be able to surpass it. Writing conversations and anecdotes down was a hard task: there was so much speed and rhythm and vividness in the way people talked that the pen could hardly keep up. And how to put something so lively on paper? Later, in Finland, I would take all that material and work with it, translate, type and edit. My first novel is mostly a gathering of those old notebooks.

It was an interesting metamorphosis, from Romanian into Finnish, the latter being my literary language. The distinctive features regarding grammar, structure and sounds would leave their Latin base and be transformed into the agglutinative Finno-Ugrian language with no genders, articles or prepositions. When moving from one language to another, the mind has to bend to a different way of thinking, framed by different grammatical rules and syntax. As a child I did not pay attention to this translation process: it happened as naturally as if no linguistic shift even existed. Only when I started writing a novel did stylistic questions such as tone arise. What to do with all the Romanian diminutives? And the exclamations? The laughter and sarcasm, which pervaded the way my relatives spoke? I would work obsessively with tone and rhythm and voice, so the reader would be able to *hear* the text as something new and familiar at the same time. From this strange translation process also came what an editor called my 'ungrammatical' Finnish – I think he meant it as a compliment.

Elias Canetti talks about a different kind of translation, but one that also took place unconsciously. As a child he lived in Ruschuk, an old, multicultural port town on the Danube (now known as Ruse). His parents would speak Ladino to him and German to each other. The maids of the house would tell Canetti fairy tales in Bulgarian. At the age of seven, Canetti moved to Vienna and learnt German, the language which replaced his previous languages, and which he describes as his belated mother tongue.[5] He would always vividly remember the fairy tales heard in Ruschuk: 'Every detail of them is present to my mind, but not in the language I heard them in. I know them in German; this mysterious translation is perhaps the oddest thing that I have to tell about my youth.'[6] The stories did not need a specific language to impregnate his memory.

_____

In oral interviews the Argentinian writer Jorge Luis Borges often talks about his 'boyish readings', meaning those childhood books a writer always returns to, seeking to create the same feeling they conjured in them as a reader. For Borges these books were the novels of Robert Louis Stevenson and *The Thousand and One Nights*.

For me, more than any specific book, it is a certain atmosphere and a position to which I owe most as a writer, and that is the stuff of which my literary memories are made: the combination of two worlds, Romania and Finland, and the shuttling between them. A Finnish typewriter is being used for important matters in a Romanian village, and villagers are gathering to watch *Scarface*, brought from the same place as the typewriter, which is to say it has subtitles in Finnish – these are places of unexpected associations and different worlds intertwining.

It is stimulating to shift between traditions, languages and cultures. One is more surprised, more alert, when not always surrounded by the continuity of the familiar. This kind of movement also creates a useful distance to one's mother tongue. Silvia Hosseini, a Finnish Iranian essayist, writes beautifully about how one's relationship to one's mother tongue changes abroad: one travels away from it at the same time as one draws closer to it. The mother tongue becomes like a room whose interior you start to examine more carefully. From its ordinariness surprising details are revealed, as are connections, colours and textures.[7]

I still look for those moments where I am at the edge of a language, just one foot inside the country, listening to what is being told. Those moments seem to possess a quality akin to the experience of childhood. I do not necessarily have to go to Romania, nor back in time, to find it. Whenever I am in a situation where I do not speak the same language as others, or as well as others, I find myself in a familiar and comfortable place. This is not in the least because those moments tend to bring the oral storytelling back. As a literature student in Scotland, where I had the opportunity to develop English as an academic and literary language, my best friends were Greeks who would spontaneously translate into English their favourite poems from Giorgos Seferis and C. P. Cavafy. From my Spanish-speaking friends I've received detailed narrations of Juan Rulfo and Federico Falco's extraordinary short stories. I enjoy literature as a shared experience: receiving a poem or a short story through the other person's interpretation (often a more or less approximative one), which stands in stark contrast to the still and organized experience of solitary reading.

———

Writing, in addition to meaning dealing with important worldly matters (proved by my grandmother and her bureaucratic efficacity) could be powerful and even dangerous.

A family friend who was Romanian used to work as a diplomat and travelled a lot in Eastern Europe. Once he took a train from Budapest to Bucharest. He was carrying a typewriter with him, a travelling model that would close neatly into a bag. At some point after leaving Budapest he lost the key.

Typewriters were not allowed in Ceaușescu's Romania unless they were registered – such an apparatus represented the possibility of writing manifests, typing documents against the government. After passing the Romanian border, he had to change trains. On the station a colonel noticed the bag and asked him to open it. The traveller said he had lost the key. Lost! The colonel was angry and scared, but he had to grab the heavy bag and hold it in his hands. The traveller tried to explain what the bag contained, but the colonel remained suspicious and beckoned a young soldier and asked him to go to the open field behind the station and open the bag there. The traveller waited, annoyed, while his train came and left without him.

The colonel waited too, possibly for a terrible explosion, but it never came. Eventually the soldier returned with the bag he had forced open: indeed, a typewriter. The diplomat had to wait and could only continue his journey once he had been given a document that proved he really owned this dangerous machine.

13

What Did the Bear Think?

A Chat with MICHAEL ROSEN

28 April 2023

SANDER GILMAN: When you think back now on your childhood, what books do you remember reading or having read to you?

MICHAEL ROSEN: I can remember many books because my parents absolutely adored books. The house was full of books, and my mother read to me when I was very, very young, and then this changes round about the age of, I think, about eleven, and then in a rather sexist sort of way – which I can say with a bit of amusement in my voice, which is that my dad then took over. So, this is when I moved from primary school to secondary school. What happened is that my father took on the job of reading to me and my brother. When I mention my brother, I should say, he was a great reader to me as well. So, going back to the very beginning, I can remember very clearly my mum sitting on the end of my bed and reading me the Beatrix Potter books, for example, *Squirrel Nutkin* and *Peter Rabbit*, those two as they were the ones that I loved very much and asked her to read many times over.

Somewhere in my mother's background, she got the idea that it would be very good to read to me, and she shared with me books of many different cultures. Now where this came from – I mean, in her background – I can't quite piece together, but I can remember her reading me Zetta and Carveth Wells's *Raff, The Jungle Bird: The Story of our Talking Mynah* and *Miskito Boy: A Tale for Children* by the American naturalist and anthropologist Victor W. V. Hagen, with illustrations by Antonio Sotomayor, a book that we absolutely adored and re-read many times. Partly because there's this funny moment in the book where the people drink some kind of fermented banana drink and get drunk, and we giggled quite a lot about that. I can remember her reading me that.

My mother also introduced me to the books of Ernest Thompson Seton, who, while English born, made his career in Canada as a wildlife artist and author. (He was also a founder of the Woodcraft Indians in 1902, and one of the founding pioneers of the Boy Scouts of America in 1910.) Seton was hardly known in Great Britain while I was growing up, while he was, obviously, very well known in North America. I absolutely adored these books, *Krag and Johnny Bear* (1902), the tale of the rabbit, the big grizzly bear and the badger, and the feral little boy who is brought up by them. I remember her reading me those, and then me taking over from her and reading more of Thompson Seton's books. Few people today know Ernest Thompson Seton: he was a Ranger in the forests of British Columbia, and then not only wrote the books, but they were beautiful to look at with animal footprints round the pages in absolutely stunning presentations. They were books which are basically extended prose texts rather than 'illustrated'. They weren't picture books. And then alongside these she read me some of the illustrated books by Paul Faucher who adopted the pseudonym Père Castor (that is, Father Beaver) and then founded a publishing house by the same name. They had been translated into English, published by George Allen & Unwin. These were very interesting historically, because these were among the first books published in Britain using the cheap lithograph methods pioneered both in the Soviet Union and by Père Castor in France. The publishing house Père Castor was the forerunner of the Little Golden Books in the USA and Puffin Books in England. In fact, I had some of the Little Golden Books, in particular I remember *Ukelele and Her New Doll* (1951) by Clara Louise Grant in the Golden Book series, a wonderful little story about a girl who loves her doll. She's from the South Sea Islands, and the colonial settlers – if you like – arrive and give her this great, big, beautiful porcelain, very Western doll, which was not to be played with. In actual fact, she still sticks with her little homemade wooden doll from the Pacific Islands. I can remember this very, very clearly, without even going and finding it on the shelves.

I can remember a whole set of folk stories from school and Aesop's Fables. I was taught to read using a series in England called the *Beacon Readers*, written by James Hiram Fassett, which in its own way was what we might call progressive, because they very much believed in an equal balance between phonic or, as they called it then, 'phonetic', with emphasis on both phonics *and* meaning, and, in fact, in their introductory booklet for teachers they made very, very clear that you shouldn't do one at the expense of the other. This is unlike many of the practices now which suggest that you should do phonics first and 'fast', whereas the *Beacon Readers* made very clear that sure you do the phonic stuff, but boy, you shouldn't let go of the meaning. The very first of those stories was about a farmer called Old Lob, and a cow called Mrs Cuddy, and a dog called Mr Dan and a pig called Mr Willie. I loved those stories, even though my dear dad used to take the mickey out of them and sit there and say things like 'And what is Mrs Cuddy doing today, Michael?', just to tease me. But I remember those, and as you advanced, there were many retellings of traditional stories. There was obviously a clear policy of introducing those cultural stories, and I remember those quite clearly while learning to read with those *Beacon Readers*. Rather drab covers, but nice drawings inside. I've still got several of them in my office. I've bought them second-hand in order to remind myself of what they looked like.

That gives you a flavour of the first five or six years of my reading. I've mentioned Puffin picture books. These were massively important to us as a family, in that we were given two or three of them every Christmas, as they kept up with the publishing of them. Puffin would publish three or four picture books and three or four of their Puffin story books a year, and these were our gifts for Christmas. We might think of this these days as being only a very few titles. My secular Jewish parents were enjoying giving Christmas presents rather than celebrating Hanukkah. I can't quite explain that, but there you go. So yes, I've got all my Puffin picture books. I think there's about forty of them that I've got in my office and I remember many of them. I pored over them. And just so people are aware: the Puffin picture book series mixed fiction with non-fiction. So, you would have books about, say, the growth of London, about architecture or about cattle. I was very fascinated by cattle, I'm not quite sure why – but anyway, the different breeds of cattle – and I used to carry this book, *Our Cattle* (1948) by Lionel Edwards, around with me when we went into the country, so I could identify the various breeds. It's quite an interesting way in which to be introduced to the world of fact alongside fiction.

My parents were left wing, they would pick up books in particular that came in from Progress Publishers, the foreign language publisher in Moscow. They used to go to what were called *Daily Worker* bazaars and pick up books with cheap lithographic printing, some of them absolutely stunning and beautiful. In fact, there's been a very famous anthology of them by Miriam Morton and another one called *Inside the Rainbow, Russian Children's Literature, 1920–35: Beautiful Books, Terrible Times* (2013), edited by Julian Rothenstein and Olga Budashevskaya, because people have rediscovered the beautiful modernist artwork. We quite often think of the Soviet Union as this incredibly dull time, producing appalling socialist realist crap! But in fact, in that space, there was original and imaginative writing for chilen, created almost certainly by Korney Ivanovich Chukovsky, a sort of Russian Dr Seuss who wrote a famous 'Defence of Fantasy Writing', and poetry for children still read today, such as *Tarakanishche* (The Monster Cockroach), *Krokodil* (The Crocodile), *Telefon* (The Telephone) and *Moydodyr* (Wash-'em-Clean). He fought off the Stalinists, and in so doing protected a range of dissident children's authors such as the surrealist Daniil Kharms (and much later Aleksandr Solzhenitsyn). He took Kharms under his wing, as he had been under the wing of Maxim Gorky, at least in the early stages. There was anxiety within the Soviet Union about producing such children's books, but they got translated into English, such as Chukovsky's own poems, and the works of Ilya Yakovlevich Marshak, known by the pseudonym 'M. Ilin', who wrote *Black on White: The Story of Boo* (1932). Their works came under attack from Stalinist socialist realist writers of children's literature such as Agniya Barto in the 1940s as not true socialist literature. Books like this came into my hands via these *Daily Worker* bazaars.

SANDER GILMAN: In our family we read the children's books produced in the 1960s in English by Seven Seas Books in East Berlin, which were the exact equivalent of those produced in Moscow by Progress Publishing. This combination, to create something that was both American and international, answered the American-centric readers of the time, the *Dick and Jane* books, that recorded the daily lives of their two main characters created by Zerna Sharp for a series of basal readers written by William S. Gray, and which were used in schools from the 1930s to the '60s, which stressed the local over the international.

MICHAEL ROSEN: If we want to get political about it, there was a form of a directive that went out to Communist parties from the Komintern, that you could be internationalist in terms of your politics, but in terms of organization you had to be national. That's why in Britain the Communist Party produced a book called the *British Road to Socialism* (1951) and stressed what they regarded as a kind of indigenous Socialism. The result was books like Arthur Leslie Morton's *A People's History of England*, published by Victor Gollancz as part of the Left Book Club in 1938. I can remember this well. I came home from school having been asked to write an essay and my dad looking me over and saying, 'What's your essay about?' and me saying 'Oh, well, it's the Chartists' (who were part of the origins of the Labour movement in Britain and organized really the first mass movement of British workers in the 1840s and '50s). My dad said, 'What's your essay called?' and I said, 'Well, it's called "Why Chartism failed",' and my dad said, 'Failed! Chartism didn't fail! We have elections in this country, why do you think that is so?' There's my dad standing over me, circa 1960, you see, and then he pulls off the shelf Morton's *People's History of England*, and says, 'Read that' – well not quite as strict as that! I sat down aged fourteen or fifteen and read my A. L. Morton. And then wrote my essay on why 'Chartism failed *or did it*?'

My mum or dad used to take me to our local library, the local public library, funded by the local authority, not a Carnegie library at all but a local library, funded by Harrow Borough Council in the northwest London suburb where I lived in Pinner. Every Saturday my dad would go in there, and he'd choose books, and I would choose books, sometimes sitting with my friend Brian Harrison, and we would choose books, or sometimes going on my own, and then we used to borrow up to four or five books, every week or so, from the age of about six or seven through to when we moved, when I was sixteen or seventeen. It was an incredible locus for my reading. On top of the books that my parents were buying there was this steady stream of books coming in, and I followed an interest that grew in historical fiction for kids, so part of that came perhaps via the *Daily Worker* bazaar, in the fact that there was a sympathizer with the British Communist Party, Geoffrey Trease, who had, in fact, visited the Soviet Union at least once and produced a quite famous book in left-wing circles called *Bows Against the Barons* (1934), based on a Marxist reading of the legend of Robin Hood. It suggested that in some way or another this was effectively a peasant's revolt. So I read Geoffrey Trease and this led me on to the writings of Rosemary Sutcliff and Henry Treece. Whereas Geoffrey Trease was sympathetic with the left and the British Communist Party, there was another writer, Henry Williamson, who was of a much different disposition, but famous as a writer about nature. His most popular book was *Tarka the Otter: His Joyful Water-Life and Death in the Country of the Two Rivers* (1927). And I read Cynthia Harnett, who wrote a wonderful children's book called *The Wool-Pack* (1951) set in fifteenth-century England.

Thus I got very immersed in historical fiction, as well as another genre of fiction that I absolutely adored, which is very much gone into decline these days, what you might call 'animal autobiographies'. These are books written in the voice of an animal, and I really got very immersed in the then rather famous French writer René Guillot, who wrote stories like *Kpo the Leopard* (1955), an African wild-life story about a female leopard cub, as well as a whole series of others. There was a famous naturalist in Britain called Henry Mortimer Batten, the author of *The Singing Forest* (1955), *British Wildlife Stories* (1936) and *British Wild Animals* (1924). I read these alternating with his-torical fiction, and among these 'animal autobiographies' were some of Ernest Thompson Seton's books. Now I think back, there's a quite famous one, *Biography of a Grizzly* (1900), that includes the tale of a smaller Roach-back bear who climbed on a stone ledge and was able to leave a scent five feet above his usual height. Thus Wahb, the silvertip grizzly bear, comes to be fooled by the brown bears who basically push the grizzly out of their little ecosystem by cheating, because rubbing their scent cre-ated the illusion that the Roach-backs were large and ferocious. The poor old silvertip grizzly comes along, and he finds the signs of this very large, as he imagines, bear. So, he thinks he's going to skedaddle out of there.

Those are the kinds of books I was reading myself up until about eleven and twelve, until, as I said, my father took over and then said, 'Hmm, time for Dickens,' and he read to us on a camping holiday somewhere it was damp and cold. If you read Marx, I think you'll find he says somewhere that Communists must go camping in the British countryside, especially when it's wet! I can't find the exact reference, but I'm sure he said that because my parents certainly dutifully schlepped us to places in Britain that were distinctly wet at all times of the year, places like the North Yorkshire Moors. That may not mean much to a North American audience, but if you can imagine somewhere like Maine, you know, with a sort of moor landscape, and it was full of mists and has fog and rain all the time. Or the Welsh borders, as it rains a lot in Wales, and my parents definitely found the bits where it rained a lot. So, the whole summer it would rain, and my dad would read Dickens to us. He read the whole of *Great Expectations*, the whole of *Little Dorrit*; then moved on to Walter Scott and read *Guy Mannering* to us in our tents in the holidays. And I remember him saying to me, 'I think it's time for Thomas Hardy, lad,' and so I then 'discovered' Thomas Hardy and read my way through all of them until I came home with either *Jude the Obscure* or *Tess of the d'Urbervilles* and I remember him saying, 'Maybe leave those till you're a bit older, lad.' So, in fact, I didn't read those till about ten years ago, so I did leave them till I was a bit older, round about age 65. And boy, did those two knock me out, I can tell you!

I got the Thomas Hardy bug, but also the poetry bug, which hit me when I was about fifteen or sixteen. In particular, the poetry of the great American poet Carl

Sandburg. My dad was in the u.s. Army's Education Corps. He taught at the u.s. Army University from 1945 to 1947. So our house was full of very cheap u.s. books for the Education Corps. I've still got these. I've kept them, and one of them is a wonderful anthology, Louis Untermeyer's *Modern American Poetry* (first published in 1919). At the time Britain was very nationalistic; it's quite hard to explain, as poetry within the education sphere in a lot of countries is jingoistic, and in Britain even more so. I don't know why poetry is treated this way, and so, if you're in school, you find you do poetry as a link between poetry and national identity. But having this father of American origin (he was born in the States) meant that the house was full of American poetry. I was reading Carl Sandburg and other modernists like Ezra Pound, H.D. [Hilda Doolittle] and Amy Lowell, when the other people at my school weren't. But I was also reading Cleanth Brooks, Robert Penn Warren and William K. Wimsatt when I was sixteen and seventeen. This was the 'New Criticism' that had hardly been discovered in Britain at the time, but it was old hat in the States. I should say that my father's best chum was Wayne C. Booth, the author of *The Rhetoric of Fiction* (1961), because they were colleagues, comrades in the American army, and taught together. Wayne was a family friend, close family friend, as close as you can be, bridging the Atlantic. In fact, Wayne's widow is still with us in her late nineties, and I correspond with her. Wayne was a hero in our house, and I can remember the first drafts of *The Rhetoric of Fiction* coming into the house, much revered, much celebrated. Among the books that my dad had was *Understanding Poetry*, an American college textbook and poetry anthology by Cleanth Brooks and Robert Penn Warren, first published in 1938. I was reading this American poetry, you know, from about fifteen and sixteen, and realizing that it had a note and a tone that was completely different from British poetry. I'm talking here of a tradition from Walt Whitman onwards. You can see this especially in the role of the Imagists and the way in which this tradition in the end gave birth to hippie and Beat poetry, to people like Allen Ginsberg. But I was very struck by this combination already in Carl Sandburg and his so-called Proletarian poetry, and the Imagist poetry. I mingled that with the modernist poetry of D. H. Lawrence, such as his 'Man and Bat' (1923):

Dipping with petty triumphant flight, and tittering
    over the sun's departure,
I believe he chirps, pipistrello, seeing me here on
    this terrace writing:
There he sits, the long loud one!
But I am greater than he . . .
I escaped him . . .

These types of poems also led me into James Joyce, not *Ulysses* (1922) so much as *Portrait of the Artist as a Young Man* (1916), when I was fifteen or sixteen. That's when it all started to kind of click, if you like.

SANDER GILMAN: Did you imagine, at that point,

writing as a profession rather than writing as entertainment, education?

MICHAEL ROSEN: When I discovered *Portrait of the Artist as a Young Man* I didn't see this as a conversion moment. I didn't think to myself, shit I can be a writer who writes like that. I think at that precise moment I said to myself, I'm going to give this a go. And I can remember my very first pieces of writing. One was based on D. H. Lawrence's poem 'Man and Bat', and I wrote in June 1962 a poem about a moth that came into the room, in which I killed it, and then I sort of reflected on the way D. H. Lawrence did.

Moth
Last night a moth was frantically drumming
Above me on the cold hard window;
His browns and ochres merging and blurring
Above me on the cold hard window.
    I cursed
    He had intruded.
He was there again tonight, lunging and twisting
As I switched on the bright white lamp.
Round and about me, plunging and twirling
As I switched on the bright white lamp.
    Furry and insolent
    He had scared me.
He swooped low against me, knocking and brushing
As I stood with collar open, my white neck protruding;
A constant desperate flitting and rushing
As I stood with collar open, my white neck protruding.

He landed on my bed
Still and brown upon the sheet.
Sweat-anxious I trapped him, my pyjama-jacket flinging.
Alone and helpless
In his own dim thick world he lay there twitching.
Alone and helpless
I threw him out
Crushed and dry.

Yet in the close airlessness of my room,
I almost see him, still airing the gloom
Mocking my lamp, my white neck, my sheets
And my Primeval Fears.

When I'm talking with children, I explain that you can
write a commentary on yourself. Imagine yourself walking
along by the side of a swimming pool and the reflection in
the pool is you and not you at the same time. That is what
I believe the voice of the explorer does so well, particularly
in Lawrence's best-known poem, 'Snake' (1923):

And immediately I regretted it.
I thought how paltry, how vulgar, what a mean act!
I despised myself and the voices of my accursed human
    education.
. . .
And so, I missed my chance with one of the lords
Of life.
And I have something to expiate:
    A pettiness.

At one moment you're in the moment when he's kill-ing the snake. The next moment you're outside now, reflecting on it, and he does it again in 'Man and Bat'. At that moment I thought, yeah, I would like to do that. So, I wrote my poem 'Moth' in that style. At this time, I was immediately struck by the modernism you see in *Portrait of the Artist as a Young Man* – the fact that you could write in the tone of the person you were in that moment. Joyce's protagonist Stephen Dedalus writes in this broken, childlike voice when he's a little boy, and then of course, as he gets older, he was always taking the mickey out of himself as this very serious young student and so I thought, oh, I'm going to write a piece now, and it's about my very first memory from when I was two and a half, sitting on the beach at a resort on the east coast of England, called Margate. I can remember myself sitting on the beach. I remember even now 75 years later, and I'm thinking at that moment that it's too hot and the sand is too sandy. And I wrote a kind of James Joyce-type piece about me, sitting on the beach in fractured sentences, because basically I was discover-ing what had been discovered fifty or sixty years earlier, 'stream of consciousness', but I was discovering it for myself and thinking oh, I like this. And so, I remem-ber writing that, and on and off I've gone on writing stream-of-consciousness things, particularly when my life has been fractured either by trauma or indeed by a near-death experience.

I've in fact, you know, recapitulated this idea several times already, because I do sometimes find that the syntax of the thing we call 'a sentence' is too logical, too full of causation, too full of sort of self-establishing itself, if you like, to convey a very immediate emotion. I think I tapped into that when I was only fifteen or sixteen, and thought, yes, I like doing this. I had an English teacher at my secondary school and I remember her saying to me, 'You are a writer.' She was incredibly encouraging and, to the annoyance of everybody else in my class, she proceeded to read out my pieces to the rest of the class. She said, 'Michael has written something today.' She had a quite strong Northern Irish accent, which, I remember, we used to giggle at behind her back, which we shouldn't have done. There's nothing wrong with the Northern Irish accent, but we did, but I can see her in my mind, Mrs Turnbull reading out a piece that I wrote about cycling home from school. I'm not on my bike, and it is raining, and me getting wet, and so on, and she read it out to the class and said something like 'That is writing!' and I was very encouraged by that, I have to say. Not that my mum and dad, both of them teachers, both of them pedagogues, both of them going into teacher training themselves later, were *not* encouraging. They were all the time. My mum, I can see me reading stuff to her and her going 'Oh, that's lovely! Do write some more,' and my dad saying, 'Keep going! Keep going, lad.'

I don't know where he got this 'lad' thing from! My mother used to call me 'Boychik', which is sort of 'Yinglish', a mix of Yiddish and English. It's not really Yiddish, but she also called me several Yiddish things, like 'shmerel', which means a little fool. But she meant it affectionately. There was also a word that doesn't often crop up in Yiddish circles, 'muzhik', which means literally a 'little peasant'. It can be used contemptuously since you can say, what are you? What are you? Some kind of 'muzhik'? On the other hand, it can be used very affectionately. She would kiss me good night and say, 'Good night, muzhik!' I had these words in my head, but my dad he did sometimes call me 'boychik' and 'mensch', but when it came to this kind of thing where he'd say 'carry on' he used to put in this 'lad' thing, which isn't even London. People who call each other 'lads' in England tend to come from the northern part. In London it's more often 'sonny' or 'mate', and then he also had a few Americanisms from his time in the American army, so he did occasionally call people 'pal', which came in British English later.

SANDER GILMAN: When you started to write, based on what you just said, you were thinking about writing something analogous to how adult readers enjoy D. H. Lawrence, right? In other words, for people who were older than you were then. You weren't interested in writing for sixteen-year-olds?

MICHAEL ROSEN: We read books early on which are written for children, and then at some point, Dickens being the perfect example, who used to be read by children all the time, suddenly we're confronted with books which are supposed to be written by adults for adults. The transition for me was also, I'm going to be a writer, like Lawrence, like Joyce, writing serious books for serious adults.

SANDER GILMAN: Did you pursue that?

MICHAEL ROSEN: Yeah. I mean one route I took when
I was about fourteen or fifteen brought me to Geoffrey
Summerfield, who was producing his quite famous
anthologies in this country, called *Voices* (1968–74) and
then *Junior Voices*, three volumes of each. These were an
important and amazing breakthrough in the history of
poetry, writing and reading in post-war Britain, particularly within the education sphere. Geoffrey Summerfield
was a friend of my parents. He had spent some time in
the States, had 'discovered' Carl Sandburg as did my
dad, who brought him to me some years earlier, and so
in these three anthologies he included poems from all
over the world, and a huge great chunk of Carl Sandburg
and a lot of oral poetry. He selected from Willard R.
Trask's *The Unwritten Song: Poetry of the Primitive and
Traditional Peoples of the World* (1966) and he put these
in these books along with some incredible illustrations
and photographs. My parents were very involved in
the production of those incredible volumes because I
can remember him coming in with new chunks, laying
them out on the floor in our living room, and us walking around them, and as I was of the age, a little bit older
perhaps, of the intended audience, I was one of the first
guinea pigs of this anthology, so he would say, 'Hey!
What do you think this one is about?' It would be a Carl
Sandburg poem like 'Under a Telephone Pole' (1916)?
'What do you make of this one?' or 'What do you make
of this about John Godfrey Saxe and "The Blind Man
and the Elephant" where the blind guys are examining

the elephant and seeing different views of an elephant, what do you make of this one, Michael?' 'What do you make of this picture by Albrecht Dürer of a rhinoceros? Do you think that should be in, or shouldn't it be in?' So, I was this kind of editor figure alongside my parents, who were giving their pedagogic advice. That was quite an important moment, and with all the voices that I was picking up, and I'm using his term there – 'voices'! With the voices I was picking up, I very much wanted to try and write in the voice that Carl Sandburg has about children and childhood. I didn't ever think necessarily that what I wrote would be particularly of interest to children, or if they were, then it would be via people like my parents and Geoffrey or my mum.

We had an educational radio service in this country, and my mum was beginning to do radio shows on there for kids. This was called the BBC Schools Radio Service, begun in 1924, and then radically restructured during the war. These broadcasts were pumped straight into schools. People had big speakers in classrooms, in schools, and they would listen to programmes about singing or dancing. You would have the speaker up in the Assembly Hall and there'd be someone saying, 'Spread out, spread out! And now we have to dance.' And all the kiddies would do it, because it obviously added a repertoire of teaching possibilities to teachers who couldn't teach dance. Or let's say drama. In the case of poetry, there was a broadcast series called *Living Language*, 'A Series of Broadcasts Provided by the BBC for the School Broadcasting Council for the United Kingdom', that my mother used to present at about this time when I was beginning to write these little pieces a bit like Carl Sandburg's.

Why did the children
put beans in their ears
when the one thing we told the children
they must not do
was put beans in their ears? (from *The People, Yes*, 1936)

I would think, oh, I could do that, and so I'd write a little poem about my dad saying, 'If you don't put your shoes on before I count to fifteen, we're not going to the woods.' 'ONE.' 'No, no, I can't find my shoes.' I remember writing that off the back of reading Carl Sandburg. I thought in some way or another that this was either for an adult audience or maybe there was a route for my writing into education.

I didn't think it through too coherently, but my mum saw me doing some of this stuff. I remember her saying, as she was working out how to do the show, that she was always looking for a link between one poem and the next. One time she had some poem or another about kids getting their hair cut, or something like that. And I ran away and wrote a poem about getting my nails cut, my hair cut, and sort of with a kid's eye-view, thinking, well, I don't like people chopping bits off me. Funny, it's kind of like a metaphor for a *bris* (circumcision), isn't it? Secular Jews! Why did they do it? Answer: to please my *Bubbe* (grandmother)? We'll leave that to one side. I think they argued about it. I think.

So, I remember writing that poem about cutting my nails and my hair. And then mum saying, 'Oh, yeah, that would fit in my show.' So, I thought, oh, well, very good. (I must have been aged about seventeen or eighteen, probably in what we then called the Sixth Form or maybe I'd already started at university, and was back for the vacation) and I was writing these things, and mum was saying, 'Oh, they'd fit in.' By the time I was about 23 or 24 the woman who was producing the *Living Language* shows – her name was Joan Griffiths – said to me 'Michael, would you like to do one of these shows?' I should say that by then I just had a play, *Backbone*, on in an off-West End theatre called the Royal Court in 1968. It dealt with the difficult courtship of a boy from a liberal, permissive, Jewish family and a girl from a rigidly conventional Anglo-Saxon Protestant family. Joan Griffiths had been to see that play and said 'Oh, Michael, seems like you're a writer,' so maybe she used the fact that I'd got a little bit of fame from this play being on. My play had a fortnight's run there, and so off the back of that Joan commissioned me to do a couple of these programmes. You can see, I was building up a pile of poems that were largely about my childhood, mostly with the kind of ironic twist that you get in a dramatic monologue. I should explain something here: when I was about fourteen, a teacher at school had introduced us to Robert Browning's dramatic monologues, and showed us the idea that you could write a monologue where the person speaking is not aware of the ironies of what it is they're saying, and I got quite excited by that. We meet it, of course, in Shakespeare many times over. I quite liked the idea that you could write something where the writer's voice doesn't indicate that they know what's happening. But then – ha ha – we, the readers, do know. Again, that's also in Sandburg, with a very light touch. They come, as you know, from *The People, Yes* (1936), which was a real eye opener for me. I had a little stash now of poems written in this tone of voice, if you like, and started to hawk it around publishers. I was around 23, 24, about that age.

From the time I began putting this stuff in front of publishers to this very day, particularly in the world of children's poetry, there was always attention to the role of the poem in the child's mental life. Editors or critics are always asking a question that, in effect, goes like this: Are you trying to elevate the children or are you sinking to their level? And that tension is expressed in a variety of ways. I got letters, 'You know the children are already in the gutter. There's no need to join them there, you know,' stuff like that. It's quite ironic that Robert Louis Stevenson, in his wonderful *A Child's Garden of Verses* (1885), very much enters the child's imagination at play. That's what fascinated him. He even wrote an essay, 'Child's Play' (1878), where he describes him and his brother playing with their porridge and imagining kingdoms in the porridge. His poetry is not only for children but cast in their voices, as hidden in his beautiful poem 'Where Go the Boats':

Dark brown is the river.
Golden is the sand.

It flows along for ever,
    With trees on either hand.
Green leaves a-floating,
    Castles of the foam,
Boats of mine a-boating –
    Where will all come home?

On goes the river
    And out past the mill,
Away down the valley,
    Away down the hill.

Away down the river,
    A hundred miles or more,
Other little children
    Shall bring my boats ashore.

Remember the volume was called *A Child's Garden of Verses*, so Stevenson was going towards a prelapsarian, Edenic notion of childhood. And then along comes somebody like me, or indeed Carl Sandburg, suggesting childhood is full of all sorts of other stuff that won't quite fit into a garden! They might be living in a city, and they might be mooching about and being rude to each other or rude to their parents. Their parents might be whopping them, and there might be all sorts of tensions, and so on. And there might be expressions of emotions that some might think of as unacceptable, emotions that they were trying to train children out of. So, there is this idea that not only should we take children from this position of not being very nice, and that we should be elevating them, but also that the language itself should elevate them. So, we shouldn't have slang in children's poetry, or we shouldn't be imitating their voices.

Here, with this, you've got an idea that their ideal poetry world should be Edenic, but also that children are born with original sin, this hangover from Christianity of the idea that all human beings are born with the first stain of the act of disobedience by Adam and Eve in the Garden of Eden. Educators then (and we must remember, of course, the first educators in the Western world, the global North, were clerics) had the job of beating out original sin, which they did sometimes physically, but also through inculcating children through the works of somebody like John Bunyan and his *Divine Emblems, or Temporal Things Spiritualized, Fitted for the Use of Boys and Girls* (1686), or indeed Isaac Watts's *Divine Songs: Attempted in Easy Language for the Use of Children* (1715), both of which were poetry books for children written explicitly to *reform* children. The intent is to elevate them out of a state of sin.

The next phase that you get in the development of poetry comes with William Wordsworth and his 'Ode: Intimations of Immortality from Recollections of Early Childhood', where he suggests that 'The child is father of the man;/ And I could wish my days to be/ Bound each to each by natural piety' (1807). He's suggesting that there is a special innocence about childhood. So here we flip from original sin, which you had seen in John Bunyan, to the notion that children are natural and beautiful and wonderful, and children can teach us how to improve because, for us adults, 'The world is too much with us; late and soon,/ Getting and spending, we lay waste our powers; –/ Little we see in Nature that is ours', as Wordsworth put it in 1807, but in actual fact the child is father to the man. Wordsworth is saying that we adults can learn the beauty of the rainbow from the child, and indeed you get 'The Star' (1806), written by Jane and Anne Taylor at that point:

Twinkle, twinkle, little star,
How I wonder what you are!
Up above the world so high,
Like a diamond in the sky.

That's the important point: children still have 'wonder' but we adults, as we've all become boring and corrupted, have lost wonder. Thus, Jane and Anne Taylor, very much influenced by Wordsworth, Keats and Shelley, sat there saying, in effect, we can show children the wonder of the stars. On the one hand, they seem to be imitating children, because they ask, do you see wonder still in children? Or they're saying that children are the kind of humans that say 'Wow! Look at that! It's a rainbow. Isn't that exciting?' On the other hand, they aimed at improving children so that they don't sink into the sewer of naughty books. Even John Bunyan was very worried about children reading about Jack the Giant Killer.

SANDER GILMAN: Or in your case, Thomas Hardy's *Jude the Obscure*!

MICHAEL ROSEN: Yes! In my dad's case! And yet there was my dad blaspheming away like hell. God knows why he thought he had to save me from *Jude*! Maybe he was worried that I'd get upset by the deaths of the children. That tension persists to this day between original sin and Wordsworth's romantic ideas, all wound up with notions of what's appropriate language for children. That is what's quite interesting about Carl Sandburg and the American poets of his ilk. Carl Sandburg is a Populist, and you know that the word 'proletarian' sometimes applies to his writing as he was trying to find the genius of a people. That's why it's *The People, Yes*! He was part of FDR's New Deal and a rethinking of what the people really meant in politics and poetry. So, the view that I was influenced by *The People, Yes* shocked people when my first book came out, and they sometimes still are. They sometimes say things like, 'My goodness, why did you write about *that* in a children's book?' It still goes on. Today, if you want to write a sensationalist article in the popular press, all you have to do is just find some book, not necessarily mine, and say, 'My God, this is the sort of stuff that's in a children's book, how is this possible?'

SANDER GILMAN: By the way, you have just described the state of America in 2023 vis-à-vis public censorship of children's books, you know. I wish again we lived in a time where 'the arc of the moral universe is long, *but it bends toward justice*', but it doesn't. Let me ask a question because it really bothers me. When writers like Judy Blume reinvented young adult fiction in the 1970s, one of the things that they did is present a problem, a problem that nobody's talked about in children's or young adult fiction before, but that problem, then, is resolved. We never leave the characters in the novel with the problem still being centre stage. It strikes me that this is just a kind of conservative rewriting of the traditional Victorian model but with otherwise banned topics. We as adults must resolve the problems for the fictional kids because we know better than they do.

MICHAEL ROSEN: I personally don't find that wrong. I've reviewed a good few Judy Blume books. I've even interviewed her a couple of times, and I take my hat off to her. She wrote about teenage and pre-teen 'problems' in an incredibly accessible way. She deals with interiority in a really profound and beautiful way. And I think *Forever...* (1975), her novel dealing with teenage sexuality, for example, is a beautiful book, and I don't have a problem with this matter of a resolution. I know some people do, but, if you like, you've defined the genre. If we say, what is children's literature? What is young adult literature? Why is it different from adult literature? It is usually conservative with a small 'c'. It resolves, it redeems, it solves the problem, and of course sometimes in quite arch, or not necessarily totally satisfactory ways. Let's give credit to the kids who can get to the end of the book. They can feel good or, on the other hand, they can say, 'Shit, life ain't like that, I know that' – that's okay. They can distance themselves. Sometimes the ending is, yeah, unsatisfactory.

But then, let's think for a moment, how does *Hamlet* end? How does *Othello* end? You get these guys coming on resolving the Senecan tragedy problem by someone saying, 'Oh, by the way, it's going to be okay.' 'What? It's going to be okay? We shouldn't worry about it?' Who remembers Fortinbras's speech after all the major characters except Horatio are dead, when Fortinbras enters and announces that Claudius's supposed orders to execute Rosencrantz and Guildenstern have been carried out? And then claims the throne! Who remembers, you know, the very end of *Romeo and Juliet*, when the prince takes the group away to discuss these events, pronouncing that 'never was a story of more woe/ Than this of Juliet and her Romeo', but now it's all going to be okay. Is it that the Capulets and Montagues are really going to stop fighting it out? Adult literature has got its own kind of phony resolutions, if you like, and we've sat with these for the last four hundred years, and by and large nobody quibbles.

I haven't got a problem with that, because the meat and potatoes of these stories is in the telling and we are back to Wayne Booth. It's the telling. And in the *how* of the telling, the unfolding, the flow of emotions we've had with and against characters; with and against the resolutions of individual little scenes as they go by. Our urging on that the good guy will do the right thing. Sometimes, maybe secretly, we illicitly urge on the bad guy, in order to see how it all resolves. It kind of does or doesn't matter. That's my, that's my own feeling.

SANDER GILMAN: You're implying that children are smart readers.

MICHAEL ROSEN: I'll always do that, and some of them will be gratified. Some of them will say, 'Well, thank goodness, there's a way out of that.' This is what we find in the words of Beverley Naidoo, in her 1985 *Journey to Jo'burg: A South African Story*. She is a fantastic novelist, who was one of the first children's authors to write about the Black child's experience in apartheid South Africa for children. Her argument is, and I've listened to this quite carefully, talking along these lines: 'Sure I resolve these things within the novel, and I'll tell you why. It's because I want to give kids hope.' Now, that's what she says. *Journey to Jo'burg* is a tough, tough novel, describing really difficult things for a family, a mother and the child, split by apartheid. The mother is forced to look after a white kid she is hired to care for and is unable to look after her own kid. This was born out of Beverley's own experience of being a white, Jewish girl in a family with a Black maid, and she realized that the Black maid was doing more looking after of her than of looking after her own child, or at least that's how she felt about it. This is tough stuff for kids. Family life broken on the back of segregation and apartheid, yet it applies across all of the world in various forms of social inequities. It's not just restricted to that particular time and place. She said that, you know, sure her novels resolve. But she doesn't want to abandon the child reader or the young adult reader with a sense of despair that nothing can be done now. She didn't say, we can immediately solve the problems of the world. But she definitely wanted to say that she wants to put hope on the agenda.

SANDER GILMAN: I've always worked on the assumption that the reason we tell stories – I'm going to say that writing is telling stories whether you're sitting around a fire, you know, telling stories in the Neolithic or whether you're listening to Michael Rosen read a poem – has to do with the notion that one is in some way interacting with another human being, even if the other human being is one removed, is not present physically, but present virtually in in the book itself, in the voice of the book, and I think that's one of the reasons we do this. Why not call that hope?

MICHAEL ROSEN: Exactly. Let's look at the *Odyssey*. Odysseus, you know he screws up. It's fine that he got rid of Polyphemus, or thought he had, but then he screwed up: he boasts about it. 'I did it. I, Odysseus, did it.' So, we have that. We will have all experienced that moment where we've gone over the edge, gone over the bar, when we shouldn't have done what we did. We screwed up one way or another, so we have there a model of this guy who's nominally a great warrior, a Greek hero, who had to face a lot of stuff, but he's enraged Poseidon, the sea god, so he's then got a lot of shit to deal with. He's got all these monsters and people who are trying to do him down, and in the end they do for all of his crew, and he's just left on his own. BUT he gets home, and only just in time because Penelope was just on the cusp of maybe getting off with this guy who she didn't like, really. So, it all resolves. So, what did that do for people who heard these stories, when they heard that for the first time, bards telling these bits of stories, fragments of stories, linking it all together with a great long story? It was a way of showing people what's possible, showing people that people can change, showing people that life isn't easy, that you're going to face many kinds of things. You're going to try and find your way through them. Some people are quite clever, and they can think of tricks like getting themselves tied to the masthead so that they can hear the Sirens' beautiful singing, and not end up drowning in the sea. Or you can get out of being turned into a pig by Circe. You kind of know if someone wants to turn you into a pig, you know you can get out of these things. So, there's lots of possibilities, notions of change. And we come back to this word *hope*. Odysseus gets home, it doesn't just end with a sense of hopelessness.

I think those of us as adults, we can read Franz Kafka, and we could go, 'Gorblimey, God! Ain't the world shitty?' Look at Joseph K. in *The Trial* (1914–15). You know, he never finds out what he was accused of. In a children's book it wouldn't end that way, you know. Tom Cruise would have to come in and defend your rights, and then he would crack the case for you. The case would break because Tom Cruise would plead on your behalf in the court.

SANDER GILMAN: Or as Joe Pesci does in *My Cousin Vinny* (1992).

MICHAEL ROSEN: Yeah, that's right! Joe Pesci would plead, and you'd be fine. Joseph K. would get off and he would expose the rotten underpinnings of the system. Kafka, though, can leave you in a sense of complete and utter despair that he experienced in his own life. We learn something from the despair I think, but that's a very adult way of viewing what fiction is supposed to do. We might think that there is a right way of addressing the problem. This leaves you, the reader, needing to figure out what is the right way to get out of the problem described by the book. I've written non-fiction about the Holocaust in my book *The Missing: The True Story of My Family in World War II* (2020). What can you say about the Holocaust? That there's hope, is there? Well, you know, twixt you and me, I mean there ain't no hope to be found in it. I mean, you can find stories of resistance. You can find stories of survival. You can find stories of commemoration. You try and make the book itself a story of commemoration. And you say this is why I'm doing it, which is what I did in *The Missing*. I said, I'm doing this because the motive of Hitler was not only to create, to exterminate, a 'race' as he called it. He also wanted to extirpate them from history, to extirpate *us* from history. By writing about it you, in a sense, push back a tiny bit, a *bissel*, against it. That was, that's the idea. But we know, historically, there ain't no hope in it. It was one of the most horrific times in history.

We know that African Americans, Afro-Caribbeans face exactly the same with narrating the slave trade and plantation life under slavery. How did they create something? How do they tell children what this was? But we can't leave them with this terrible sense of just nothing can be done. I think the way we do it comes from the fact of life going on. I've seen, for example, in Australia, non-fiction books for children about the aboriginal experience in Australia and the tone of it has changed over the years. The ones that I saw when I was there thirty years ago, people were writing, for example, about survival. They wrote 'In spite of all this, we survived.' But today there is a culture of resistance. 'Look at me! I am an aboriginal person from Tasmania, or the Outback, look at the culture that I'm putting together, our dance, our song, our textiles, whatever it is, this is what we're doing now.' And that's the way hope comes into the story.

SANDER GILMAN: People keep on confusing writing about the Holocaust with the lived experience of the Holocaust. We're back to the act of reading, the act of being read to, as well as the notion that the act of reading presents you to and with other people. Not as a purely private act, but rather telling tales around the fire. We are not at that moment in the presence of Anne Frank. We are in the presence of a story which we are reading and it's both a very private and a very public act. But for me it is also connected with the physical nature of a book, a three-dimensional, solid object that feels different, smells different from other objects in the world. I like pictures in books, just like Alice does in Wonderland. Are we now moving towards the end of the book. Are we all going to be reading texts that are infinitely recyclable in new forms? Authored by Chatbots. We don't need authors anymore.

MICHAEL ROSEN: We're at some sort of cusp. Obviously, we don't need the book to have a text. If you say to me, 'Oh, Michael, could you just lay your hands on Macbeth's soliloquy, "Tomorrow, and tomorrow, and tomorrow, Creeps in this petty pace from day to day, To the last syllable of recorded time."' You know as well as I do that I go, 'Just hang on one moment,' and right away I'm online on a computer, and I type in 'Macbeth tomorrow', and it pops up in a second, and that actually saves me schlepping all the way over to the bookcase and pulling down my copy of the *Complete Works of Shakespeare*, and looking for Macbeth's soliloquy on 'Tomorrow', saying to myself, 'Which scene is that? Is that Act I scene two? No, it's later. It's after he's heard Lady Macbeth has died.' We just type 'Macbeth tomorrow', and it comes up straight away. I'm not going to get sentimental. Sure, I've got my *Complete Shakespeare*, and I used to use it as a reference. And now I use the computer and you know it's a fantastic tool. It does the job for me, so that for me, just in terms of me being a bibliophile and someone living in this *Republic of Letters*, as Marc Fumaroli and Emile Zola called it, has been a huge advance. This lightweight machine that I'm talking to you on, it's got it all in there. Millions of books!

The bloody library that I've got sitting in my office I know to a certain extent is better, but the reach is more limited. At the same time, just to bring it back down to children, you sit in a classroom, and you see a group of kids around a pile of books, getting up and sitting down, pulling a book off the shelf. Three of them, you know, huddling over a picture book, turning over the pages of Maurice Sendak's *Where the Wild Things Are* (1963) and laughing at the wild things. When it first came out, people said they're too horrific to give to kids. They'll all run and hide. The reality is kids read it together and argue about the last page. Less likely as an e-book, I think.

Remember I read Thompson Seton's books on nature in British Columbia, on badgers and bears, as a child. If we're going on a bear hunt, do we have to know what the bear is thinking? Because Helen Oxenbury, the illustrator to my *We're Going on a Bear Hunt* (1989) has left it there, ambiguous. We spoke of unresolved endings. What did the bear want: Did the bear want to play with the kids? Is the bear lonely? Does the bear want to go swimming? What does the bear do? And you'll see four-year-olds arguing with passion as to what they believe the bear is thinking. Well, yes, I suppose you could do that on a computer. But while the three kids are doing that with *We're Going on a Bear Hunt*, there's now another three kids over there doing it with *Where the Wild Things Are* and other kids over there doing it with Julia Donaldson's *The Gruffalo* (1999). While they're all doing it in different places in a classroom, in terms of pedagogic surroundings that's a tremendous momentum with children reading apart, reading together, with autonomy, around the book, both sharing and being separate at the same time. That's very powerful.

I notice people on our London Underground trains split half and half. I was counting it the other day on the train. There are people on there with Kindles and about the other half are reading books. If I want to make notes on a book that I'm reading, I find that I want a book. With some books I do scribble in cheap paperbacks. If I'm doing radio interviews, I know it's a professional thing, but you know if I've got to interview a guy about, say, the language of grief, or something like that on a BBC radio show called *Word of Mouth*, I get the book and scribble on it. I make some notes in the back, and these are the briefs for my questions to the author.

I notice that a lot of books pass between professionals these days. You know I've got a stack of books here that people have sent to me because they want me to read it for me to respond. I send them books, and there's a sort of exchange. Another kind of elite, do you suppose, where we pass books between us? Yet if it is purely the question of storytelling, of the narrator, of the narrative (all that Wayne C. Booth stuff!), I don't think there's much difference between reading a Kindle and reading a book. Of course, the advantage of books is that they are very cheap in contrast to the electronic media.

As far as Chatbots are concerned, well, as it happens, the very last radio show I just did on *Word of Mouth* was about Chatbots. One of my questions was, 'Can Chatbots write my poems for me?' And then the profound professor based in California who I was interviewing said, 'No.' I think she was being optimistic, because in actual fact it does not do a bad job! I might look at it and go, yeah, it's just about okay. It's missing a little bit here or missing some sort of little personal quirks, or something like that, but in terms of little rhymes and quite simple things, it can do it. Even now, when I look for a rhyme for a word, I go to RhymeZone online. Take a difficult word, like 'system'. I think, oh gosh! How many rhymes for system are there? System, victim in system, victim, hmmm, sort of all right. It depends whether I want it to be a close rhyme, or, of course, these days with rap there are very,

very loose rhymes. After all, Wilfred Owen invented the half-rhyme, which was a beautiful and wonderful thing. So, you know, maybe we can get away with it. I put up a little tweet the other day asking whether people could tell me any songs that don't rhyme. I think the example I gave was the chorus of 'You Can't Always Get What You Want' by the Rolling Stones on their 1969 album *Let It Bleed*. It's got some assonance in it. 'You can't always get what you want . . ./But if you try sometimes you might find/ You get what you need.' It's assonance, it's not rhyme. The chorus doesn't really rhyme.

SANDER GILMAN: If we're going to say there is something distinct about the human imagination from a computer program that is, after all, only working off databases, that's all we can do. We say there's a database and AI will merge it with other databases to create something that looks like it is different and therefore creative.

MICHAEL ROSEN: Then, somehow or other, we have got to, as you say need to, do better. I mean Christopher Ricks as T. S. Eliot's editor discovered, without the use of a computer, that the multiple 'allusions' in some of Eliot's early poems were what we would these days call a mash-up. He was translating, chopping bits up, moving them round and creating something new. Maybe Eliot was one of the first Chatbots! But of course, Ricks wasn't saying, 'Is he a shitty writer because of it?' He was saying, well, that was the game he was playing. People do the same with Bob Dylan: sit and listen to *Highway 61 Revisited* (1965). Joan Baez said about Dylan at that time that he was spending almost 24 hours a day obsessively reading people like Eliot and Jack Kerouac. He was pouring this into the lyrics without necessarily knowing that's what he was doing. He was doing a kind of mash-up. So, when they go back to 'Just like Tom Thumb's Blues' and find the line 'Up on Housing Project Hill it's either fortune or fame', critics find that he has taken that from Kerouac's autobiographical novel of 1965, *Desolation Angels*, and they say, 'Wow! That's true creativity, real intertextuality!' Chatbot, anyone?

SANDER GILMAN: Michael. Thank you so much. This has been fun.

14

Words After

SANDER L. GILMAN

There is an apocryphal tale told about William Faulkner
concerning an event that took place after he was awarded
the 1949 Nobel Prize 'for his powerful and artistically unique
contribution to the modern American novel'. The following
year the Department of English at the University of Virginia
– Thomas Jefferson's university – scheduled a conference recognizing this as an honour to southern literature, as Faulkner
was in residence. The topic was to be the most enigmatic of all
Faulkner's tales, 'The Bear' (1942), first published in the *Saturday
Evening Post* and then expanded later that year in his volume of
short stories *Go Down, Moses*. By the 1950s this was the most
widely taught of all of Faulkner's often difficult and always prob-
lematic texts. The tale of Isaac McCaslin and his coming of age
in pursuit and eventual killing, over a decade, of Old Ben, the
last of the Grizzlies left in the east, pits civilization against an
ever-vanishing nature, a 'doomed wilderness', which includes
both dying former slaves and vanishing indigenous peoples.
What was and is enticing about the tale is its overt set of symbolic
references, a sort of children's bear tale for adults. After a number
of learned papers on a 'close' or a 'Marxist' or a 'psychoanalytic'

reading, Faulkner was asked to respond. 'At his very first UVA session Faulkner was asked about ... this tale but admitted in his reply that "I don't remember the story too well."'[1] Okay, maybe not so apocryphal after all. You can listen to this exchange online and it is really quite different from the tale I just told, except in the author's verbal refusal to engage with his own text. My apocryphal account had Faulkner say: 'Hell, I don't know; I only wrote the thing.' Is my story a counterfactual reading as a riff on our longstanding anxiety about knowing and inter-preting on the part of both author and critic alike? Writers, it is claimed, are in the main the worse readers of their own prod-ucts, especially when confronted with other readings. And yet their readings have a sort of innate veracity, right or wrong, that needs to be taken seriously, especially when they claim that they don't remember. And the tales that we tell about them may be apocryphal but they too reveal much about our own prejudices and desires.

Faulkner's 'real' response seems to me also the shrugging of the author's metaphoric shoulders in the bright light of analysis. My own experience was too similar. I got to know the Holocaust-survivor novelist Jurek Becker in the 1980s and, after his death, wrote his biography.[2] Becker was the most important survi-vor-author in the German Democratic Republic and then after 1977, when he was exiled in West Berlin, one of the most import-ant writers both for television and 'high' culture in a reunited Germany until his death in 1997. In one exchange, after an intense argument about what being Jewish meant to him, he wrote to me that I was an ornithologist; he was a bird. And he did not mean that kindly. I categorized and organized and made clear (or at least tried to). He was in and of the 'real' world. Me, not so much. But of course, I was very much of the world but writing in a different register for an audience that clearly over-lapped with his. I was an academic PR agent, giving his work status as part of a canon that, as with Faulkner, got them taught in schools and universities, giving them a sort of serious cachet that they would have anyway, but now with an institutional imprimatur. But I was also engaged with his readings of his own works. When he spent a term as a visiting professor at Cornell, I planned a course in which, for the first half of the term, my students and I read his major novels. When he arrived mid-term, we 're-read' the books with his participation. Our interest was not so much his readings providing an authentic account through which to correct our interpretations. Rather, we sought to have a second tier of primary texts, now his readings of his works in an American academic context, as the focus of our future inter-pretations of the books. Not truer in their interpretations but providing new insights with which the critic now had to grapple. That is certainly one reason why Faulkner was at Charlottesville; why Becker and I met regularly in Ithaca and in Berlin. In com-plex ways a writer without a critical reader is the ultimate of George Berkeley's paradox: 'If a tree falls in a forest and no one is around to hear it, does it make a sound?' (Of course, Berkeley is only supposed to have said this. It is an attributed quote that may or may not paraphrase bits of his *A Treatise Concerning the Principles of Human Knowledge*, published in 1710. But one that haunts all of our imaginations, nevertheless.) Berkeley's answer was that God hears the sound; for us today, again not so much: the artist or the writer would only hear the echo of their work retreating into the distance if it were not for the engaged reader or viewer. And critics are both such readers as well as unpaid PR agents. But writers are readers too, and that is at the core of this quite unusual project of having critics and writers alike read their own childhood reading.

The key to our volume is that the readings that each and every one of our authors re-reads are embedded in their sense of their own childhood. Here another Jurek Becker story: Becker was born of Jewish parents in Łódź in 1937. Like many of his parents' generation after the re-establishment of the post-First World War Polish state, they opted to speak Polish, rather than Yiddish, in the home and baby Jerzy (Jurek is a childhood nickname for the very Polish name Jerzy) heard only Polish. After his liberation from Auschwitz in 1945, his father rescued him from the hospital that the Red Cross had created in what had been the Ravensbrück concentration camp for women and children, where his mother had died shortly before the Russians liberated the camp on 30 April 1945. He was then brought to East Berlin, where his father's choice was to speak only German. Jurek's family and then literary language became the German of the GDR. After he was exiled in West Berlin and then remarried, he and his new wife had a son. Well established and seriously middle class, they hired a nanny for the baby, who turned out to be a young Polish woman. One day she was suddenly dismissed. When I asked Jurek why, he was very close-mouthed, very unusual for him in our exchanges. His wife, Christine, with whom I later spoke about this, told me that one evening he overheard the nanny singing a lullaby to their baby in Polish, of course. He was completely freaked that not only could he understand what she was singing, but that he anticipated all the words in the song well in advance of her singing them. Was this the return of a repressed memory of his mother's voice or, perhaps, more simply, the omnipresence of our childhood, repressed or not, evoked in moments over which we have little control, a childhood omnipresent in our psyche? Sigmund Freud made this point in his 1930 essay 'Civilization and Its Discontents', noting that the core of our psychological distress is the very fact that

> the meaning of the evolution of civilization is no longer obscure to us. It must present the struggle between Eros and Death, between the instinct of life and the instinct of destruction, as it works itself out in the human species. This struggle is what all life essentially consists of, and the evolution of civilization may therefore be simply described as the struggle for life of the human species. And it is this battle of the giants that our nurse-maids try to appease with their lullaby about Heaven.[3]

The final line is Freud's creative misreading of Heinrich Heine's account of returning to the German-speaking world from Paris, in his *Germany: A Winter's Tale*. As he was crossing the Rhine in the winter of 1843, where there had been, at least in fairy tales, the dangerous Lorelei, luring men to death with her singing, today there was only the political simulacra now chanting a lullaby of religion ('*Das Eiapopeia vom Himmel*') that lulls its German listeners into forgetting the trauma of the day in the sweet sounds of promised salvation. Yet such lullabies are all the extension of the parent's narcissistic fantasy into the lives of their children. They fantasize that

> The child shall have a better time than his parents; he shall not be subject to the necessities which they have

recognized as paramount in life. Illness, death, renunciation of enjoyment, restrictions on his own will, shall not touch him; the laws of nature and of society shall be abrogated in his favour; he shall once more really be the centre and core of creation – 'His Majesty the Baby', as we once fancied ourselves.[4]

When such narcissism is re-enforced, such as in the moment of holding, caring and listening to the lullaby, the infant is at one with its expectations of the world. But, of course, that is always disrupted as the infant expects the world to be totally the world of the lullaby, and often it is not. The caring, the fulfilling of every need is normally denied. Yet this takes on a different cast when death intervenes, where the absence is total, and the telling and singing lost.

Jurek's reality reversed Heine's irony: his Polish childhood was framed by the innocence of Polish lullabies before 1939 and then the daily struggles and horrors, ending with the death of his Polish-speaking mother in 1945 when he was seven. Such are the forces that play on our remembering our childhood. But we can also add that such topics are also then quickly assimilated into children's literature. By 1987 over three hundred children's books had been published in the United States alone on the Second World War, the Holocaust, and war in general, across a range of genres.[5] Today, the numbers worldwide are exponentially more. Indeed, as survivors such as Jurek Becker died, the numbers of children's books about the Holocaust have overtaken the number of survivors.

And if William Faulkner's 'The Bear' is no longer taught in English departments across the world, indeed, as Faulkner is no longer read, bears continue to haunt the fantasy of children's writing (as distinct to Faulkner writing about children). We discussed *Winnie-the-Pooh* in our introduction, but his direct descendants, such as the refugee bear from 'darkest Peru' in Michael Bond and Peggy Fortnum's *A Bear Called Paddington* (1958), remain staples on children's bedside tables and in the cinema – and indeed as friends eating marmalade sandwiches with the late Queen celebrating her Platinum Jubilee. That is not too far from Becker and the Holocaust, as the bear was modelled on the refugee children of the Kindertransport, brought to England in order to escape death in Central Europe. 'Paddington, in a sense, was a refugee, and I do think that there's no sadder sight than refugees,' Michael Bond reiterated in 2014, when the status of refugees was becoming an increasingly volatile political issue in Britain.[6]

A child's memories of reading and listening are always conflicted. And those conflicts are never superficial. The psychoanalyst Naomi Schlesinger recounts the case of Miss F., whose mother had died when she was nine, after a two-year battle with cancer, and noted that her father had remarried three years later:

> Early on, in response to Miss F.'s persistently requesting stories about her mother, she described being told by her father that her mother was beautiful and intelligent, a woman who always had a book in her hands, who had an extraordinary vocabulary and always knew 'exactly the right word to use'. Miss F.'s only fond personal memory was that of her mother reading to her when she was a little girl, especially when she was sick and home from school. She recalled her mother reading children's literature,

stories such as *Charlotte's Web* and *Heidi*. During the last year of her mother's life, her mother had isolated herself, deciding that it would be easier for everyone to deal with her death if she withdrew from them. At the time, this was experienced by Miss F. as grave rejection, convincing her that she was unloved and unlovable.[7]

When such fragmentary memories are unleashed in the course of the analysis, more and more nuance is given to the analysand's memories of her mother. Her father's insistence that any mention of her mother was an insult to her new stepmother came to be the censor that had controlled her memories, except for the moment of the solace of being read to. Yet the texts remembered, E. B. White's *Charlotte's Web* (1952) and Johanna Spyri's *Heidi* (1880), deal directly with death and displacement at their core, even if in the fictions both are sublimated into narratives of salvation and rescue. White's animal fable centres on the rescue of Wilbur, a pig raised for slaughter, by Charlotte, a literate barn spider, whose death heralded new life for her porcine friend as well as her future multitudinous offspring. Both of Heidi's parents die when she is five, her father in a work accident and her mother by the shock of his death; she is then abandoned by her aunt and sent into the mountains to live with her misanthropic grandfather. Typical of children's tales of rescue and succour in modernity.

Johanna Spyri's novels were hugely popular in Victorian England, where the stage was already set for the appropriation of death as merely a function of culture. In his controversial essay of 1899, the Anglo-Jewish ethnologist Joseph Jacobs commented anonymously on 'The Dying of Death':

Death as a motive is moribund. Perhaps the most distinctive note of the modern spirit is the practical disappearance of the thought of death as an influence directly bearing on practical life. We insure our lives, it is true, but having done so think no more of the matter, except in the spirit of William Micawber when he signed a promissory note. There are no skeletons at our feasts nowadays, or at worst they are living ones. Death has lost its terrors.[8]

But not its presence in the world of texts, perhaps especially in those for children.

In *The Gift of Death*, Jacques Derrida notes that 'narrative is genealogical, but it is not simply an act of memory. It bears witness, in the manner of an ethical or political act, for today and for tomorrow. It means first of all thinking about what takes place today.'[9] There is no theme that better fits Derrida's formula concerning the collapse of a hierarchy of ethics in the modern world than narratives of sacrifice and dying. Modernity no longer has the comfort of the sort of transcendental hierarchy of sacrifice as found in Søren Kierkegaard. In modernity, an individual may have complex and contradictory affiliations and therefore be unable to 'respond responsibly' to any given situation. Ambiguity and doubt result. It is the text itself that harbours immortality as well as mourning. 'Et in Arcadia ego,' says Death, but as Virgil shows in his memento mori in the *Eclogues* (v.42) it is art in all its forms that seizes the moment of death and freezes it in a denial of death. The key to children's reading is that it ameliorates or frames the fear of abandonment and death for a child still very dependent on the parent's succour but also intuitively aware of its fragility.

Sigmund Freud, hiking in the Dolomites 'in the summer before the war', presents his high Victorian (or perhaps better, Imperial Austrian) view, already present in his concern with the universality of death as the prime driver of the ego, in a debate with two much younger compatriots:

> Transience value is scarcity value in time. Limitation in the possibility of an enjoyment raises the value of the enjoyment. It was incomprehensible, I declared, that the thought of the transience of beauty should interfere with our joy in it . . . The beauty of the human form and face vanish forever in the course of our own lives, but their evanescence only lends them a fresh charm. A time may indeed come when the pictures and statues which we admire to-day will crumble to dust, or a race of men may follow us who no longer understand the works of our poets and thinkers, or a geological epoch may even arrive when all animate life upon the earth ceases; but since the value of all this beauty and perfection is determined only by its significance for our own emotional lives, it has no need to survive us and is therefore independent of absolute duration.[10]

But the 'young but already famous poet' (Rilke, perhaps) and the friend (perhaps the author and psychoanalyst Lou Andreas-Salomé) who accompany him cannot agree.[11] They, living at the moment when death is not beautiful, but ambivalent, counter his argument:

> These considerations appeared to me incontestable; but I noticed that I had made no impression either upon the

poet or upon my friend. My failure led me to infer that some powerful emotional factor was at work, which was disturbing their judgment, and I believed later that I had discovered what it was. What spoilt their enjoyment of beauty must have been a revolt in their minds against mourning. The idea that all this beauty was transient was giving these two sensitive minds a foretaste of mourning over its decease; and, since the mind instinctively recoils from anything that is painful, they felt their enjoyment of beauty interfered with by thoughts of its transience.[12]

For the young at the turn of the twentieth century beauty evoked transience, death and loss. A melancholy for the loss of an object not quite real to them, a fictive and static object of death. It is not mourning, with our fluid memories of lived experience, but the melancholic, repetitive evocation of death as it is in reading about death: never altered, always constant, regardless of the circumstances. We may change; the words never do. As Freud noted, this sense antedated the Great War, for 'a year later the war broke out and robbed the world of its beauties . . . It robbed us of very much that we had loved, and showed us how ephemeral were many things that we had regarded as changeless.'[13]

The function of such a modernist destabilization at the core of children's writing becomes a literary theme too. Time distorted is time remembered, as in Ian McEwan's 1987 *The Child in Time*, which also provides a model for the fictionalization of the act of writing children's books, as writing them becomes the protagonist Stephen Lewis's refuge having rejected teaching children as a role. Becoming a well-known writer of children's books, he owes his success to 'a clerical error, a moment's inattention in the operation of the internal post' at his publishers, 'which had brought a parcel of typescript onto the wrong desk'. He 'remained the author of children's books, and half forgot that it was all a mistake . . .' The trigger for the novel, the horrific kidnapping and disappearance of his three-year-old daughter Kate two years earlier, shapes both the reader's sense of the instability of relationships, as his marriage disintegrates, and the impossibility of guaranteeing succour to any child except through reading fairy tales. But in McEwan's tale literature is itself always a watered-down version of lived experience. When, returning from a trip to rethink his life, Stephen Lewis tries to turn his fantasy of a sexualized, drug-filled hippie holiday experience in Turkey into a novel entitled *Hashish*, 'Stephen came to write a novel based on a summer holiday he had spent in his eleventh year with two girl cousins, a novel of short trousers and short hair for the boys, and Alice bands and frocks tucked into knickers for the girls', a domestic tale set in Reading, not Istanbul, entitled *Lemonade*.[14] His friend and publisher Charles Darke attempts to console him with an observation that 'the distinction between adult and children's fiction was indeed a fiction itself. It was entirely false, a mere convenience . . . that the greatest so-called children's books were precisely those that spoke to both children and adults, to the incipient adult within the child, to the forgotten child within the adult.'[15] And yet when his daughter vanishes all he can do is to fall into a depressive reverie; no magic moment when life becomes art. Stephen muses:

> I remember Kate, my daughter . . . but no . . . the written
> word can be the very means by which the self and the

world connect, which is why the very best writing for children has about it the quality of invisibility, of taking you right through to the things it names, and through metaphors and imagery can evoke feelings, smells, impressions for which there are no words at all. A nine-year-old can experience this intensely. The written word is no less a part of what it names than the spoken word – think about the spells written round the rim of the necromancer's bow, the prayers chiselled on the tombs of the dead . . .[16]

His most intense memory is of 'sitting on the edge of Kate's bed reading to her'. His fantasy, however, is of 'an image of his daughter, older than he had known her, sitting up in bed engrossed in a novel. She turned a page, frowned. Turned back. It could have been a book he had written for her.'[17] No writing of the great book, indeed no writing at all, just a fantasy of a child lost now returned. Indeed, at least one reviewer noted that 'Kate's disappearance provides a terrible illustration of the loss of innocence, depicted in Stephen's first book, as well as a heavy-handed metaphor for his own inability to retrieve his youth.'[18] And perhaps, like Miss F., the memories of succour transgressed.

Writing for children means also remembering one's readings as a child. In Sir Salman Rushdie's essay 'Ask Yourself Which Are the Books You Truly Love' (2021) the very adult themes are death and loss, a loss of place and its rescue in storytelling.[19] For 'I grew up in Bombay, India, a city that is no longer, today, at all like the city it once was and has even changed its name to the much less euphonious Mumbai, in a time so unlike the present that it feels impossibly remote, even fantastic. In that far-off Bombay, the stories and books that reached me from the West seemed like true tales of wonder.' The tales told seemed timeless and contextless, even the religious narratives of Hinduism come to be children's fairy tales for the young Muslim child. And Rushdie recognizes that writing comes secondarily to listening to such tales, shaped only by their parental teller:

> Before there were books, there were stories. At first the stories weren't written down. Sometimes they were even sung. Children were born, and before they could speak, their parents sang them songs, a song about an egg that fell off a wall, perhaps, or about a boy and a girl who went up a hill and fell down it. As the children grew older, they asked for stories almost as often as they asked for food.

And the key was not merely repetition, but as Freud noted, the need for repetition to reinforce the sense of the child's self. 'The children fell in love with these stories and wanted to hear them over and over again . . . The act of falling in love with stories awakened something in the children that would nourish them all their lives: their imagination.' And here we can quote Paul in 1 Corinthians 13:11: 'When I was a child, I spake as a child, I understood as a child, I thought as a child: but when I became a man, I put away childish things.' Rushdie amends this to observe that 'they went on growing up and slowly the stories fell away from them, the stories were packed away in boxes in the attic, and it became harder for the former children to tell and receive stories, harder for them, sadly, to fall in love.' Our adult narcissism gives way to a compartmentalizing of story-listening and a path to storytelling for all the wrong reasons.

And yet Rushdie's essay centres on death and storytelling as certainly as any other account for his exemplary storyteller is that of *The Thousand Nights and One Night*, more a Western invention in its received French version by Antoine Galland (titled *Les mille et une nuits*, finished in 1717), one reflecting a Persian or Arabic tale-telling, and its heroine, Scheherazade. Rushdie's account stresses the Bluebeard-like aspect of the tale-telling, which culminated in the death of women. 'King Shahryar and King Shah Zaman duly took their revenge on faithless womankind. For three years, they each married, deflowered and then ordered the execution of a fresh virgin every night. Scheherazade's father, Shahryar's vizier, or prime minister, was obliged to carry out Shahryar's executions himself . . . At any rate, the final count of the dead was three thousand, two hundred and sixteen. Thirteen of the dead were men.'

Rushdie's flight into the world of a 'West-East Divan', to use Goethe's phrase, is also a flight back into and away from his own childhood reading. For it is the adult reader who stops looking within his own experience, that of the little Muslim boy in a multi-ethnic, multilingual, post-colonial city now lost in the Hindutva of modern India, and flees into reading, reading tales about tales, tales about death. I'll stop here for a moment and again recall my own first reading of *Midnight's Children* (1981) with its magical protagonist Saleem Sinai, born at the moment of partition, midnight 15 August 1947, endowed, like all of the children born at that moment, with extraordinary powers – his being telepathy and an extraordinary nose for scents. Switched at birth with Shiva, a poor Muslim infant, in Rushdie's reworking of Mark Twain's *Pudd'nhead Wilson* (1894), it is not race that is suddenly indistinguishable, but religion and class. Our narrator is born as a natural teller of fairy tales, to whom, as a sickly child, lullabies were sung by adults giving him succour. All of the cast of characters have magical powers that do not seem to really shield them from the historical reality through which they pass.

Not quite a magic fairy tale, but close enough for me was in 1981 when I was living for the moment in London with my family. We had a flat in Blackheath and were acclimatizing ourselves to a new city, new schools and for the first time, we thought, to a London, for which 'rivers of blood' had been prophesized by Enoch Powell in 1968, that had become somewhat more accommodating to foreigners.

What Rushdie's novel brought home was that the notion of 'rivers of blood' was not a metaphor and that the radical, involuntary rendering of a subcontinent, caused by the collapse of post-war British flight, meant that London now was the home not only to a generation carrying that trauma with them, but to new magical voices able to tell their stories. Many years ago, my friend J. Edward Chamberlin wrote an important book about oral history and indigenous land rights, entitled *If This Is Your Land, Where Are Your Stories?*[20] Now London became the space where the stories told were not of permanence, but of flux; not of continuities, but of disruption. And blood and death and fantasy were everywhere in texts such as *Midnight's Children*. And, this is what is so strange in retrospect, WE WANTED MORE! One could not wait for his next book or his next or his next. We haunted the bookshops, just as the critics echoed our desire in print. A new Scheherazade now writing about Scheherazade's tales.

Yet who is Rushdie's pre-eminent storyteller, the model for all such tellers of tales, since at least the Enlightenment in the West:

Consider Scheherazade, whose name meant 'city-born' and who was without a doubt a big-city girl, crafty, wisecracking, by turns sentimental and cynical, as contemporary a metropolitan narrator as one could wish to meet. Scheherazade, who snared the prince in her never-ending story. Scheherazade, telling stories to save her life, setting fiction against death, a Statue of Liberty built not of metal but of words.

Scheherazade, who insisted, against her father's will, on taking her place in the procession into the king's deadly boudoir. Scheherazade, who set herself the heroic task of saving her sisters by taming the king. Who had faith, who must have had faith, in the man beneath the murderous monster and in her own ability to restore him to his true humanity, by telling him stories.

She is the 'big-city girl, crafty, wisecracking, by turns sentimental and cynical' now at another court. She is, Scheherazade before Scheherazade, Hadassah. Ah, a name you don't know? Try 'Esther' on for size. The heroine in one of the only two books in the Hebrew Bible in which the name of God does not appear. (The other, complementary to this, is the erotic *Song of Songs*, sung to praise the woman loved, not a God who made her.) You may vaguely remember the tale of the young woman, drafted, with the connivance of her cousin Mordecai to replace the banned (but not murdered) Persian queen Vashti who had in turn displeased Ahasuerus the king. A plot unravels; Esther, now again self-consciously the Jewish Hadassah, narrates at a series of banquets over three nights the tale of the viceroy Haman's perfidy in planning to murder all of the Jews in Persia to revenge himself on Mordecai's snub. Central to this is her evoking of tales of the past, such as Mordecai's rescue of the king. The evil Haman is overthrown, and here 'death', echoing Scheherazade's ruler and his brother, enters fully into the tale. For if Haman's desire is to murder all of the Jews in the kingdom of Ahasuerus,

> Then said Esther, if it please the king, let it be granted to the Jews which are in Shushan to do tomorrow also according unto this day's decree, and let Haman's ten sons be hanged upon the gallows. And the king commanded it so to be done: and the decree was given at Shushan; and they hanged Haman's ten sons. For the Jews that were in Shushan gathered themselves together on the fourteenth day also of the month Adar, and slew three hundred men at Shushan; but on the prey they laid not their hand (Esther 9:13–15).

Over 75,000 people are eventually killed by the Jews, who are careful to take no plunder, only to murder their persecutors. The peripety of the plot, the lost rescued, the villain destroyed, is however more than that. It was the tales told that succeeded in melting the king's heart, to persuade him to kill many more than the 'three thousand, two hundred and sixteen' dead of Scheherazade's tale.

Rushdie's take is that this world was shaped, perhaps as in Esther's city of Shushan; it was 'a conspiracy between the daughter and the father' Is it possible that Scheherazade and the vizier had hatched a secret plan? For, thanks to Scheherazade's strategy, Shah Zaman was no longer king in Samarkand. Thanks to Scheherazade's strategy, her father was no longer a courtier and unwilling executioner but a king in his own right, a well-beloved king and, what was more, a wise man, a man of peace, succeeding a bloody ogre. And then, without explanation, Death came, simultaneously, for Shahryar and Shah Zaman. Death, the 'Destroyer of Delights and the Severer of Societies, the Desolator of Dwelling Places and the Garnerer of Graveyards, came for them, and their palaces lay in ruins, and they were replaced by a wise ruler, whose name we are not told.' Was this Ahasuerus, Xerxes the Great of Persia, by another name? In storytelling all is possible.

We return to mass death, to Jurek Becker's Ravensbrück, to Esther/Hadassah's Shushan, to the Baghdad of Scheherazade. We return to the stories of childhood, half-remembered as tales of redemption, not tales of loss. As Rushdie observes, 'The fantastic is neither innocent nor escapist. The wonderland is not a place of refuge, not even necessarily an attractive or likeable place. It can be – in fact, it usually is – a place of slaughter, exploitation, cruelty and fear.' And yet, we thrive on these tales, on the fictions of everything at the end working out alright, if not perfectly. As Rushdie notes about fairy tales,

> we know, when we hear these tales, that even though they are 'unreal', because carpets do not fly and witches in gingerbread houses do not exist, they are also 'real', because they are about real things: love, hatred, fear, power, bravery, cowardice, death. They simply arrive at the real by a different route. They are so, even though we know that they are not so. The truth is not arrived at by purely mimetic means. An image can be captured by a camera or by a paintbrush. A painting of a starry night

is no less truthful than a photograph of one; arguably, if the painter is Van Gogh, it's far more truthful, even though far less 'realistic'.

As are, as we know, all fictions no matter how embedded in history. They are told to us to shield us even as they expose us to lived experience, an experience whose end is absolute but articulated only through tales about redemption. And the teller of the tale – always and in perpetuity – outlives their subject, who is fixed in the text, always the same and yet always different the moment the cover of the book is opened.

REFERENCES

Setting the Scene

1 Alberto Manguel, *A History of Reading* [1996] (New York, 2014), p. 6.
2 It is salutary to remind ourselves of the power and freedom of literacy. Henry Louis Gates Jr recounts how Rebecca Cox Jackson, an African American visionary and Shaker eldress, miraculously learned to read. She opened the Bible and discovered that she could read. At first frightened and angrily queried by her family members, she later served as a model for others to emulate. She attributed this ability to God's grace. Jackson's suddenly found skill emphasizes the potentially revolutionary power literacy has. Henry Louis Gates Jr, *The Signifying Monkey: A Theory of African-American Literary Criticism* (Oxford, 1989), p. 249.
3 Maryanne Wolf, *Reader, Come Home: The Reading Brain in a Digital World* (Toronto, 2018), p. 83.
4 Meghan Cox Gurdon, *The Enchanted Hour: The Miraculous Power of Reading Aloud in the Age of Distraction* (Toronto, 2019), p. 49.
5 Wolf, *Reader, Come Home*, pp. 22–3.
6 Maria Tatar, *Enchanted Hunters: The Power of Stories in Childhood* (New York, 2009), pp. 3–4.
7 Lewis Carroll, *Alice's Adventures in Wonderland* [1865] (London, 1994), pp. 3–4.
8 Ibid., p. 47.
9 Ibid., pp. 147, 148–9.
10 Quoted in Tatar, *Enchanted Hunters*, p. 4.
11 Barbara Sicherman, *Well-Read Lives: How Books Inspired a Generation of American Women* (Chapel Hill, NC, 2010), p. 119.
12 Zohar Shavit, *Poetics of Children's Literature* (Athens, GA, and London, 1986), p. 70. Shavit holds that in many books the so-called implied

reader, the postulated recipient that is rhetorically embedded in the text, is the child. Thus, she argues that the dual structure is not found in all books for children.

13 A. A. Milne, *Winnie-the-Pooh* [1926] (London, 2004), pp. 7–8.
14 Manguel, *A History of Reading*, p. 27.
15 Milne, *Winnie-the-Pooh*, p. 29.
16 Maryanne Wolf, *Proust and the Squid: The Story and Science of the Reading Brain* (Toronto, 2007), p. 3.
17 Ibid., p. 12.
18 Milne, *Winnie-the-Pooh*, p. 9.
19 A. A. Milne, *The House at Pooh Corner* [1928] (London, 2004), pp. 173, 179.
20 Tatar, *Enchanted Hunters*, p. 4.
21 Milne, *Winnie-the-Pooh*, p. 29.
22 Milne, *The House at Pooh Corner*, p. 56.
23 J. A. Appleyard, *Becoming a Reader: The Experience of Fiction from Childhood to Adulthood* (Cambridge, 1990), pp. 3–9.
24 Ibid., p. 15.
25 Louise Rosenblatt, *Literature as Exploration* [1938] (New York, 1995), p. 1.
26 Appleyard, *Becoming a Reader*, p. 39.
27 Rosenblatt, *Literature as Exploration*, p. 1.
28 Appleyard, *Becoming a Reader*, p. 83.
29 Ibid., pp. 67–9.
30 Tatar, *Enchanted Hunters*, pp. 18–21.
31 Rosenblatt, *Literature as Exploration*, p. 109.
32 Ibid., p. 140.
33 Appleyard, *Becoming a Reader*, p. 123.
34 Adrienne Kertzer, 'The Politics of Children's Reading', *Ariel*, XXIII/4 (1992), pp. 113–20.
35 Jonathan Culler, 'The Closeness of Close Reading', *ADE Bulletin*, 149 (2010), pp. 20–25 (p. 20).
36 Paul Ricoeur, *Freud and Philosophy*, trans. Denis Savage (New Haven, CT, 1970), pp. 26, 32.
37 Milne, *Winnie-the-Pooh*, p. 61.
38 Rita Felski, *Uses of Literature* (Oxford, 2008).
39 Shoshana Felman, *What Does a Woman Want? Reading and Sexual Difference* (Baltimore, MD, and London, 1993), pp. 5–6.

40 We will not go into alternative reading tactics such as surface reading; see, for example, Stephen Best and Sharon Marcus, 'Surface Reading: An Introduction', *Representations*, CVIII/1 (2009), pp. 1–21.
41 Elaine Castillo, *How to Read Now: Essays* (London, 2022), p. 64.
42 Frederick Clarke Prescott, *The Poetic Mind* (New York, 1922), p. 84.
43 Simon O. Lesser, *Fiction and the Unconscious* (Chicago, IL, 1975), p. 218.
44 Wolf, *Proust and the Squid*, p. 143.
45 Daniel R. Schwarz, *In Defense of Reading: Teaching Literature in the Twenty-First Century* (Oxford, 2008), p. 15.

3 The Dream of an Intenser Experience

1 Henry James, 'Preface to *The American*', in *Literary Criticism*, ed. Leon Edel, vol. II (New York, 1984), p. 1063.
2 Jean-Paul Sartre, *La Nausée* [1938], trans. Lloyd Alexander (New York, 2007), p. 40.
3 Robert Louis Stevenson, *Treasure Island* [1883] (New York, 2012), p. 57.
4 See Marthe Robert, *Roman des origines et origines du roman* (Paris, 1973).
5 Stevenson, *Treasure Island*, p. 79.
6 Ibid.
7 Ibid., p. 99.
8 Ibid., p. 136.
9 Ibid., p. 173.
10 Ibid., p. 204.
11 Ibid., p. 265.
12 See Sartre, *La Nausée* [1938] (Paris, 1957), p. 207.
13 For a fuller discussion, see Peter Brooks, *History Painting and Narrative: Delacroix's 'Moments'* (Oxford, 1998).
14 See Kirsty Nichol Findlay, ed., *Arthur Ransome's Long-Lost Study of Robert Louis Stevenson* (Woodbridge, Suffolk, 2011).
15 Arthur Ransome, *Swallows and Amazons* [1930] (Boston, MA, 1985), p. 203.
16 Ibid., p. 209.
17 Arthur Ransome, *Swallowdale* [1931] (Boston, MA, 1985), p. 60. It appears that *Peter Duck* was in fact written, at least as a draft, before *Swallowdale*, but published after.
18 *The Autobiography of Arthur Ransome*, ed., with prologue and epilogue, Rupert Hart-Davis (London, 1976).

19 Lewis Carroll, *Alice's Adventures in Wonderland* [1865] (Chicago, IL, 1998), p. 144.

20 Jean-Jacques Rousseau, *Confessions; autres textes autobiographiques* (Paris, 1962), p. 41.

21 James, 'Preface to *The American*', p. 1063.

5 A Life in Literature

1 For my experience of Shakespeare from age ten, see 'No "I" in Shakespeare', in *Shakespeare and I*, ed. William Mckenzie and Theodora Papadopoulou (London, 2012), pp. 201–20.

2 Thomas Hardy, *The Mayor of Casterbridge* [1886] (London, 1974), chap. 40.

3 George Eliot, *Daniel Deronda* [1876] (London, 1967), chap. 32.

4 D. H. Lawrence, *The Rainbow* [1915] (London, 1949), chap. 8.

5 D. H. Lawrence, *Fantasia of the Unconscious* [1922] (London, 1971), chap. 13.

6 Reading (in) My Father's Shadow

1 Matthew 13:13.

2 Charlotte Brontë, *Jane Eyre*, ed. Richard J. Dunn (New York, 2019), p. 270.

3 Galit Atlas, *Emotional Inheritance: Moving Beyond the Legacy of Trauma* (London, 2022), p. 19.

4 Benjamin G. Ogden and Thomas H. Ogden, *The Analyst's Ear and the Critic's Eye: Rethinking Psychoanalysis and Literature* (London, 2013), p. 15.

7 Reading in Times of War

1 The essay was later published in English in a collection of writers' responses to the invasion of Ukraine, 'Day 5, Day 9, Day 16: Responses to the Invasion of Ukraine', *London Review of Books*, XLIX/6 (24 March 2022).

2 Ibid.

3 Kateryna Kalytko, Люди з дієсловами (People with Verbs) (Chernivtsi, 2022), p. 94.

4 Serhiy Zhadan, 'Хай це буде текст не про війну' (May this Text Be Not about War), speech at the 2022 Frankfurt Book Fair, 23 October 2022, available at https://chytomo.com.

5 Ibid.

6 Pascale Casanova, 'Combative Literatures', *New Left Review*, 72 (2011), pp. 123–34.

7 Kateryna Hlushchenko, 'Як мова визначає пам'ять' (How Language Defines Memory), lecture notes from the conversation between Volodymyr Rafeyenko and Marianna Kianovska, Lviv, 19 August 2019, available at https://zbruc.eu.

8 Volodymyr Rafeyenko, *Mondegreen: Songs about Death and Love* (Cambridge, MA, 2022), p. 17.

9 A curious detail: it's the girl's father who's forced to take her out to the forest, where he finds a hut of an old man who shelters the girl. But both men then leave her when it gets dark and the forest beasts emerge. Mare's head appears and, because the girl has been kind to her and offered food and shelter, the head makes the girl rich so that she can go live in the city. So the tale is in a way about one female figure helping the other to get financial independence and climb the class ladder.

10 Ibid., p. 24.

11 Hlushchenko, 'Як мова визначає пам'ять' (How Language Defines Memory).

12 Rafeyenko, *Mondegreen*, p. 17.

13 Hlushchenko, 'Як мова визначає пам'ять' (How Language Defines Memory).

14 While this might seem like an unusual word (from the German, *Protuberanz*), for a Ukrainian reader this would be a very familiar image, popularized by high school reading of the 1960s poets and, in this case, Ivan Drach's well-known poem 'Protuberances of the Heart' (1965). Protuberances are a solar phenomenon, usually translated into English as 'solar prominences', which manifest as large loop-shaped extensions of plasma and magnetic field from the Sun's surface.

15 Rafeyenko, *Mondegreen*, p. 16.

16 Ibid., p. 18 (emphases in original).

17 Ibid., p. 19.

18 Take, for example, the news media who, all of a sudden, had to report on the invasion along the joint border between Ukraine and Russia (1,974 kilometres), as well as the joint border with Belarus (1,084 kilometres),

in the mode of a live broadcast. The situation along the sea coast was even more uncertain.

19 I am grateful to Matti Kangaskoski for this observation.

20 The semiotic structure of utopia, if we follow Fredric Jameson, is built around an identification, unity and double negation of opposites: Utopia is neither a good nor non-existent place but it retains both terms in their mutual negation of each other and thus allows us 'to grasp the moment of truth of each term'. Fredric Jameson, 'The Politics of Utopia', *New Left Review*, 25 (2004), p. 50.

10 Reading from the Spine

1 Siri Hustvedt, 'I responded viscerally to De Beauvoir's The Second Sex', *The Guardian*, 26 November 2021.

2 Gertrude Stein, *Tender Buttons* [1914] (San Francisco, CA, 2014), p. 35.

3 Gertrude Stein, *The Autobiography of Alice B. Toklas* (London, 1933), p. 152.

4 Virginia Woolf, *To the Lighthouse* [1927] (London, 1938), p. 129.

5 Katherine Mansfield, *The Garden Party and Other Stories* [1922] (London, 1997).

6 Laura Oulanne, 'Containment and Empathy in Katherine Mansfield's and Virginia Woolf's Short Stories', in *Narrating Nonhuman Spaces: Form, Story, and Experience Beyond Anthropocentrism*, ed. Marco Caracciolo, Marlene Karlsson Marcussen and David Rodriguez (New York, 2022), pp. 19–35.

12 A Typewriter's Travels

1 Jean-Paul Sartre, *Les Mots* (Paris, 1964), p. 30.

2 Ingmar Bergman, *The Magic Lantern* (New York, 1988), p. 5.

3 Joseph Brodsky, *On Grief and Reason: Essays* (New York, 1995), p. 5.

4 Vladimir Nabokov, *Speak, Memory: An Autobiography Revisited* (New York, 2012), p. 10.

5 Elias Canetti, *The Tongue Set Free: Remembrance of a European Childhood* (New York, 1979), p. 82.

6 Ibid., p. 10.

7 Silvia Hosseini, *Tie, totuus ja kuolema* (Helsinki, 2021), p. viii.

14 Words After

1 'Faulkner at Virginia', https://faulkner.lib.virginia.edu, accessed 2 May 2023.
2 Sander L. Gilman, *Jurek Becker: A Life in Five Worlds* (Chicago, IL, 2003).
3 Sigmund Freud, 'Civilization and Its Discontents', in *The Standard Edition of the Complete Psychological Works of Sigmund Freud*. trans. James Strachey et al., 24 vols (London, 1953–74), vol. XXI, p. 121.
4 Sigmund Freud, 'On Narcissism: An Introduction', in *The Standard Edition*, vol. XIV, p. 91.
5 Barbara Harrison, 'Howl Like the Wolves', *Children's Literature*, XV (1987), pp. 67–90 (p. 67).
6 Michelle Pauli, 'Michael Bond: "Paddington stands up for things, he's not afraid of going to the top and giving them a hard stare"', *The Guardian*, 28 November 2014.
7 Naomi J. Schlesinger, 'Loss to Legacy: The Work of Mourning Early Parental Death', *Psychoanalytic Social Work*, XXI/1–2 (2014), pp. 75–89 (p. 78).
8 Joseph Jacobs, 'The Dying of Death', *Fortnightly Review* (August 1899), pp. 264–9 (p. 264).
9 Jacques Derrida, *The Gift of Death*, trans. David Wills (Chicago, IL, 1996), p. 35.
10 Sigmund Freud, 'On Transience' (1916), in *The Standard Edition*, vol. XIV, pp. 305–6.
11 Hannah S. Decker, *Freud, Dora, and Vienna 1900* (New York, 1991), p. 133.
12 Sigmund Freud, 'On Transience', p. 306.
13 Ibid., p. 307.
14 Ian McEwan, *The Child in Time* (London, 1987), p. 26.
15 Ibid., p. 30.
16 Ibid., p. 88.
17 Ibid., p. 89.
18 Michiko Kakutani, '*The Child in Time*', *New York Times*, 26 September 1987.
19 Salman Rushdie, 'Ask Yourself Which Books You Truly Love', *New York Times Magazine*, 24 May 2021. This is a redacted version of the opening chapter, 'Wonder Tales', in his volume of essays, *Languages of Truth: Essays, 2003–2020* (New York, 2021).

20 J. Edward Chamberlin, *If This Is Your Land, Where Are Your Stories? Finding Common Ground* (New York, 2003). Recently he has turned to the power of storytelling in general to shape not only where we are but who we expect ourselves to be in that place in his Storylines. *How Words Shape Our World* (Madeira Park, BC, 2023).

WORKS CITED

Setting the Scene

Appleyard, J. A., *Becoming a Reader: The Experience of Fiction from Childhood to Adulthood* (Cambridge, 1990)

Best, Stephen, and Sharon Marcus, 'Surface Reading: An Introduction', *Representations*, CVIII/1 (2009), pp. 1–21

Carroll, Lewis, *Alice's Adventures in Wonderland* [1865] (London, 1994)

Castillo, Elaine, *How to Read Now: Essays* (London, 2022)

Culler, Jonathan, 'The Closeness of Close Reading', *ADE Bulletin*, 149 (2010), pp. 20–25

Felman, Shoshana, *What Does a Woman Want? Reading and Sexual Difference* (Baltimore, MD, and London, 1993)

Felski, Rita, *Uses of Literature* (Oxford, 2008)

Gates, Henry Louis Jr, *The Signifying Monkey: A Theory of African-American Literary Criticism* (Oxford, 1989)

Gurdon, Meghan Cox, *The Enchanted Hour: The Miraculous Power of Reading Aloud in the Age of Distraction* (Toronto, 2019)

Lesser, Simon O., *Fiction and the Unconscious* (Chicago, IL, 1975)

Manguel, Alberto, *A History of Reading* (New York, 2014)

Milne, A. A., *Winnie-the-Pooh* [1926] (London, 2004)

——, *The House at Pooh Corner* [1928] (London, 2004)

Pullman, Philip, *His Dark Materials: The Complete Trilogy* (London, 2015)

Ricoeur, Paul, *Freud and Philosophy: An Essay on Interpretation*, trans. Denis Savage (New Haven, CT, 1970)

Rosenblatt, Louise M., *Literature as Exploration* (New York, 1995)

Schwarz, Daniel R., *In Defense of Reading: Teaching Literature in the Twenty-First Century* (Oxford, 2008)

Shavit, Zohar, *Poetics of Children's Literature* (Athens, GA, and London, 1986)

Sicherman, Barbara, *Well-Read Lives: How Books Inspired a Generation of American Women* (Chapel Hill, NC, 2010)

Tatar, Maria, *Enchanted Hunters: The Power of Stories in Childhood* (New York, 2009)

Thompson, E. P., *The Making of the English Working Class* (London, 1963)

Winnicott, D. W., 'Transitional Objects and Transitional Phenomena', *International Journal of Psychoanalysis*, XXXIV (1953), pp. 89–97

Wolf, Maryanne, *Proust and the Squid: The Story and Science of the Reading Brain* (Toronto, 2007)

——, *Reader, Come Home: The Reading Brain in a Digital World* (Toronto, 2018)

1 Portable Magic

Barker, Pat, *The Silence of the Girls* (New York, 2018)

Bloom, Paul, *Against Empathy: The Case for Rational Compassion* (New York, 2016)

Breithaupt, Fritz, *The Dark Sides of Empathy* (Ithaca, NY, 2019)

Campbell, Joseph, *The Hero with a Thousand Faces* (New York, 1949)

Carroll, Lewis, *Alice's Adventures in Wonderland* (London, 1865)

Carter, Angela, *The Bloody Chamber* (New York, 1979)

Didion, Joan, 'Why I Write', *New York Times Magazine*, 5 December 1976, repr. in *Let Me Tell You What I Mean* (London, 2021), pp. 45–57

Eliot, George, *Middlemarch* (Edinburgh and London, 1871)

Gottschall, Jonathan, *The Story Paradox: How Our Love of Storytelling Builds Societies and Tears them Down* (New York, 2021)

Haynes, Natalie, *A Thousand Ships* (New York, 2019)

Horta, Paulo, ed., *The Annotated Arabian Nights* (New York, 2021)

Lahiri, Jhumpa, *The Namesake* (New York, 2003)

Mann, Thomas, *Der Zauberberg* (Frankfurt am Main, 1924)

Miller, Madeline, *Circe* (Boston, MA, 2020)

Milton, John, *Areopagitica* (London, 1644)

Mott, Jason, *Hell of a Book* (New York, 2022)

Nabokov, Vladimir, *Lectures on Literature* (New York, 1980)

Rousseau, Jean-Jacques, *Emile: or, On Education*, trans. Allan Bloom (New York, 1979)

Serpell, Namwali, 'The Banality of Empathy', *New York Review of Books*,
  2 March 2019
Tatar, Maria, *The Heroine with 1,001 Faces* (New York, 2021)
VanArendonk, Kathryn, 'The Limits of the Women's Redemption Plot',
  Vulture, www.vulture.com, 25 February 2022

3 The Dream of an Intenser Experience

Brooks, Peter, *History Painting and Narrative: Delacroix's 'Moments'*
  (Oxford, 1998)
Carroll, Lewis, *Alice's Adventures in Wonderland* [1865] (Chicago, IL, 1998)
Findlay, Kirsty Nichol, ed., *Arthur Ransome's Long-Lost Study of Robert
  Louis Stevenson* (Woodbridge, Suffolk, 2011)
James, Henry, 'Preface to The American,' *Literary Criticism*, vol. II (New
  York, 1984)
Ransome, Arthur, *Swallows and Amazons* [1930] (Boston, 1985)
—, *Swallowdale* [1931] (Boston, 1985)
Robert, Marthe, *Roman des origines et origines du roman* (Paris, 1973)
Rousseau, Jean-Jacques, *Confessions; autres textes autobiographiques* (Paris,
  1962)
Sartre, Jean-Paul, *La Nausée* (Paris, 1938)
Stevenson, Robert Louis, *Treasure Island* [1883] (New York, 2012)

5 A Life in Literature

Bateman, Robert, *Young Footballer* (London, 1958)
Crompton, Richmal, *Just William* (Oxford, 1922)
Eliot, George, *Daniel Deronda* [1876] (London, 1967)
Graves, Robert, *I, Claudius* [1934] (London, 1953)
Hardy, Thomas, *The Mayor of Casterbridge* [1886] (London, 1974)
Hopkins, Gerard Manley, *Poems*, ed. W. H. Gardner and N. H. Mackenzie
  (Oxford, 1970)
Kästner, Erich, *Emil and the Detectives* [1929], trans. Eileen Hall (London,
  1959)
Lawrence, D. H., *Fantasia of the Unconscious* [1922] (London, 1971)
—, *The Rainbow* [1915] (London, 1949)
Mckenzie, William, and Theodora Papadopoulou, eds, *Shakespeare and I*
  (London, 2012)

Manning, Frederic, *Her Privates We* (New York, 1930)
Middleton, Stanley, *Cold Gradations* (London, 1972)
O'Donnell, Mabel, *Janet and John: Here We Go* (London, 1949)
Suetonius, *The Twelve Caesars*, trans. Robert Graves (London, 1957)
Villeneuve, Gabrielle-Suzanne, Barbot de, *Beauty and the Beast* [1740],
    ed. Vera Southgate (London, 1968)
Yeats, W. B., *Collected Poems* (London, 1965)

6 Reading (in) My Father's Shadow

Atlas, Galit, *Emotional Inheritance: Moving Beyond the Legacy of Trauma*
    (London, 2022)
The Bible: King James Version (Oxford Text Archive)
Brontë, Charlotte, *Jane Eyre* [1847], ed. Richard J. Dunn (New York, 2019)
Defoe, Daniel, *The Life and Adventures of Robinson Crusoe* [1719], ebook
    (2016)
Ogden, Benjamin G., and Thomas H. Ogden, *The Analyst's Ear and the
    Critic's Eye: Rethinking Psychoanalysis and Literature* (London, 2013)
Suova, Maija, ed., *Joka naisen niksikirja: Käytännöllisiä neuvoja* (Every
    Woman's How To: Practical Advice) (Helsinki, 1951)

7 Reading in Times of War

Andrukhovych, Sofia, 'Day 5, Day 9, Day 16: Responses to the Invasion of
    Ukraine', *London Review of Books*, XLIV/6 (24 March 2022)
Casanova, Pascale, 'Combative Literatures', *New Left Review*, 72 (2011),
    pp. 123–34
Hlushchenko, Kateryna. 'Як мова визначає пам'ять' (How Language
    Defines Memory), lecture notes from the conversation between
    Volodymyr Rafeyenko and Marianna Kianovska, Lviv, 19 August 2019,
    available at https://zbruc.eu
Jameson, Fredric, 'The Politics of Utopia', *New Left Review*, 25 (2004),
    pp. 35–54
Kalytko, Kateryna, *Люди з дієсловами* (People with Verbs) (Chernivtsi, 2022)
«*Люди з дієсловами*: виходить нова збірка віршів Катерини Калитко
    – про війну, довіру і пам'ять» ('People with Verbs': Kalytko's New
    Poetry Collection Is Out – On War, Trust and Memory), *Meridian
    Czernowitz*, www.meridiancz.com, August 2022

Rafeyenko, Volodymyr, *Мондеґрін: Пісні про смерть і любов* (Chernivtsi, 2019), trans. Mark Andryczyk as *Mondegreen: Songs about Death and Love* (Cambridge, MA, 2022)

Zhadan, Serhiy, 'Хай це буде текст не про війну' (May This Text Be Not about War), speech at the 2022 Frankfurt Book Fair, 23 October 2022, available at https://chytomo.com

8 Reading as a Rambunctious Boy-Girl

Cooke, Donald E., *Powder Keg, or The Gunpowder Smugglers* (New York, 1971)

Dostoevsky, Fyodor, *Crime and Punishment* [1866], trans. David McDuff (London, 2003)

Fitzhugh, Louise, *Harriet the Spy* (New York, 1964)

Flaubert, Gustave, *Madame Bovary* (Paris, 1856)

Hemingway, Ernest, *The Sun Also Rises* (New York, 1926)

Konigsburg, Elaine L., *From the Mixed-Up Files of Mrs. Basil E. Frankweiler* (New York, 1967)

Lenski, Lois, *Strawberry Girl* (Philadelphia, PA, 1945)

—, *Blue Ridge Billy* (Philadelphia, PA, 1946)

—, *Judy's Journey* (Philadelphia, PA, 1947)

Lindgren, Astrid, *Pippi Longstocking*, trans. Louis S. Glanzman (New York, 1950)

O'Dell, Scott, *The Island of the Blue Dolphins* (Boston, MA, 1960)

Southhall, Ivan, *To the Wild Sky* (Sydney, 1967)

Speare, Elizabeth George, *The Witch of Blackbird Pond* (Boston, MA, 1958)

Talbot, Charlene Joy, *Children in Hiding, or Tomas Takes Charge* (New York, 1966)

Wilder, Laura Ingalls, *Little House on the Prairie* (New York, 1935)

10 Reading from the Spine

Fuchs, Thomas, 'Phenomenology of Body Memory', in *Body Memory, Metaphor and Movement*, ed. Sabine C. Koch, Thomas Fuchs, Michela Summa and Cornelia Müller (Amsterdam, 2012), pp. 9–22

Hustvedt, Siri, 'I Responded Viscerally to De Beauvoir's *The Second Sex*', *The Guardian*, 26 November 2021

Mansfield, Katherine, 'Miss Brill', *The Garden Party and Other Stories* (London, 1997), pp. 110–14
Merleau-Ponty, Maurice, *Phenomenology of Perception*, trans. Colin Smith (London, 1962)
Noë, Alva, *Strange Tools: Art and Human Nature* (New York, 2015)
Oulanne, Laura, 'Containment and Empathy in Katherine Mansfield's and Virginia Woolf's Short Fiction', in *Narrating Nonhuman Spaces: Form, Story, and Experience Beyond Anthropocentrism*, ed. Marco Caracciolo, Marlene Karlsson Marcussen and David Rodriguez (New York, 2021), pp. 19–35
Stein, Gertrude, *Tender Buttons* [1914] (San Francisco, CA, 2014)
——, *The Autobiography of Alice B. Toklas* (London, 1933)
Woolf, Virginia, *To the Lighthouse* (London, 1927)

12 A Typewriter's Travels

Bergman, Ingmar, *The Magic Lantern*, trans. Joan Tate (New York, 1988)
Brodsky, Joseph, *On Grief and Reason: Essays* (New York, 1995)
Canetti, Elias, *The Tongue Set Free: Remembrance of a European Childhood*, trans. Joachim Neugroschel (New York, 1979)
Hosseini, Silvia, *Tie, totuus ja kuolema* (Helsinki, 2021)
Nabokov, Vladimir, *Speak, Memory: An Autobiography Revisited* (London, 2012)
Sartre, Jean-Paul, *Les Mots* (Paris, 1964)

13 What Did the Bear Think?

Batten, H. Mortimer, *British Wild Animals* (London, 1924)
——, *British Wildlife Stories* (London, 1936)
——, *The Singing Forest* (London, 1955)
Blume, Judy, *Forever...* (New York, 1975)
Booth, Wayne C., *The Rhetoric of Fiction* (Chicago, IL, 1961)
Brooks, Cleanth, and Robert Penn Warren, eds, *Understanding Poetry* (New York, 1938)
Bunyan, John, *Divine Emblems, or Temporal Things Spiritualized, Fitted for the Use of Boys and Girls* (London, 1686)
Communist Party of Great Britain, *British Road to Socialism* (London, 1951)

Works Cited

Donaldson, Julia, *The Gruffalo* (London, 1999)

Dylan, Bob, *Highway 61 Revisited* [LP] (Columbia Records, 1965)

Edwards, Lionel, *Our Cattle* (London, 1948)

Fassett, James Hiram, *Beacon* [First–Sixth] *Readers* (Boston, MA, 1913–)

Grant, Clara Louise, *Ukelele and Her New Doll* (New York, 1951)

Guillot, René, *Kpo the Leopard*, trans. Gwen Marsh (London, 1955)

Hagen, Victor W. V., *Miskito Boy: A Tale for Children* (London, 1943)

Harnett, Cynthia, *The Wool-Pack* (London, 1951)

Kerouac, Jack, *Desolation Angels* (New York, 1965)

Lawrence, D. H., *Collected Poems*, vol. II (New York, 1929)

M. Ilin (Ilya Yakovlevich Marshak), *Black on White: The Story of Boo*
    (London, 1932)

Morton, Arthur Leslie, *A People's History of England* (London, 1938)

Morton, Miriam, ed., *A Harvest of Russian Children's Literature* (Berkeley,
    CA, 1967)

Naidoo, Beverley, *Journey to Jo'burg: A South African Story* (New York, 1985)

Père Castor [Paul Faucher], *Bourru, the Brown Bear,* trans. Lida and Rose
    Fyleman (London, *c.* 1940)

Potter, Beatrix, *Peter Rabbit* (London, 1902)

—, *Squirrel Nutkin* (London, 1903)

Rosen, Michael, *Backbone* (London, 1968)

—, *We're Going on a Bear Hunt* (New York, 1989)

—, *The Missing: The True Story of My Family in World War II* (London,
    2020)

Rothstein, Julian, ed., *Inside the Rainbow, Russian Children's Literature,*
    1920–35: Beautiful Books, Terrible Times (Princeton, NJ, 2013)

Sandburg, Carl, *The People, Yes* (New York, 1936)

Sendak, Maurice, *Where the Wild Things Are* (New York, 1963)

Seton, Ernest Thompson, *Biography of a Grizzly* (New York, 1900)

—, *Krag and Johnny Bear* (New York, 1902)

Stevenson, Robert Louis, *A Child's Garden of Verses* (London, 1885)

—, 'Child's Play', *Cornhill Magazine*, XXXVIII (1878), p. 352

Summerfield, Geoffrey, *Voices*, 3 vols (London, 1968–74)

—, *Junior Voices* (London, 1970)

Trask, Willard R., *The Unwritten Song: Poetry of the Primitive and*
    Traditional Peoples of the World (London, 1966)

Trease, Geoffrey, *Bows Against the Barons* (London, 1934)

Untermeyer, Louis, *Modern American Poetry* (New York, 1919)

Watts, Isaac, *Divine Songs: Attempted in Easy Language for the Use of Children* (London, 1715)

Wells, Zetta, and Carveth Wells, *Raff, the Jungle Bird: The Story of Our Talking Mynah* (New York, 1941)

Williamson, Henry, *Tarka the Otter: His Joyful Water-Life and Death in the Country of the Two Rivers* (London, 1927)

14 Words After

Chamberlin, J. Edward, *If This Is Your Land, Where Are Your Stories: Finding Common Ground* (New York, 2003)

—, *Storylines: How Words Shape Our World* (Madeira Park, BC, 2023)

Decker, Hannah S., *Freud, Dora, and Vienna 1900* (New York, 1991)

Derrida, Jacques, *The Gift of Death*, trans. David Wills (Chicago, IL, 1996)

Faulkner, William, 'Faulkner at Virginia,' https://faulkner.lib.virginia.edu, accessed 2 May 2023

Freud, Sigmund, *The Standard Edition of the Complete Psychological Works of Sigmund Freud*, trans. James Strachey et al., 24 vols (London, 1953–74)

Gilman, Sander L., *Jurek Becker: A Life in Five Worlds* (Chicago, IL, 2003)

Harrison, Barbara, 'Howl Like the Wolves', *Children's Literature*, XV (1987), pp. 67–90

Jacobs, Joseph, 'The Dying of Death', *Fortnightly Review* (August 1899), pp. 264–9

Kakutani, Michiko, '*The Child in Time*', *New York Times*, 26 September 1987

McEwan, Ian, *The Child in Time* (London, 1987)

Pauli, Michelle, 'Michael Bond: "Paddington stands up for things, he's not afraid of going to the top and giving them a hard stare"', *The Guardian*, 28 November 2014

Rushdie, Salman, *Languages of Truth: Essays 2003–2020* (New York, 2021)

Schlesinger, Naomi J., 'Loss to Legacy: The Work of Mourning Early Parental Death', *Psychoanalytic Social Work*, XXI (2014), pp. 75–89

CONTRIBUTORS

DR NATALYA BEKHTA is a research fellow at Tampere Institute for Advanced Study. She has written a pioneering study on multiple-voiced narration, *We-Narratives: Collective Story-Telling in Contemporary Fiction*, which won the Perkins Prize for the best book in narratology in 2021.

PETER BROOKS is the Sterling Professor of Comparative Literature Emeritus at Yale. Using French and English literature as examples, Brooks has discussed French literary salons, melodrama, psychoanalytic transference as pertaining to narrators and readers as well as the relationship between literature and law. Extensive reading has turned him into an author of two books of fiction, *World Elsewhere* and *The Emperor's Body*.

PHILIP DAVIS is emeritus professor of Literature and Psychology at the University of Liverpool. He was the director of the Centre for Research into Reading, Literature and Society. He provides a lovingly probing look at all things Victorian (*The Victorians, 1830–1880*) and *Why Victorian Literature Still Matters*. Also a biographer, he has recounted the lives of George Eliot and Bernard Malamud. As the editor of Oxford University Press's series The Literary Agenda on the role of literature in the world of the twenty-first century, Davis knows the current state of reading from the inside out. His *Reading and the Reader* is a modern classic on the topic.

SANDER L. GILMAN is a distinguished emeritus professor of the Liberal Arts and Sciences as well as Professor of Psychiatry at Emory University. A cultural and literary historian, he is the author or editor of well over ninety books. His widely reviewed *Stand Up Straight! A History of Posture* was published by Reaktion Books in 2018; his most recent edited volume is *The Oxford Handbook of Music and the Body* (with Youn Kim), published by Oxford University Press in 2019. He is the author of the basic study of the visual stereotyping of the mentally ill, *Seeing the Insane*, published by John Wiley & Sons in 1982 (reprinted 1996 and 2014), as well as the standard study of Jewish self-hatred, which is the the title of his Johns Hopkins University Press monograph of 1986, which is still in print.

Professor emerita LINDA HUTCHEON of comparative literature and professor emeritus MICHAEL HUTCHEON of medicine at the University of Toronto, a married couple – one a literary and cultural scholar, the other a medical docto – have turned reading into collaborative action. Together they have read and listened to countless operas, uniting their respective fields into a series of fascinating and ground-breaking studies of opera: *Bodily Charm: Living Opera*; *Opera: The Art of Dying*; and *Four Last Songs: Aging and Creativity in Verdi, Strauss, Messiaen, and Britten*.

DANIEL MENDELSOHN is a Charles Ranlett Flint Professor at Bard College. His academic speciality is in Greek (Euripedean tragedy) and Roman poetry. He has received multiple prizes for his writing such as The American Arts and Letters Harold D. Vursell Memorial Award for Prose Style (2014), The American Philological Association President's Award for Service to the Classics (2014) and The George Jean Nathan Prize for Dramatic Criticism (2002). *The Odyssey: A Father, Son, and an Epic* (2017) combines memoir and literary criticism in dealing with the participation of Mendelsohn's father in the *Odyssey* class the author taught. It focuses on the epic's father-son relationships. It was named the best book of the year by National Public Radio, *Library Journal* and *Kirkus Review*. It won the Prix Méditerranée in France in 2018. *The Lost: A Search for Six of Six Million* (2006) records Mendelsohn's five-year search for the fates of his relatives who perished in the Holocaust.

LAURA OTIS is professor of English at Emory University. She trained as a neuroscientist and literary scholar. She studies the ways that literature and science intersect. Otis has earned a BS in Biochemistry, an MA in Neuroscience, an MA and a PhD in Comparative Literature and an MFA in Fiction. She is the author of the recent academic books *Rethinking Thought: Inside the Minds of Creative Scientists and Artists* (2016) and *Banned Emotions: How Metaphors*

Can Shape What People Feel (2019), as well as the novels *Clean, Refiner's Fire, Lacking in Substance, The Memory Hive* and *The Tantalus Letters*. In 2000 she was awarded a MacArthur 'Genius' fellowship for creativity.

DR LAURA OULANNE demonstrates how objects and things animate modernist fiction in her book *Materiality in Modernist Short Fiction: Lived Things* (2021). In her many articles she traces the ways in which material things in modernist literature enable readers to have tactile experiences of literature.

HETA PYRHÖNEN is professor of Comparative Literature at the University of Helsinki. She has published two books on detective fiction, *Murder from an Academic Angle: An Introduction to the Study of the Detective Narrative* (1994) and *Mayhem and Murder: Narrative and Moral Problems in the Detective Story* (1998), and numerous articles on the genre. She studied the legacy of the 'Bluebeard' tale in the novels by British female authors in *Bluebeard Gothic: 'Jane Eyre' and Its Progeny* (2008). She has written a monograph on Jane Austen (*Jane Austen, Our Contemporary* (2014) in Finnish. With Janna Kantola, she edited a volume of essays, *Reading Today* (2019).

MICHAEL ROSEN is a British children's author, poet, columnist, broadcaster and activist. He was appointed British Children's Laureate for 2007–9. Rosen received the Fred and Anne Jarvis award in 2010 and the J. M. Barrie lifetime achievement award in 2021. He has published 140 children's books such as *We're Going on a Bear Hunt* (1989), *This is Our Home* (2009) and *I'm Number One* (2009). Rosen is an expert in how to get kids to read. His books feed children's love of language and rhyming, gripping stories, but also their hunger for knowledge. Rosen has written non-fiction for middle-school children such as *What Is Right and Wrong? Who Decides? Where do Values Come Grom? And Other Big Questions* (2021 with Annemarie Young).

SALMAN RUSHDIE is the author of fifteen novels: *Grimus* (1975), *Midnight's Children* (awarded the Booker Prize in 1981), *Shame* (1983), *The Satanic Verses* (1988), *Haroun and the Sea of Stories* (1990), *The Moor's Last Sigh* (1995), *The Ground Beneath Her Feet* (1999), *Fury* (2001), *Shalimar the Clown* (2005), *The Enchantress of Florence* (2005), *Luka and the Fire of Life* (2010), *Two Years, Eight Months and Twenty-Eight Nights* (2015), *The Golden House* (2017), *Quichotte* (2019) and *Victory City* (2023).

Rushdie has also written a book of stories and four works of non-fiction. *Midnight's Children* was named The Best of the Booker – the best winner in the award's forty-year history – by a public vote. Rushdie's books have been translated into over forty languages.

Rushdie is a Fellow of the British Royal Society of Literature. He has received, among other honours, the Whitbread Prize for Best Novel (twice), the Writers' Guild Award, the James Tait Black Prize and the European Union's Aristeion Prize for Literature. He holds honorary doctorates and fellowships at six European and six American universities, is an Honorary Professor in the Humanities at MIT and University Distinguished Professor at Emory University.

CRISTINA SANDU is of Romanian and Finnish descent. Her debut novel *Valas nimeltä Goliat* (The Whale Called Goliath, 2017) was nominated for the Finlandia Prize and has been translated into Catalan, French and Romanian. Her second novel, *Vesileikit* (2019), won the Toisinkoinen Prize for the best second book in Finland. It was translated by the author into English and published in Britain two years later as *The Union of Synchronized Swimmers*, after which it was shortlisted for the Oxford-Weidenfeld Prize in 2022. Her third novel, *Tanskalainen retkikunta* (The Danish Expedition), will be published in 2024.

PAJTIM STATOVCI is a Finnish-Albanian author. Statovci has woven the lore of his childhood into his passionate books. *Kissani Jugoslavia* (2014; *My Cat Yugoslavia*, 2017) won the best first book prize in Finland. *Tiranan sydän* (2016) won the Toisinkoinen Prize in 2017. Translated as *The Crossing* (2019), the book was a finalist for the National Book Award in the category of translated literature and for the Kirkus Prize in fiction in 2019. Statovci's most recent book, *Bolla*, was awarded the Finlandia Prize, the country's most prestigious literary prize, in 2019. Bolla was also shortlisted for the Nordic Council Literature Prize. The novel was published in the United States in 2021 and was a finalist for the Kirkus Prize for fiction. In 2022 *Bolla* won Statovci the Italian Premio Grinzane Literature Award.

MARIA TATAR, the John L. Loeb Professor of Germanic Languages and Literatures at Harvard, is an expert on how oral tales have been turned into the written fairy-tale tradition in Western cultures. She is the author of books on the Brothers Grimm (*The Hard Facts of the Grimms' Fairy Tales*, 1987) and *Off with Their Heads!* (1993). Her latest books include *Secrets beyond the Door* (2004) and *The Heroine with 1,001 Faces* (2021).

PERMISSIONS